HOW TO MAKE
2x4
FURNITURE
FOR INDOORS AND OUTDOORS

HOW TO MAKE
2x4
FURNITURE
FOR INDOORS AND OUTDOORS

The Family Workshop

DOUBLEDAY

NEW YORK LONDON TORONTO SYDNEY AUCKLAND

PUBLISHED BY DOUBLEDAY
a division of Bantam Doubleday Dell Publishing Group, Inc.
666 Fifth Avenue, New York, New York 10103

DOUBLEDAY and the portrayal of an anchor with a dolphin
are trademarks of Doubleday, a division of Bantam Doubleday Dell
Publishing Group, Inc.

Created by The Family Workshop, Inc.
Editorial Director: Janet Weberling
Editors: Suzi West, S.P. Bob
Art Director: Wanda Young
Production Artists: Roberta Taff, Julie Barrett
Illustrator: Janice Harris Burtsall
Typography: Suzi West
Project Designs: D.J. Olin, April Bail, Ed and Stevie Baldwin
Photography: Bill Welch, C. Forrest Brokaw III
Photo Stylist: April Bail

The information in this book is correct and complete to the best of
our knowledge. All recommendations are made without guarantees
on the part of the authors or Doubleday, who disclaim all liability
in connection with the use of this information.

Library of Congress Cataloging-in-Publication Data
The Family Workshop
   How to make 2x4 furniture for indoors and outdoors.
   1. Furniture making–Amateurs' manuals.
II. Title.
TT195.B35   1987   684.1'04   86-11664
ISBN 0-385-19710-1 (pbk.)
ISBN 0-385-24149-6

Dedicated with love to Bob Young & Bev Smart.

Preface

At last – handsome, solid-wood furniture that can be reproduced in the home work-shop with just a few basic tools and no advanced skills!

We call it "2 x 4 furniture," because it is made primarily of 2 x 4 and other standard dimensional lumber available at reasonable prices in every lumberyard in the nation. Many of the projects in this book require only that you cut the boards to length and assemble with nails or screws. Others are slightly more complex, but all are far less expensive than similar furnishings available at retail stores.

We've included furniture for every room in your house and for your yard and patio – from very simple items, such as the convertible couch and tables, conversation pit, picnic table, hammock stand, porch swing and modular bookcase; to items that require a little more time, such as the easy chair and hassock, the classic butcher block and the charming latticework corner pantry.

Even if you're a novice in the woodshop, you'll find it easy to produce furniture you'll be proud to display. The plans for each project include a complete materials list, cutting layouts and illustrated step-by-step instructions, including special notes pointing out where it's easy to make an error.

The opening section of woodworking tips and techniques provides basic information on wood selection, materials, tools, cutting and joining procedures. We know you'll enjoy the section of color photographs.

We'd like to offer special thanks to Black & Decker and to Shopsmith, who provided tools used in the production of the furnishings in this book.

Contents

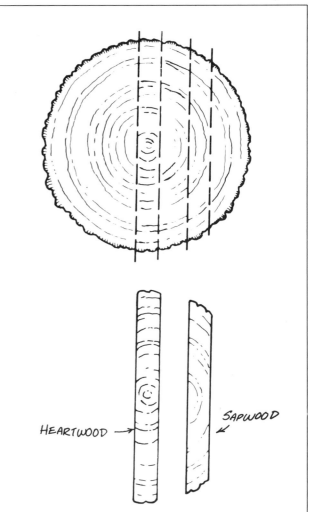

Tips & Techniques

Selecting Wood

Hardwood comes from deciduous trees (they shed their leaves annually). Softwood comes from conifers (evergreens). Hardwood is more difficult to cut and work with and usually is more expensive, but it also is more sturdy and long-lasting. Common hardwoods include oak, ash, pecan and maple; common softwoods include pine, fir, redwood and cedar. Pine is available in both white (finer grain) and yellow (coarser grain). Douglas is a particularly good fir.

Softwoods vary widely in their tendency to shrink, swell and warp. Those least likely to do so are redwood, white pine and cedar. Newly cut lumber contains quite a bit of sap and is seasoned (partially dried by air or in a lumber kiln) before it is sold to the consumer. Wood that is not sufficiently seasoned will warp, crack and shrink much more than properly dried wood. Unfortunately, there is no sure way to assess the amount of sap still left in the wood that you buy.

When you are choosing lumber, examine the end grain of each board (see **Figure A**). Heartwood is highly rot-resistant. It may become thinner as it loses moisture, but is not as likely to warp and crack. Sapwood is cut farther from the center of the tree, is more vulnerable to rot and insect damage and is more likely to warp and crack as it loses moisture.

Lumber is graded according to overall quality. Here is a rundown of the grading system for pine and other softwoods. Keep in mind that for rustic outdoor projects you can often get by with a much lower grade than what would be appropriate for fancy indoor furnishings. If you are in doubt as to which grade to use, show your lumber dealer the plans and ask his opinion.

Regular Board Grades:

#3 common – Small knotholes are common and knots are easily dislodged while you work. Prone to check.

#2 common – Free of knotholes, but contains some knots. Often used for indoor flooring and paneling. We use this grade for many of our outdoor projects.

#1 common – Top quality of the regular board grades. Contains small knots and other insignificant imperfections, but should have no knotholes.

Better Board Grades:

D select – The lowest quality of the better board grades. Comparable to #1 common, but better seasoned.

C select – A few small blemishes may appear on one side of the board, but it should be almost perfect on the other side.

1 and 2 clear – The best and most expensive grades. These should be used only for the finest indoor and outdoor furniture.

When using lower grades of lumber, buy more than called for so that you can eliminate the worst knots and cracks. You can repair by filling small cracks and gouges with wood putty or a mixture of glue and sawdust. Tap all knots to see which ones will fall out. Glue them back in place. If a board is badly cracked at the ends, it's best to cut off the cracked portions, because the cracks may worsen and split the entire board. Minor cracks should be filled. Warped boards can be weighed down and straightened, but this takes time.

We specify the types and amounts of lumber that we used for each of our projects. Amounts include a waste allowance of about ten percent.

Figure B

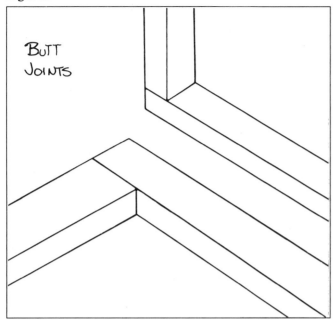

BUTT JOINTS

Lumber Sizes

Softwoods are available in the standard sizes shown here, called "dimensional" lumber. Because of differences in softwoods, the planing required to surface the lumber yields slight differences in thickness. Dimensional lumber is sold in standard lengths: 4-foot, 6-foot, 8-foot, 10-foot, etc.

Nominal Size	Actual Size
1 x 2	¾ x 1½ inches
1 x 4	¾ x 3½ inches
1 x 6	¾ x 5½ inches
1 x 8	¾ x 7¼ inches
1 x 10	¾ x 9¼ inches
1 x 12	¾ x 11¼ inches
2 x 2	1½ x 1½ inches
2 x 4	1½ x 3½ inches
2 x 6	1½ x 5½ inches
2 x 8	1½ x 7½ inches
2 x 10	1½ x 9¼ inches
2 x 12	1½ x 11¼ inches
4 x 4	3½ x 3½ inches
4 x 6	3½ x 5½ inches
6 x 6	5½ x 5½ inches
8 x 8	7¹⁄₂₄ x 7½ inches

The production limitations of hardwood require that each board be cut as wide and as long as the log will allow. Boards are then trimmed just enough to make the edges and ends square. This method of cutting yields the maximum amount of wood, limits waste and helps reduce the cost of hardwood.

Because of the manner in which hardwoods are cut and surfaced, they are almost always offered in random widths and lengths and priced per board foot. One board foot represents a piece of lumber 1 inch (or less) thick, 12 inches wide and 1 foot long. Hardwood thicknesses are measured in quarter inches. Standard thicknesses are ¾, ⁴⁄₄, ⁵⁄₄, ⁶⁄₄ and ⁸⁄₄. Depending upon what is available, your dealer may have to split boards to supply a specific thickness, which will cost extra. For boards more than 1 inch thick, the board foot measurement is doubled (to account for the double thickness).

Preservatives and Finishes

For indoor projects, we use a penetrating stain and sealer combination called Danish oil, which requires no additional finishing product unless you want a high gloss.

For children's toys and furnishings, we strongly suggest that you use non-toxic finishing products. Plain vegetable oil rubbed into the wood gives a nice, clear finish. Salad-bowl finish is a non-toxic commercial finish.

For outdoor projects a preservative will help delay insect and rot damage. Commercial preservatives such as zinc and copper naphthenates will help protect the wood, but are highly poisonous to both plant and animal life. Read the labels carefully and follow the directions! You can pour the product into a bucket and soak the cut ends of the boards and you can also brush it onto the surfaces.

If your project is a planter, picnic table, birdhouse or similar project on which you don't want to use a toxic preservative, you can seal cut ends and edges with waterproof glue. Several coats of waterproofing sealer will also help.

For finishing of outdoor projects, use exterior paint, a combination stain and sealer or a clear penetrating sealer. For extra protection, add a final coat or two of clear synthetic marine-grade varnish. Thin it for the first coat and use it full-strength for subsequent coats.

Adhesives

We recommend both glue and fasteners (nails, screws or bolts) for all joints, unless you want to be able to disassemble the joint. Aliphatic resin, commonly sold as carpenter's wood glue, is what we use for indoor projects. For outdoor projects you may wish to use a waterproof marine glue or a two-part epoxy that must be mixed and used immediately.

Fasteners and Hardware

For indoor projects, common "mild steel" hardware is perfectly acceptable. Outside, mild steel eventually will deteriorate and produce a black stain that is absorbed into the wood...not an attractive sight on your handmade furnishings!

Galvanized hardware is more rust-resistant and is commonly available at reasonable prices. Better yet is hardware made of brass, bronze or alloyed stainless steel, although it is more expensive than the galvanized variety.

Cutting and Joining

Butt Joints: A butt joint connects one piece to another with no interlocking surfaces (**Figure B**). It is an extremely weak joint and should be strengthened with glue blocks, splines, nails, screws, dowels or other reinforcement.

Figure C

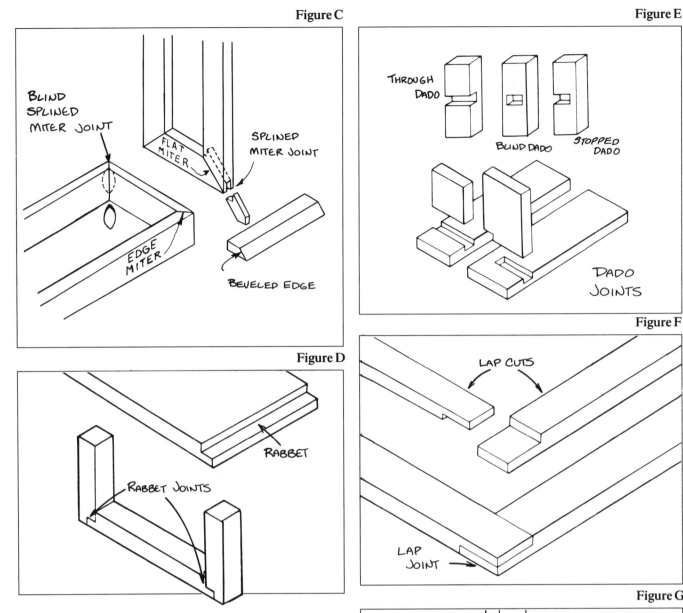

BLIND SPLINED MITER JOINT

FLAT MITER

SPLINED MITER JOINT

EDGE MITER

BEVELED EDGE

Figure D

RABBET

RABBET JOINTS

Figure E

THROUGH DADO

BLIND DADO

STOPPED DADO

DADO JOINTS

Figure F

LAP CUTS

LAP JOINT

Figure G

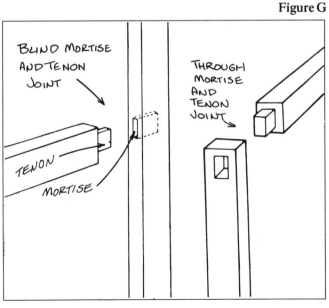

BLIND MORTISE AND TENON JOINT

THROUGH MORTISE AND TENON JOINT

TENON

MORTISE

Miters and Bevels: A miter joint connects two angle-cut ends (**Figure C**) and can be reinforced using splines, dowels or fasteners. The most common miter is a 45-degree, which is used to construct right angles. A flat miter is cut across the width of the board. An on-edge miter is cut across the thickness. A bevel is an angle cut made along an edge or surface.

Rabbets: A rabbet is an L-shaped groove (**Figure D**). It provides a greater surface area for glueing, thus creating a stronger joint. A rabbet has other uses such as recessing the inner surface of a door so that it will fit into the door opening.

Dadoes: A dado is a groove (**Figure E**) and can be used to make a strong joint.

Lap Joints: A lap joint normally is used to form right angles, with both surfaces flush (**Figure F**). This is a relatively strong joint, providing a large surface to be glued.

Mortise and Tenon Joints: Basic mortise and tenon joints are shown in **Figure G**. This is an extremely strong joint if the members are cut carefully. A pegged (or pinned) mortise and

Figure H

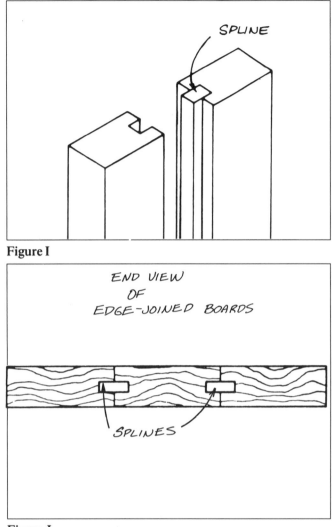

SPLINE

Figure I

END VIEW
OF
EDGE-JOINED BOARDS

SPLINES

Figure J

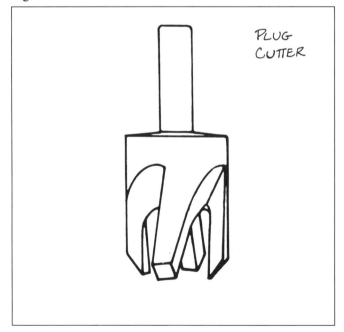

PLUG
CUTTER

tenon is one in which the tenon extends out beyond the mortise and is itself mortised to accommodate a peg. Left unglued, the pegged mortise and tenon is very handy for projects you wish to be able to disassemble.

Splines: A spline is a thin strip of wood used as a connecting member between two boards (**Figure H**). It fits into grooves cut into the edges to be joined and can be used to strengthen almost any type of joint. (**Figure C** shows miter joints reinforced by splines.) A through spline reaches from end to end. A blind spline is stopped short of both ends and can not be seen once the joint is assembled.

If you are working with standard 1-inch lumber (which actually measures about ¾ inch thick), the grooves should be cut ¼ inch wide and just slightly deeper than ⅜ inch. The easiest way to cut them is to use a dado blade with your table saw. Otherwise, use a router with a ¼-inch straight bit or make a couple of passes with a normal table-saw blade. The spline should be cut ¼ inch thick, ¾ inch wide and the same length as the grooves. Spline joints may be left unglued if the assembled boards will be secured at the ends or edges. Unglued splines allow the boards to expand and contract with changing atmospheric conditions and help prevent warping and cracking.

Whenever you edge-join two or more boards (whether you use splines or not), turn every other board so that the ray patterns are alternated (**Figure I**), to avoid warping.

Screws and Nails: To prevent splitting the wood, drill a pilot hole for each screw, using a drill bit slightly smaller than the screw shank. For a nice finish, use a combination pilot-countersink bit to drill the pilot hole. The countersunk screw heads can be covered with wooden plugs or wood filler. Plugs will be almost invisible if you cut them from matching stock that has been reduced to about ¼ inch thick. A plug-cutter attachment for your drill press or hand-held power drill (**Figure J**) makes plug cutting a breeze. Plugs can also be cut from dowel rod, but they present end grain and will be much more apparent, particularly if the wood is stained. Finishing nails should be recessed and covered with filler.

Toenailing: When you wish to secure a joint but can not drive a nail straight because of board width or other considerations, toenail at the ends, as shown in **Figure K**. Screws also can be angled in this manner.

Pegged Joints: Many joints normally secured with screws can be secured with dowel pegs instead. Follow these steps: Glue and clamp the joint and allow the glue to dry. Drill a socket into the joint. To make the peg, cut a length of dowel rod (the same diameter as the socket). Chamfer both ends and cut grooves along the length (**Figure L**). The grooves will allow excess glue to escape from the socket. Glue the peg into the socket, tapping with a hammer to make sure it is seated securely. Trim the end flush with the surrounding wood.

As a general rule, the socket should be the same length as the screw you would otherwise use in that joint. The peg should be cut a little longer. If there is room, most joints should be secured with two or more pegs (or screws) rather than just one.

If you wish to conceal the end grain of the peg, cut it about ¼ inch shorter than the socket and install as described above. Then cut a covering plug from stock that matches the surrounding wood (as described under the heading "Screws and Nails," above). Glue the plug into the socket over the recessed end of the peg. Sand the plug flush with the wood.

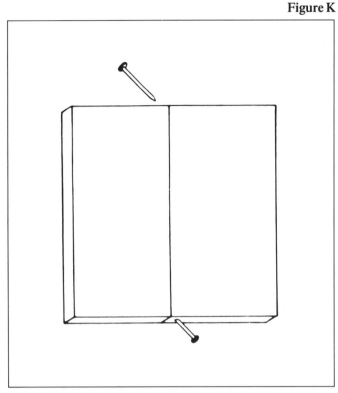

Figure L

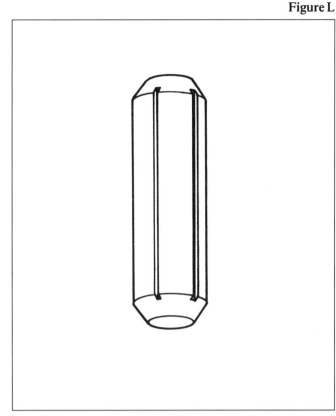

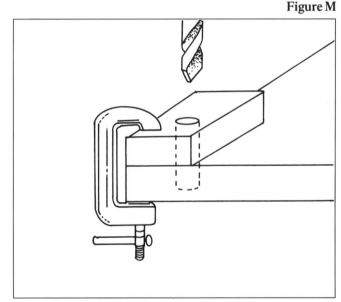

Clamping: Most glued joints should be clamped, but not so tightly as to force out most of the glue. Thirty minutes is normal clamping time. Those that will be under a great deal of stress should be clamped overnight. Joints secured with power-driven screws need not be clamped at all.

Drilling

You may find it difficult to drill a hole or socket that is perfectly square with the wood stock. A small homemade jig (**Figure M**) will be helpful in these cases. Cut a small, perfectly square block of wood. Drill a hole straight through it, using a bit of the same diameter as the hole to be drilled into the stock. Double check to be sure that the hole is perfectly square with the block. You may have to make several attempts, using a new block each time, to achieve a perfectly drilled block. Now clamp the jig to the stock, as shown. The jig will keep the bit from straying off course. Make a similar jig for each different size drill bit and you'll have them on hand whenever you need to use one.

To achieve correct depth of a socket, mark the desired depth on the drill bit, using fingernail polish, chalk or a pencil. (If you are going to use a drilling jig, the measured distance should equal the desired depth plus the thickness of the jig.)

Patterns

Enlarging Scale Drawings: A scale drawing appears on a background grid of small squares and includes a legend at the top that specifies the scale: 1 square = 1 inch. There are several ways to enlarge the drawing to full size:

Pantograph – A pantograph is a tool containing several joined rods and two styli (pencil leads). As you trace the scale drawing, using the guide stylus, the secondary stylus draws the full-size pattern on another sheet of paper.

Opaque Projector – Place the scale drawing in the projector and aim it at a flat wall. Move the unit forward or backward until the projected squares of the grid measure exactly 1 inch square. Tape paper to the wall and trace the outlines of the patterns.

Grid Paper – For this method you'll need paper containing a grid of 1-inch squares (drafting paper or dressmaker's pattern

Figure N

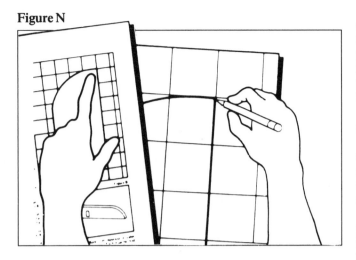

paper). To make the full-size pattern (**Figure N**), work one square at a time as you reproduce onto the full-size grid the lines that appear on the scale drawing.

Half-Patterns: The center line on a half-pattern is clearly marked. To make a complete full-size pattern, turn the half-pattern right side down and trace the outlines onto another sheet of paper. Cut out the traced half-pattern and tape it to the original one, carefully matching the center lines. Or, use the half-pattern as is by placing it on the wood stock and tracing the outlines; then turn it right side down, matching the center line to the traced center line on the wood, and draw the mirror-image half by tracing the outlines again.

Circular Patterns: There are at least two easy methods of drawing circles:

Method 1 – Drive a brad halfway into the stock. Tie a string to the brad. Measure along the string a distance equal to the radius of the circle. Tie a pencil to the string at the measured distance. Rotate the pencil around the brad as you draw the circle, keeping the string taut and the pencil straight.

Method 2 – Drill a tiny hole through a length of lath or a yardstick, close to one end. Measure along the yardstick from the hole a distance equal to the radius and drill a second small hole. Drive a brad through the first hole into the stock. Insert a pencil point through the second hole and rotate the yardstick around the brad as you draw the circle.

Identical Parts: Use the pattern, cutting diagram or specified dimensions as a guide to cut only the first one. Then use the resulting wooden part as a guide to cut all of the others. This is especially helpful when you must drill holes that require perfect alignment between the identical parts.

Latticework Corner Pantry

This terrific corner pantry has lots of storage capacity yet takes up very little floor space. It is sturdy enough to last for ages, but the latticework door panels give it a light and airy look. It measures 40 inches across the front, 22 inches deep and 75 inches tall.

Materials

Pine 2 x 4: four 6-foot lengths
Pine 2 x 2: two 8-foot lengths
Pine 1 x 8: 120 linear feet
½-inch wooden dowel rod: one 3-foot length
Eight ornamental hinges, about 2½ inches long with ½-inch-wide flanges
Four wooden door knobs, about 1 inch in diameter
Flathead wood screws in 1¼-, 1½- and 2½-inch lengths
⅝-inch-long wire brads
Carpenter's wood glue; and paint in your choice of colors or other finishing materials

The corner pantry is easy to build, based on frame-and-panel construction. It is built as two separate cabinets, which share a dividing shelf. There are two shelves in the upper cabinet and one in the lower. The main frame members are grooved lengths of 2 x 4 into which the wall panels fit. The doors frames are rabbeted to accommodate the latticework panels.

Figure A

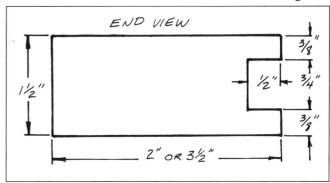

Figure B

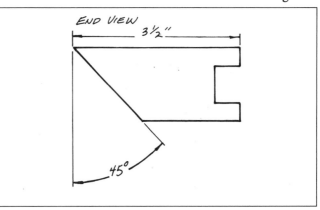

Figure C

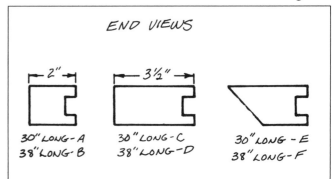

Cutting the Parts

1. The main frame members are cut from the four 6-foot 2 x 4s. Rip one 2 x 4 to 2 inches wide. All four 2 x 4s are now grooved to accommodate the wall panel boards, as shown in the end-view diagram, **Figure A**. Cut or rout a ¾ x ½-inch groove, centered along one long edge of each 2 x 4 (including the one that was ripped to 2 inches wide).

2. Cut from each of the grooved 2 x 4s one 30-inch length and one 38-inch length.

3. Four of the wider 2 x 4s from step 3 must now be ripped at a 45-degree angle along the edge opposite the groove, as shown in the end-view diagram, **Figure B**. Rip two of the 30-inch lengths and two of the 38-inch lengths as shown.

4. For reference during assembly, label each grooved frame member with the appropriate code letter, as shown in **Figure C**.

Figure D

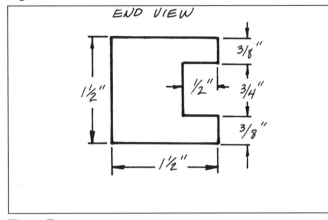

END VIEW

Figure E

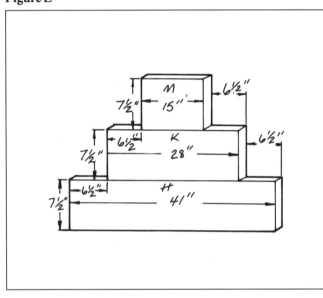

Figure F

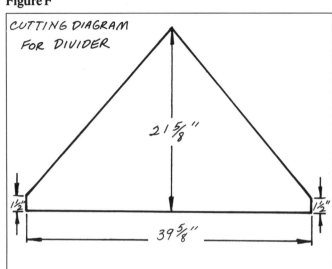

CUTTING DIAGRAM FOR DIVIDER

Figure G

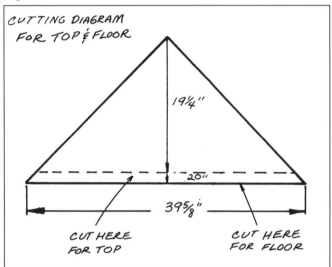

CUTTING DIAGRAM FOR TOP & FLOOR

CUT HERE FOR TOP

CUT HERE FOR FLOOR

Figure H

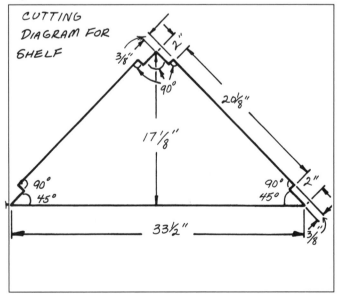

CUTTING DIAGRAM FOR SHELF

5. Cut from pine 2 x 2 eight 20⅛-inch lengths and label each one **G**. These will also be frame members. Cut or rout a ¾ x ½-inch groove, centered along one edge of each length, as shown in the end-view diagram, **Figure D**.

6. Cut from pine 1 x 8 the parts listed in this step and label each one with its code letter. All parts are the full ¾-inch thickness of the 1 x 8 stock.

Code	Dimensions	Quantity
H	7¼ x 41 inches	6
J	7¼ x 35¾ inches	6
K	7¼ x 28 inches	6
L	7¼ x 27¾ inches	6
M	7¼ x 15 inches	6
N	3½ x 39⅞ inches	4
P	3½ x 38⅛ inches	2
Q	2¼ x 35½ inches	4
R	3½ x 30⅛ inches	2
S	2¼ x 27½ inches	4
T	2¼ x 17 inches	8
U	2¼ x 6 inches	2
V	⅞ x 20 inches	6

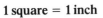

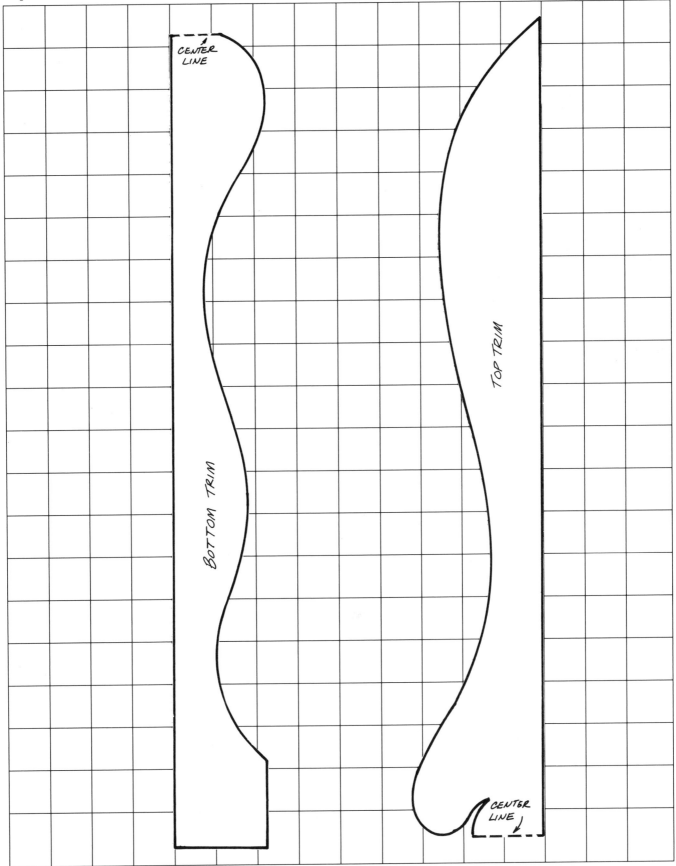

CENTER
LINE

TOP TRIM

BOTTOM TRIM

CENTER
LINE

LATTICEWORK CORNER PANTRY

Figure J

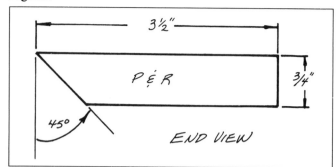

3½″

P & R

¾″

45°

END VIEW

Figure K

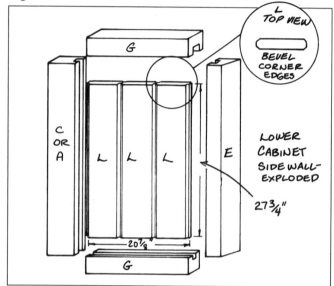

L TOP VIEW

BEVEL CORNER EDGES

G

C OR A

L L L

E

LOWER CABINET SIDE WALL-EXPLODED

27¾″

20⅞″

G

Figure L

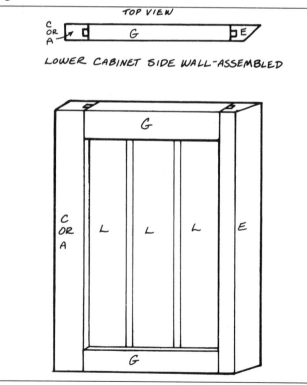

TOP VIEW

C OR A

G

E

LOWER CABINET SIDE WALL-ASSEMBLED

G

C OR A

L L L

E

G

7. The pantry contains six triangular parts: the three shelves, the floor, the top and the divider between the upper and lower cabinets. These parts are cut from splined lengths of 1 x 8, which you cut in step 6. Align one H, one K and one M board, as shown in **Figure E**. Spline them together edge-to-edge, as shown (see Tips & Techniques), and clamp while the glue dries. Spline together five more identical assemblies, using the remaining H, K and M boards.

8. Cutting diagrams for the divider, top, floor and shelves are provided in **Figures F, G and H**. We suggest that you make a full-size pattern for each one, as the stability and correctness of the structure depends on these parts being right. Cut from the step 7 splined assemblies one divider, one top, one floor and three shelves. Label each with its name.

9. Scale drawings for the top and bottom trim are provided in **Figure I**. Enlarge them to full size (see Tips & Techniques). Use the top trim pattern as a guide to contour one N board from step 6. Use the bottom trim pattern as a guide to contour another N board.

10. The P and R boards are ripped at a 45-degree angle along one long edge, as shown in **Figure J**.

11. Cut from the remaining pine 1 x 8 five 20-inch lengths. Rip all five boards into ⅛-inch-wide strips, for the latticework door panels (each strip should measure ⅛ x ¾ x 20 inches). You should be able to get twenty-nine strips from each board.

Lower Cabinet Assembly

1. There are two side walls in the lower cabinet and two in the upper. The six L boards form the walls of the lower cabinet. Place three L's edge-to-edge and measure the total width. Rip one or more of them to reduce the width so that the total measurement across the three boards is 20⅞ inches (**Figure K**). We used a hand plane to bevel the four corner edges along the entire length of each board, as shown in the top-view detail diagram, **Figure K**. The bevels should be very shallow – you don't want to remove too much material, or there will be large gaps between the boards. Repeat this step to prepare the three remaining L boards for the second side wall.

2. For one side-wall frame you will need one C, two G's and one E, as shown in **Figures K and L**. Assemble the frame members around the three wall boards, as shown. We did not glue the wall boards together, but we did glue them into the top G frame. The frame members should be glued together and clamped while the glue dries. We secured each corner with two long screws inserted through the vertical frame member into the horizontal one. When inserting the screws into the E frame be sure to drill a recess for the screw head, because it should not extend beyond the beveled edge of the E frame. Assemble the second side wall in the same manner, using one A, two G's and one E for the frame; and the three remaining L wall boards.

3. Place the two side walls on the triangular floor, as shown in **Figure M**. Note that A and C are butted together, flush with the back corner of the floor. The frames are flush with the side edges of the floor. Glue A and C together and glue the frames to the floor. Insert screws through C into A and through the floor into the frames.

4. Place one shelf inside the walls (**Figure N**). The spacing is up to you – we placed it about 15 inches above the floor. The

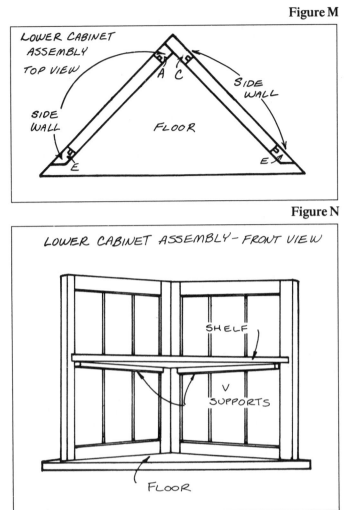

Figure M

LOWER CABINET ASSEMBLY TOP VIEW

SIDE WALL

SIDE WALL

A C

E E

FLOOR

Figure N

LOWER CABINET ASSEMBLY - FRONT VIEW

SHELF

V SUPPORTS

FLOOR

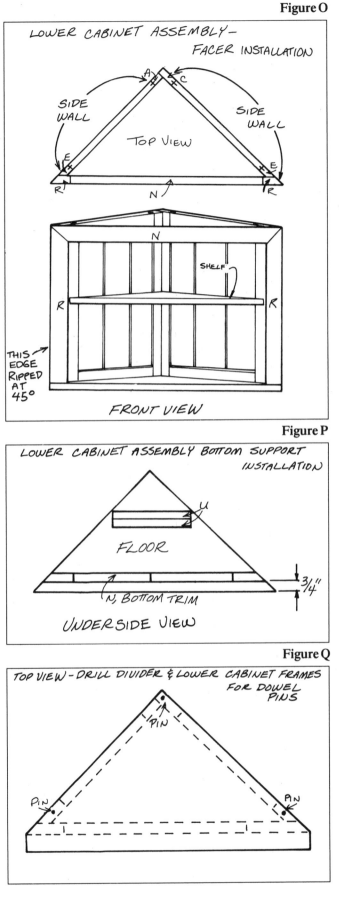

Figure O

LOWER CABINET ASSEMBLY - FACER INSTALLATION

SIDE WALL

SIDE WALL

A C

TOP VIEW

E E

R' R

N

N

SHELF

R R

THIS EDGE RIPPED AT 45°

FRONT VIEW

Figure P

LOWER CABINET ASSEMBLY BOTTOM SUPPORT INSTALLATION

U

FLOOR

N, BOTTOM TRIM

3/4"

UNDERSIDE VIEW

Figure Q

TOP VIEW - DRILL DIVIDER & LOWER CABINET FRAMES FOR DOWEL PINS

PIN

PIN

PIN

notched corners of the shelf should fit around the side-wall frames. Check to be sure it is level and mark the position of the bottom surface on each side wall. Remove the shelf. The V strips serve as the shelf supports. Attach a V support to each side wall between the front and back frame members, aligning the top of the support with the shelf placement line. Insert three screws through each support into the wall boards. We did not countersink or plug the screws but you may wish to. Place the shelf on top.

5. The facers that form the opening for the doors are shown in **Figure O**. Use an N board for the top horizontal facer and a beveled R board for each vertical facer. Flat miter both ends of the top facer and one end of each vertical facer at a 45-degree angle so they will fit together as shown. Before you cut the miters, check the measurements against the partially assembled cabinet – the top edge of the N facer should be flush with the tops of the side-wall frames. Note that each R facer is turned with its beveled long edge facing outward, flush with the corner of the floor. The R facers rest on the floor, flush with the front edge, and butt against the front edge of the shelf. Glue the facers in place and secure with screws.

6. The contoured N bottom trim and the two U boards support the lower cabinet (**Figure P**). Edge miter both ends of the bot-

Figure R

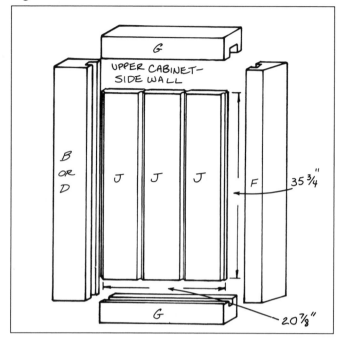

Labels in figure: G, UPPER CABINET—SIDE WALL, B OR D, J, J, J, F, 35¾", G, 20⅞"

tom trim at a 45-degree angle toward the same side of the board (don't confuse it with the similar **N** top trim). Glue together the two **U** boards to form a single piece 1½ x 2¼ x 6 inches. Placement of the trim and **U** support on the underside of the lower cabinet floor is shown in **Figure P**. Note that the trim is ¾ inch from the front edge. It is turned so the mitered ends match the floor edges. Attach the **U** support as close to the back corner as possible, but it should not extend beyond the floor. Secure each support with glue and screws.

Upper Cabinet Assembly

1. Place the divider on top of the lower cabinet, flush at the back corner and along the side walls. It will extend out beyond the facers at the front (**Figure Q**). Do not use glue, but clamp the divider to the lower cabinet temporarily. Use a ½-inch bit to drill down through the divider into the 2 x 4 frame member at each corner, as shown in **Figure Q**, to accommodate a dowel pin. Drill to a depth of about 1½ inches.

2. Cut three 3-inch lengths of ½-inch dowel for the pins. Chamfer and groove them, as described in Tips & Techniques. Insert a pin into each socket (do not use glue) and trim the tops flush with the top surface of the divider. Remove the divider from the lower cabinet and glue the pins into the sockets in the frame members. The upper cabinet is assembled separately, with the divider as the floor, and it is then reattached to the lower cabinet via the dowel pins.

3. The upper cabinet is assembled in the same manner as the lower cabinet. For each side wall (**Figure R**), trim and bevel three **J** wall boards. Use one **B**, one **F** and two **G** frames for one upper-cabinet side wall; and one **D**, one **F** and two **G**'s for the second one.

4. Attach the two assembled side walls to the divider, flush

at the back corner and along the side edges, as you did for the lower cabinet. (Refer to **Figure M** – where **A** and **C** butt together in the lower cabinet you will have **B** and **D** butting together in the upper cabinet. The front **F** frames of the upper cabinet correspond to the **E**'s shown for the lower cabinet and should be turned the same way in relation to their beveled edges.)

5. Install the two remaining shelves between the walls of the upper cabinet, spacing them as you like. We placed one about 13 inches above the divider and the second one about the same distance above. Use two **V** supports to secure each shelf, as for the lower cabinet.

6. For the front, use the remaining **N** board as the horizontal top facer and the two beveled **P** boards as the vertical facers (**Figure S**), as you did for the lower cabinet. Again, you will have to measure the partially assembled upper cabinet before flat mitering the facers to fit together at the upper corners – the top edge of the horizontal facer should be flush with the tops of the side-wall frames. Remember that each **P** facer should be turned with the beveled edge facing outward, flush with the side edge of the divider.

7. The contoured **N** top trim and the triangular top complete the basic upper cabinet assembly (**Figure S**). Glue the top trim in place along the upper edge of the horizontal facer, flush at the front and ends. Place the triangular top over the wall frames, flush at the back corner and along the sides. It should butt against the back of the contoured trim. Glue it in place and secure with screws. Secure the trim to the front edge of the top, using a few countersunk screws.

8. To join the upper and lower cabinets, first spread glue on the dowel pins that are glued into the lower cabinet. Hoist the upper cabinet and lower it carefully, guiding the tops of the dowel pins into the holes in the divider.

Door Assembly

1. The **Q**, **S** and **T** boards will serve as the door frames for the upper and lower cabinets. First, cut or rout a ½ x ½-inch rabbet along one long edge of each one, as shown in **Figure T**. (There are four **Q**'s, four **S**'s and eight **T**'s – rabbet all of them.)

2. Two **Q**'s and two **T**'s form the frame for each upper cabinet door, as shown in **Figure U**. Measure and flat miter both ends of each one at a 45-degree angle; overall dimensions of the frame should be 16¼ x 34⅜ inches, as shown. **Note** that all four members should be turned with the rabbets facing center, on the same side of the frame. Do not glue the corners just yet. Measure and miter the **Q**'s and **T**'s for the second upper cabinet door in the same manner.

3. Two **S**'s and two **T**'s form the frame for each lower cabinet door, as shown in **Figure U**. Measure and flat miter the **S**'s and remaining **T**'s so that the overall dimensions of each frame are 16¼ x 26⅜ inches, as shown. Do not glue the corners yet.

4. The corner joints of each door frame are splined for greater strength. To accommodate the splines, cut or rout a stopped dado, centered along both ends of each **Q**, **S** and **T** frame, as shown in **Figure V**. Note that the dado is stopped ¼ inch short of the outer corner. Each dado should be ¼ inch wide by ⅜ inch deep, as shown.

5. Rip and cut from leftover pine stock sixteen splines, each ¼ x ¹¹⁄₁₆ x 2⅛ inches.

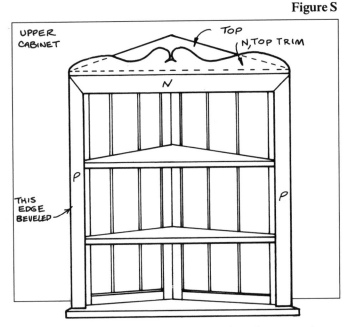

UPPER CABINET

TOP

N, TOP TRIM

N

P

P

THIS EDGE BEVELED

Figure V

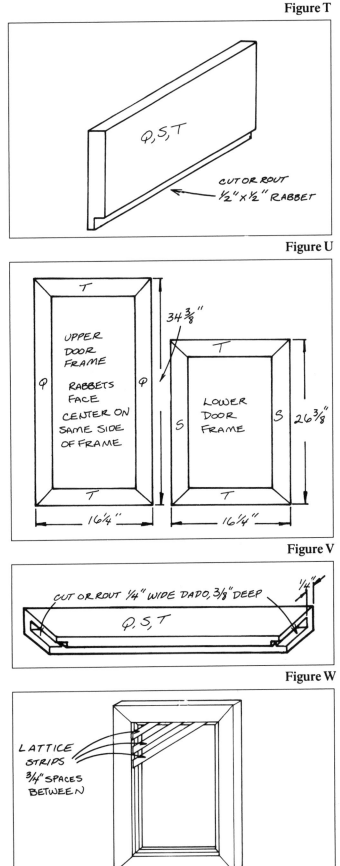

Q,S,T

CUT OR ROUT ½" X ½" RABBET

UPPER DOOR FRAME

RABBETS FACE CENTER ON SAME SIDE OF FRAME

T

Q   Q

T

16¼"

34⅜"

LOWER DOOR FRAME

T

S   S

T

16¼"

26⅜"

CUT OR ROUT ¼" WIDE DADO, ⅜" DEEP

Q,S,T

¼"

LATTICE STRIPS ¾" SPACES BETWEEN

6. Glue together two upper-cabinet door frames and two lower-cabinet door frames, as shown in **Figure U**, glueing a spline into each corner joint. The splines should be butted against the stopped ends of the dadoes; they should not extend into the rabbets at the center-facing edges of the frame. Be sure that each frame member is turned correctly, with the rabbets on the same side. Clamp while the glue dries.

7. To assemble the latticework panel, place one upper-cabinet door frame rabbeted side up on a flat work surface. Gather the lattice strips that you ripped and cut earlier. Trim one strip and miter both ends at a 45-degree angle so that it will fit into the door frame near the upper left-hand corner, as shown in **Figure W**. The ends of the strip should rest in the rabbets, butting against the edges. Glue the ends into the rabbets. Continue to trim, miter and glue lattice strips into the frame in this manner, allowing a ¾-inch space between each two strips, as shown. (An easy way to achieve even spacing is to use a spare lattice strip as a spacer.) Work all the way down to the lower right-hand corner. Now begin at the upper right-hand corner and add a second layer of strips, perpendicular to the strips of the first layer. Work all the way down to the lower left-hand corner.

8. To secure the panel, rip and cut from leftover pine stock two ¼ x ½ x 30⅞-inch strips and two ¼ x ½ x 11¾-inch strips. Glue them to the latticework along the edges and ends, butted against the edges of the door-frame rabbets. Secure the strips with wire brads.

9. Repeat steps 7 and 8 to assemble a latticework panel inside the second upper-cabinet door frame. Repeat step 7 to assemble a latticework panel inside each lower-cabinet door frame. For these doors, cut the step 8 strips ¼ x ½ x 21⅞ inches and ¼ x ½ x 11¾ inches.

10. Use two hinges to attach each door to the adjacent vertical facer on the front of the pantry. We did not use cabinet catches inside, as the doors fit together tightly enough to stay closed. You may prefer to use catches. Drill through the center vertical frame member of each door and install a knob.

11. Paint or stain the pantry as you like.

LATTICEWORK CORNER PANTRY

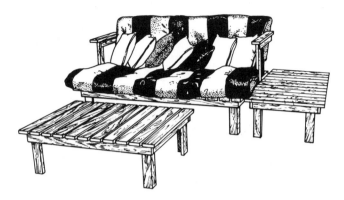

Convertible Couch & Tables

This contemporary couch and cocktail tables set makes a very comfortable bed! The futon-style cushion serves both the couch and bed arrangement.

Materials

Note: The amounts listed here are for a couch and two tables that make up into a queen-size bed, 60 x 80 inches. Please refer to the instructions if you want to make a different size.

For the couch and two tables:

Pine 1 x 4: eleven 10-foot lengths
Pine 1 x 6: one 6-foot length, two 8-foot lengths and three 10-foot lengths
1¼-inch-long flathead wood screws

For the futon cushion:

If you want to make a solid-color cushion, you'll need 7½ yards of 60-inch-wide fabric. If you want to make a two-color striped cushion, you'll need 7 yards of 44-inch-wide fabric in each of two colors.

Thread to match the fabric
To stuff the cushion, you'll need eight or ten layers of quilt batting, each 60 x 120 inches. Batting comes in packages or by the yard, so make your choice according to what will give you the best buy.

This attractive slat-style suite consists of a couch and two cocktail tables. It makes a wonderful addition to a living room or den. With the two tables placed against the front of the couch and the futon cushion unfolded, it makes a queen-size bed. Overall dimensions of the queen-size couch are 64 x 31 x 40 inches. One cocktail table measures 49 x 30 x 13 inches.

Cutting the Parts

1. Cut from pine 1 x 6 the parts listed in this step and label them with their code letters, for reference during assembly. A cutting layout is provided in **Figure A**, showing how we used the lengths of 1 x 6 specified in the materials list. All parts are the full ¾-inch thickness of the stock. Quantities are for one couch and two tables, which will make up a queen-size bed. For a different size, please refer to step 3 of the cutting instructions.

Code	Dimensions	Quantity
A	2½ x 55½ inches	2
B	2½ x 57 inches	2
C	2½ x 35½ inches	2
D	2½ x 12 inches	12
E	2½ x 9½ inches	1
F	1¾ x 12 inches	10
G	1¾ x 30 inches	2
H	2½ x 30 inches	2
J	2 x 54 inches	1
K	2½ x 59¾ inches	1
L	2½ x 5⅝ inches	2
M	2½ x 18⅛ inches	2
N	2½ x 16¼ inches	2
P	2½ x 37 inches	4
Q	2½ x 25½ inches	4
R	5 x 40 inches	1

2. Cut from pine 1 x 4 the lengths listed in this step and label with their code letters. All parts are the full thickness and width of the stock – ¾ x 3½ inches. We cut three T's from each of five 10-foot 1 x 4s; four U's from each of five 10-foot 1 x 4s; and the two S's and the remaining two U's from the remaining 10-foot 1 x 4.

Code	Length	Quantity
S	23 inches	2
T	40 inches	15
U	30 inches	22

3. If you wish to make the sofa-bed wider or narrower than queen size (60 inches wide), please refer to the assembly diagrams and make notes on how much longer or shorter you will need to cut the A's, B's, J and K for the couch; and the Q's and U's for the tables. You will also have to cut more or fewer T slats for the couch, but the length will remain the same.

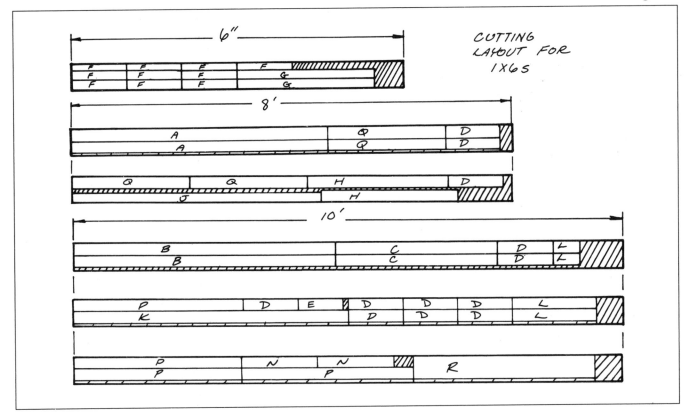

CUTTING LAYOUT FOR 1X6S

Couch Assembly

All joints should be glued and secured with countersunk screws. The screw heads that will show on the finished assembly should be covered with plugs.

1. The basic support frame for the couch is shown in **Figure B**. Glue together the B's and C's, as shown, with the B's covering the ends of the C's. Insert the A brace, centered between the two B's. Secure all joints.

2. There are three different types of leg assemblies, as shown in **Figure C**. Assemble a single center leg by sandwiching an E between two D's, flush at the lower ends, as shown in diagram 1. Secure with a few screws from each side. Assemble one front leg by attaching a D to one long edge of an F, flush at top and bottom and the resulting wide side, as shown in diagram 2. Assemble another identical front leg. The two back legs are longer versions of the front legs, as shown in diagram 3. Assemble two back legs, using a G and an H for each one.

3. The legs are attached to the support frame, as shown in **Figure D**. First, fit a front leg into each front corner of the frame, flush at the top and with the D member of the leg against the long B member of the frame. Glue and secure with screws. Fit the uneven upper end of the center leg around the A frame member, as shown, centered between the ends. Secure with glue and screws. Finally, fit a back leg into each back corner of the frame, with the H member of the leg against the long B frame member. Before you secure the back legs, make sure they extend below the frame about 12 inches; adjust them so that the couch sits evenly and does not rock.

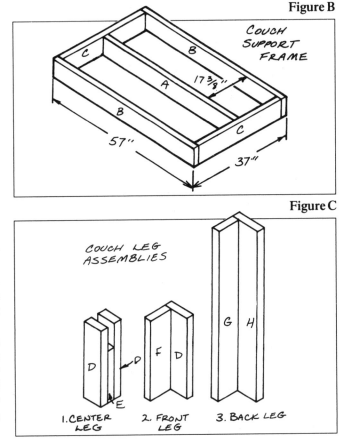

Figure B

COUCH SUPPORT FRAME

17 3/8″

57″

37″

Figure C

COUCH LEG ASSEMBLIES

1. CENTER LEG   2. FRONT LEG   3. BACK LEG

Figure D

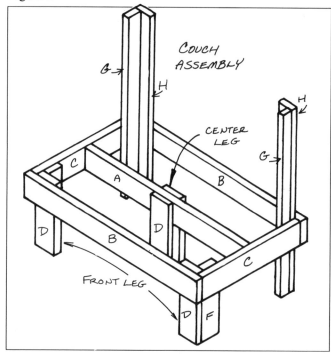

COUCH ASSEMBLY

G
H
H
CENTER LEG
G
C
A
B
D
D
B
C
FRONT LEG
D F

Figure F

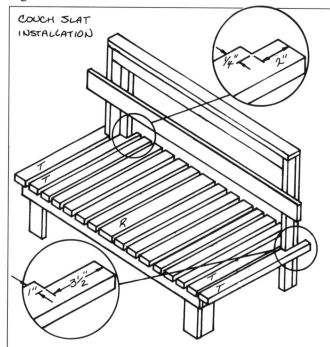

COUCH SLAT INSTALLATION

¼" 2"

T
T
R
1" 3½"
T
T

Figure E

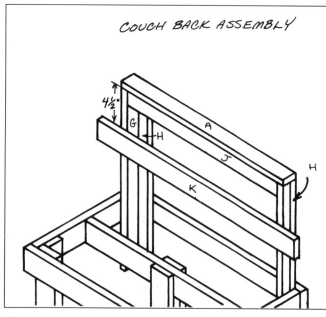

COUCH BACK ASSEMBLY

4½"
G
H
A
J
K
H

Figure G

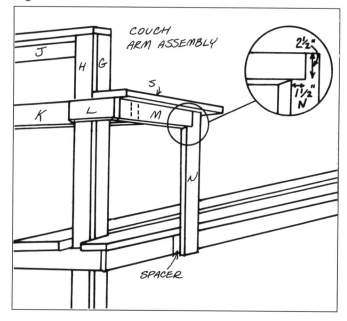

COUCH ARM ASSEMBLY

J
H G
2½"
S
1½"
K L M
N
N
SPACER

4. The tops of the back legs are stabilized, as shown in **Figure E**, using the J, K and remaining A parts. **Note:** Use temporary holding nails only (no glue) to attach the K brace flat against the front edges of the two legs, 4¼ inches below the tops, as shown. (When you have completed step 6, you can remove the nails and secure the brace with glue and screws.) The A and J braces can be permanently attached at this time, as shown. Note that the J support is inserted between the G members of the two legs, flush with the tops of the legs. The A top piece sits flat on top of the legs, flush at both ends and along the front edge.

5. The fifteen T slats and the single wider R slat are attached to the top of the frame (**Figure F**), with ⅜ inch between slats. Note that four of the T slats must be notched to fit around the back legs, as shown in the detail diagrams. Use the wider R slat near the center. **Note:** The back ends of all slats should be flush with the back frame member; they will extend 2¾ inches beyond the front. The two outside slats should extend 1½ inches beyond the end frame members. Secure each slat with a screw inserted into the back frame member, another into the front and another into the center.

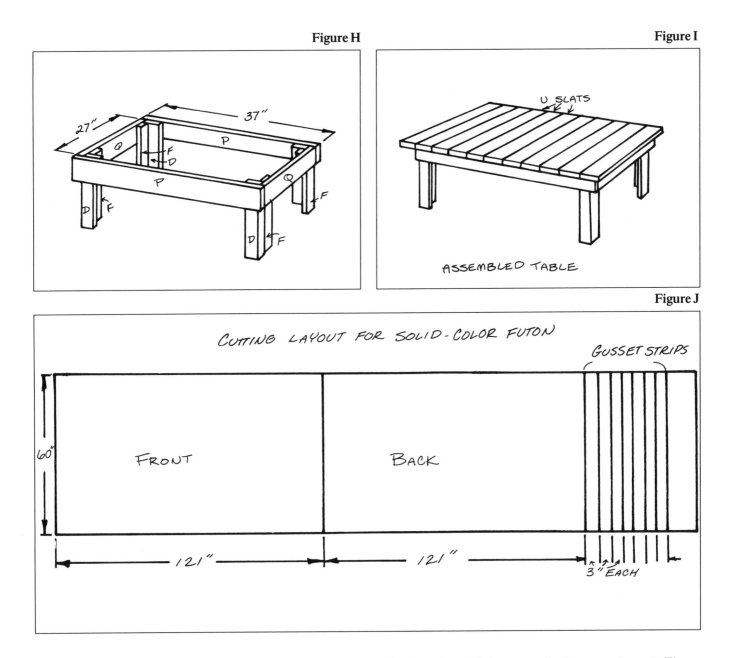

Figure H — 27", 37", Q, P, F, D

Figure I — U SLATS / ASSEMBLED TABLE

Figure J — CUTTING LAYOUT FOR SOLID-COLOR FUTON / GUSSET STRIPS / 60" / FRONT / BACK / 121" / 121" / 3" EACH

6. The arm assembly is shown in **Figure G**. First, notch the two **N** front posts (1½ x 2½-inch notch), as shown. Assemble the parts for each arm – you will have to cut from leftover pine a spacer block to fit between each **N** front post and the adjacent end member of the couch support frame. Ours were ¾ x 2½ x 1½ inches. It may be necessary to adjust the placement of the **K** brace so that it fits just under the armrests, as shown. Permanently attach the **K** brace at this time.

Table Assembly

1. The basic support frame, with legs attached, is shown in **Figure H**. Attach the **P**'s over the ends of the shorter **Q**'s.

2. Assemble four identical legs, using an **F** and a **D** member for each one, exactly as you did the front legs for the couch (see **Figure C**, diagram 2). Install the legs in the inside corners of the table frame, flush at the top, as shown in **Figure H**.

3. Place eleven **U** slats across the frame, as shown in **Figure I**, with a space of about ½ inch between slats. Both ends of each slat should extend 1½ inches beyond each long **P** frame member. The two outside slats should extend about 1½ inches beyond the **Q** end frame members. Secure each slat with glue and screws.

4. Assemble a second, identical table.

5. Place the two tables side by side and end-on against the front of the couch. This is the arrangement when the suite is being used as a bed. To keep the three pieces from working their way apart, use two or three clamps.

Making the Futon

Notes: All seams are ½ inch wide unless otherwise specified. If you are making a solid-color futon, follow the instructions in steps 1 and 2; then skip to step 5. If you are making a striped

Figure K

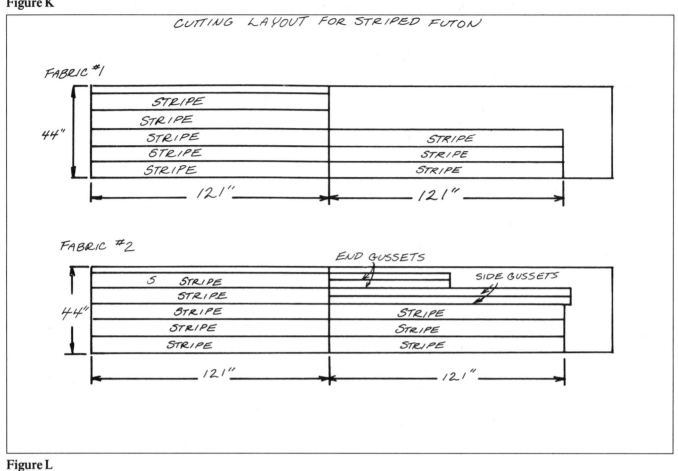

CUTTING LAYOUT FOR STRIPED FUTON

FABRIC #1

44"

| STRIPE |
| STRIPE |
STRIPE	STRIPE
STRIPE	STRIPE
STRIPE	STRIPE

|← 121" →|← 121" →|

FABRIC #2

END GUSSETS

SIDE GUSSETS

44"

| S STRIPE |
| STRIPE |
STRIPE	STRIPE
STRIPE	STRIPE
STRIPE	STRIPE

|← 121" →|← 121" →|

Figure L

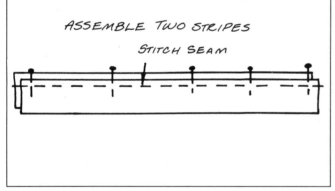

ASSEMBLE TWO STRIPES

STITCH SEAM

Figure M

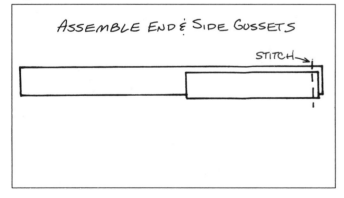

ASSEMBLE END & SIDE GUSSETS

STITCH

futon, skip steps 1 and 2 and follow all of the remaining instructions. If you wish to make a different size, alter the width by the same amount as you did the couch and tables.

1. For a solid-color queen-size futon, cut the fabric pieces listed in this step. Refer to the cutting layout. **Figure J.**

   Front/Back — 60 x 121 inches, cut two
   Gusset Section — 3 x 60 inches, cut seven

2. Place two gusset sections right sides together and stitch the seam across one end. Press open. Repeat to stitch together all of the sections to make one tremendously long strip. Cut from the long strip two 122-inch lengths and label them side gussets. Cut two 61-inch lengths and label them end gussets.

3. For a striped futon, cut the fabric pieces listed in this step, referring to the cutting layout provided in **Figure K.**

Fabric #1:
   Stripe — 8½ x 121 inches, cut eight
Fabric #2:
   Stripe — 8½ x 121 inches, cut eight
   Side Gusset — 3 x 122 inches, cut two
   End Gusset — 3 x 62 inches, cut two

4. To assemble the front of the striped futon, first sew together a stripe of each color in the following manner: Place the two stripes right sides together, even along both ends and both edges. Pin them together along one long edge only. Stitch the seam along the pinned edge (**Figure L**). Press the seam open.

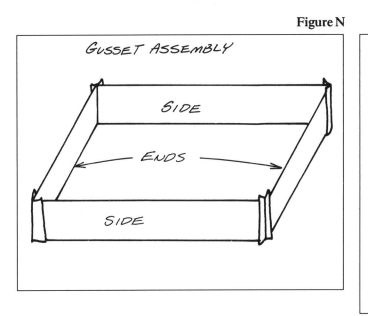

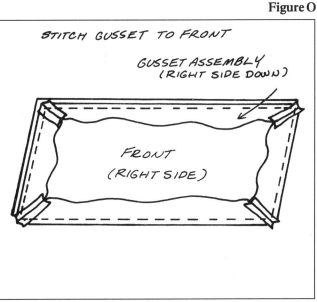

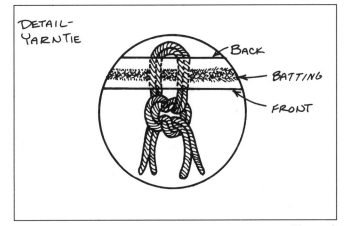

Follow the same procedures to add six more stripes to the assembly, alternating colors. When you have sewn together eight stripes, the futon front is complete. Repeat these procedures to assemble an identical futon back, using the remaining four stripes of each color.

5. Cut eight or ten layers of quilt batting, 59 x 120 inches (for a solid futon) or 60 x 120 inches (for a striped futon).

6. The gusset assembly consists of the two end gussets and the two side gussets sewn together end-to-end, as shown in **Figure N**. Place an end gusset and a side gusset right sides together, even at one end, and stitch the seam along the aligned ends, as shown in **Figure M**. Press the seam open. Sew the second end gusset to the free end of the attached side gusset in the same manner. Sew the second side gusset to the free end of one end gusset in the same manner. Finally, sew together the free ends of the assembly, placing right sides together and making sure the fabric is not twisted. Press all seams open.

7. The gusset assembly is now sewn to the futon front. Place the front right side up on a flat surface. Turn the gusset assembly so that the right sides of the pieces face center. Place it on top of the futon front, as shown in **Figure O**. Pin and then baste the layers together along each edge. Stitch the seam along each edge and remove the basting threads.

8. Stitch the futon back to the free edges of the gusset assembly in the same manner, leaving one end open. Clip the corners and turn the futon right side out. Press the seam allowances to the inside along the open end.

9. Arrange the layers of quilt batting into an even stack and tack them together at the center and near each corner. Insert the stack into the futon through the open end, working it into the corners. Whipstitch or blindstitch the opening edges together.

10. Make yarn ties to keep the batting in place inside the futon, as shown in **Figure P.**

11. To use the futon as a couch cushion (**Figure Q**), place one end on the couch, pushed all the way to the back. Fold the futon at the front of the couch slats; then fold it upward at the back. Lap the top of the futon over the back of the couch frame, as shown. Because of the depth of the couch seat, we suggest that you use additional throw pillows along the back.

Couch & Chairs

You'll love how easy and inexpensive it is to build this couch and chairs. And you can vary the design of the side panels to make completely unique furnishings!

Materials

For the couch:
Pine 2 x 4: five 6-foot lengths and one 10-foot length
Pine 2 x 2: one 6-foot length
Pine 1 x 2: four 10-foot lengths and eight 6-foot lengths
10 square feet of standard 1-by pine, in whatever width is on sale or readily available (We used one 8-foot length and one 10-foot length of 1 x 8.)

Figure A

Cushions: The most inexpensive solution is to use two standard patio lounge cushions. If you can't find cushions you like, purchase enough fabric to cover them or purchase the materials to make the cushions from scratch. To cover two standard lounge cushions you'll need 4½ yards of 60-inch-wide fabric. To make the cushions from scratch you'll need the same amount of fabric plus the following: forty upholstery buttons (optional), 24 yards of piping (optional), two packages of quilt batting and thread to match the fabric.

For one chair:
Pine 2 x 4: two 10-foot lengths and one 8-foot length
Pine 1 x 2: one 8-foot length and three 6-foot lengths
8 square feet of standard 1-by pine, in whatever width is on sale or readily available (We used one 8-foot length and one 6-foot length of 1 x 8.)
Cushion: The most inexpensive solution is to use one standard patio chair cushion (about 24 x 46 x 3 inches). If you can't find a cushion you like, purchase fabric to cover one or purchase the materials to make the cushion from scratch. To cover one standard chair cushion you'll need 1½ yards of 60-inch-wide fabric. To make the cushion from scratch you'll need the same amount of fabric plus the following: eight upholstery buttons (optional), 8 yards of piping (optional), one package of quilt batting and thread to match the fabric.

Miscellaneous:
3d finishing nails
Flathead wood screws in 1-, 1½- and 2-inch lengths
Carpenter's wood glue; Danish oil or other finishing materials

THE COUCH

Overall dimensions of the couch are 6 feet long by 37 inches tall by 31 inches deep. If you want to alter the size, please read through the section on cutting the parts and refer to the assembly diagrams (**Figures I** through **K**). Make notes on how much longer or shorter you will have to cut the following parts: The A's, B's and H's determine depth; the E's and F determine length; the C's, D's and G's determine height.

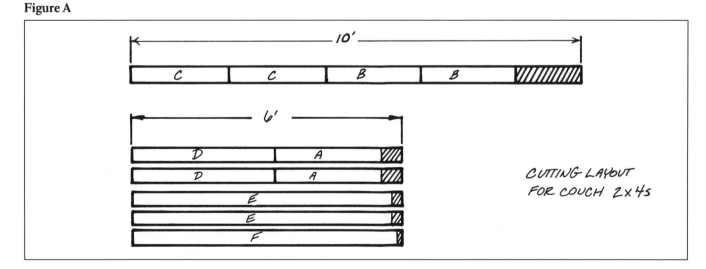

CUTTING LAYOUT FOR COUCH 2x4s

Cutting the Parts

1. Cut from pine 2 x 4 the parts listed in this step and label each one with its code letter. All parts are the full thickness and width of the stock – 1½ x 3½ inches. A cutting layout is provided in **Figure A**, showing how we used the lengths of 2 x 4 specified in the materials list.

Code	Length	Quantity	Description
A	29⅛ inches	2	Top Rail
B	25⅜ inches	2	Bottom Rail
C	26 inches	2	Front Leg
D	38 inches	2	Back Leg
E	70 inches	2	Lower Span
F	73 inches	1	Upper Span

2. Modify one **A** top rail, as shown in the side- and bottom-view diagrams, **Figure B**. First, flat miter one end at a 10-degree angle. Cut a half lap at each end, making both cuts on the same side of the board. Follow the 10-degree miter when you cut the half lap at that end. Now refer to the bottom-view diagram. Cut or rout a dado along the center of the lower edge, ¾ inch wide by ½ inch deep, as shown. This dado will accommodate the upper ends of the boards that form the panel (see **Figure I**). Modify the second **A** top rail in the same manner, but make it a mirror image of the first one (see **Figure J**).

3. The **B** bottom rails are modified in the same manner as the top rails. The dado is cut into the upper edge, 19 inches long, to accommodate the lower ends of the boards that form the panel (see **Figure I**). Repeat step 2 to miter each **B** rail, cut the half laps and cut or rout the dado. Take care that you cut the dado into the correct edge and that you make the two bottom rails mirror images of each other.

4. The **C** front legs are modified, as shown in **Figure C**. On what will be the outer side of the board, make a lap cut at the upper end and another 1 inch from the lower end. Each lap is ¾ inch deep and 3½ inches wide. On the opposite side of the board, cut or rout a dado 10½ inches from the lower end, as shown in the second diagram, **Figure C**. The dado should be ¾ inch deep and 1½ inches wide, as shown. Modify the other **C** front leg in the same manner.

5. The **D** back legs are modified, as shown in **Figure D**. First cut a 1½ x 3½-inch notch across the upper end, centered between the side edges. Measure 11½ inches from the upper end along one edge and mark this point. Draw guide lines and cut or rout an angled lap cut across the surface of the board, as shown. Note that it is ¾ inch deep by 3½ inches wide and is cut at an 80-degree angle to the edge. Measure 18½ inches from the lower edge of the lap cut and mark the position of the lower lap cut. Cut or rout the lower lap. This will be the outside surface of the board. Flat miter the lower end of the board at a 10-degree angle. Finally, round off the two upper corners – we used the radius of a 25-cent piece as a guide.

6. On the opposite surface of the **D** back leg, cut or rout an angled dado across the surface, 10½ inches from the lower end (measured along the shorter edge, as shown in the second diagram, **Figure D**). Be sure to angle this dado the correct way in relation to the laps on the opposite side. When you modify the second **D** back leg, make it a mirror image of the first one.

7. The two **E** lower spans are rabbeted along one long edge,

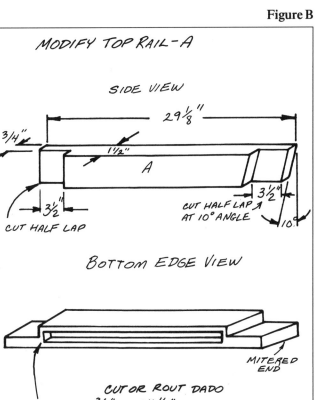

Figure C

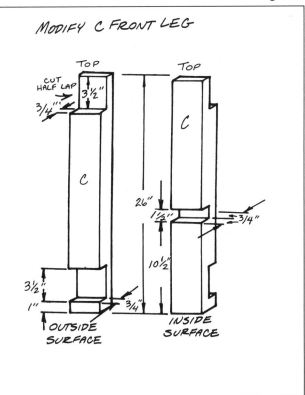

Figure D

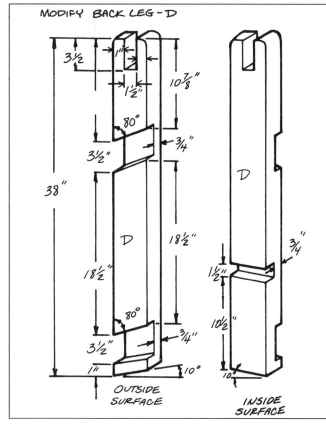

MODIFY BACK LEG-D

OUTSIDE SURFACE

INSIDE SURFACE

Figure E

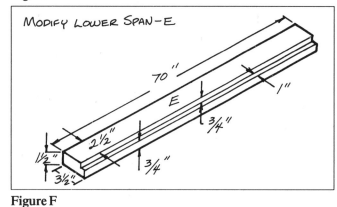

MODIFY LOWER SPAN-E

Figure F

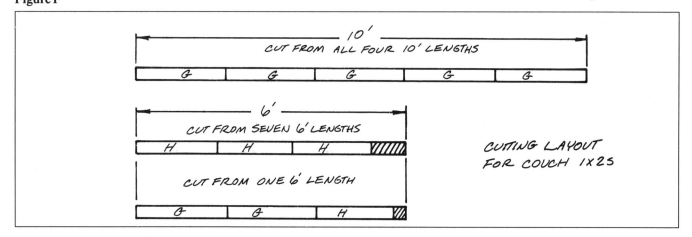

10'

CUT FROM ALL FOUR 10' LENGTHS

| G | G | G | G | G |

6'

CUT FROM SEVEN 6' LENGTHS

| H | H | H | |

CUT FROM ONE 6' LENGTH

| G | G | H | |

CUTTING LAYOUT FOR COUCH 1X2S

as shown in **Figure E**. Cut or rout a ¾ x 1-inch rabbet along each E Span, as shown. In addition, cut the same size rabbet along the F upper span.

8. Cut the lengths of pine 1 x 2 listed in this step. Label each part with its code letter. Each one is the full thickness and width of the stock – ¾ x 1½ inches. Refer to **Figure F** for our suggested cutting layout.

Code	Length	Quantity	Description
G	24 inches	22	Back Slat
H	21 inches	22	Seat Slat

9. Trim the 6-foot-long 2 x 2 to 68½ inches in length. Label it J lower support. The remaining parts will be cut later.

Assembly

The couch consists of two frame-and-panel sides (**Figure I**), which are connected by three long spans (**Figure J**). The design of the side panels is repeated across the front of the couch (**Figure K**). Back and seat slats support the cushions.

Note: You can make your couch very different and unique simply by altering the design of the panels in the side sections and along the front. Our panels are made of vertically aligned 1-by boards, which were beveled along the corner edges to resemble tongue-and-groove. You might prefer to align the boards diagonally, leave spaces between them, use latticework instead of 1-bys, use plywood with decorative cutouts or any number of other variations.

1. The panel for each side section consists of 1-by boards aligned edge-to-edge and contained within the 2 x 4 frame members (**Figure I**). A cutting diagram showing overall size of the panel for each side section is provided in **Figure G**. (You will have to revise it if you altered the couch size.) Cut as many 18⅞-inch lengths of 1-by lumber as you need to make up the 21½-inch width. (We used 1 x 8, so we cut three lengths.) To make a panel that resembles tongue-and-groove, we beveled all four long corner edges of each board, as shown in **Figure H**. Clamp the boards together edge-to-edge and even at both ends. Refer to the cutting diagram in **Figure G** and draw the outlines on the clamped boards. Trim the assembly to match the outlines. You need not glue the boards together, as the frame will hold them in place. Make a second side-section panel in the same manner.

2. An assembled side section is shown in **Figure I**. Match the

Figure I

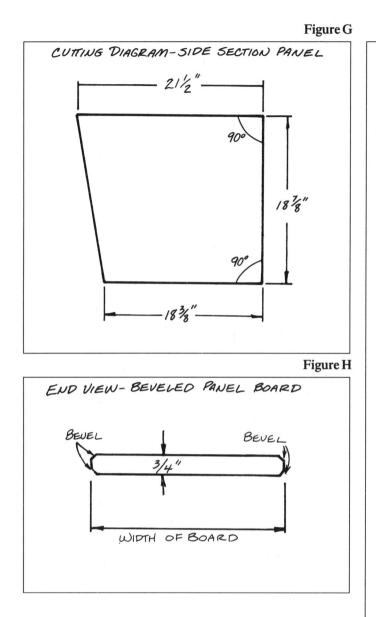

Figure H

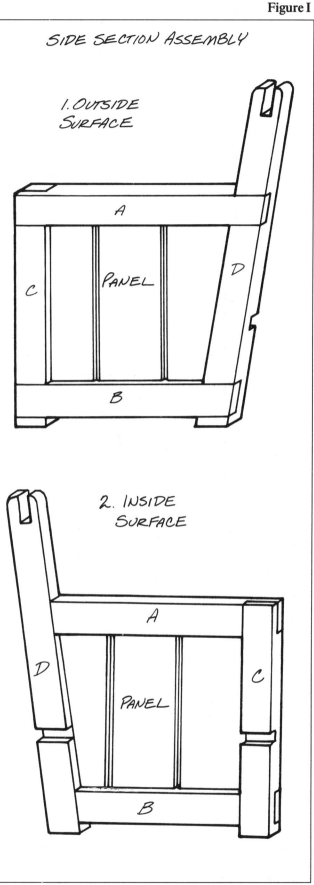

lap cuts in the 2 x 4 A, B, C and D rails and legs, assembling them around the panel, as shown. The upper and lower ends of the panel will fit into the dadoed edges of the A and B rails, but the side edges of the panel simply butt up against the inner edges of the C and D legs. Glue the frame joints and secure with screws inserted from the outer side of the assembly. Countersink the screws and cover the heads with plugs. Assemble a second side section, making it a mirror image of the first one.

3. The two side sections are joined by the E and F spans, as shown in **Figure J**. Note that the two E lower spans fit into the dadoes on the inside surfaces of the C front legs and D back legs. The lower spans are turned so that the rabbeted edge of each one is at the top, facing the center of the couch. The F upper span fits into the notches at the tops of the D back legs; its ends should be flush with the outer surfaces of the back legs. It should be turned so that the rabbeted edge is at the bottom, facing the center of the couch. Cut two small filler blocks to fit into the ends of this rabbet, where it shows on the outside surface of each back leg. Secure the lower spans by inserting

Figure J

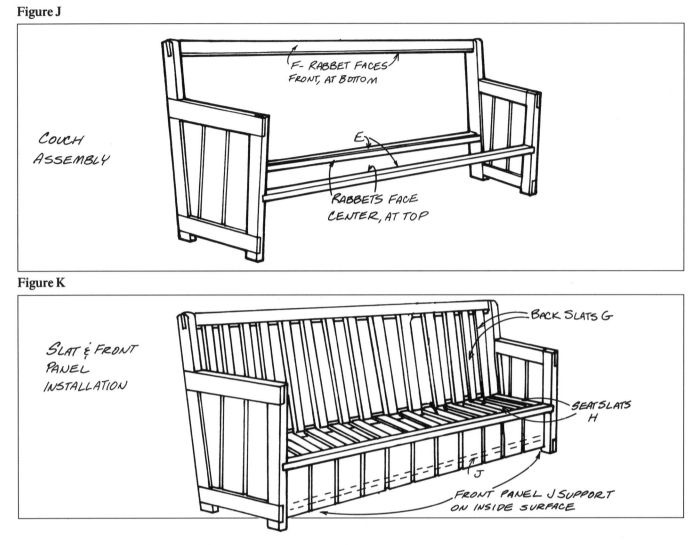

COUCH ASSEMBLY

F - RABBET FACES FRONT, AT BOTTOM

E

RABBETS FACE CENTER, AT TOP

Figure K

SLAT & FRONT PANEL INSTALLATION

BACK SLATS G

SEAT SLATS H

J

FRONT PANEL J SUPPORT ON INSIDE SURFACE

screws through the front and back legs into the ends of the spans. Secure the upper span by inserting screws through the back edge of each back leg. Countersink the screws and cover with plugs.

4. The front panel that runs along the bottom of the couch is similar to the side panels, consisting of 1-by boards joined edge-to-edge (**Figure K**). These boards should be cut 9⅜ inches long (unless you altered the height of the lower span). This will leave a gap of about 1¾ inches below the front panel. Cut from the 1-by stock as many boards as necessary to fit between the front legs. (On our couch, the overall width was 68½ inches. We used nine lengths of 1 x 8 plus one narrower length.) Again, we beveled the corner edges of each board, to duplicate the design of the side panels (see **Figure H**). Align the boards edge-to-edge, even at both ends, and glue the J lower support to them about ½ inch from one long edge. Secure with screws inserted through the support into the boards. Glue the assembled front panel between the front legs, butted against the underside of the front lower span (**Figure K**), with the support on the inside. The panel should be recessed about 1¼ inches behind the front edges of the front legs and span.

5. Glue the **G** back slats and **H** seat slats in place, fitting the ends into the rabbets in the spans, as shown in **Figure K**. Secure each end of each slat with a screw.

6. Sand and stain the couch frame. If you purchased patio lounge cushions, place one on the seat and the other against the back, on top of the seat cushion. If you are making cushions, please continue reading the next section.

Making the Cushions

Instructions are provided in this section for making the cushions from scratch. If you purchased cushions and wish to cover them with different fabric, follow the instructions in this section, omitting the quilt batting. Just stuff the covers with the purchased cushions.

1. Cut the fabric pieces listed in this step and label each one. A cutting layout is provided in **Figure L**. Quantities are for two identical cushions: one for the seat and one for the back. (**Note:** If you are covering purchased cushions, it may be necessary to alter the cutting dimensions slightly. Measure the cushions. Cut the front and back pieces 1½ inches wider and longer. Cut the side gussets 1 inch longer than the front and back. Cut the

Latticework Corner Pantry
(page 15)

Convertible Couch & Tables
(page 22)

Convertible Couch & Tables
(page 22)

Couch & Chair
(page 28)

Couch & Chair
(page 28)

Bunk Beds
(page 35)

Chopping-Block Kitchen Center
(page 44)

Microwave Cart
(page 52)

end gussets 1 inch longer than the width of the front and back pieces. Cut the side and end gussets 1½ inches wider than the thickness of the cushions.)

Description	Dimensions	Quantity
Front & Back	24 x 76 inches	4
Side Gusset	3½ x 77 inches	4
End Gusset	3½ x 25 inches	4

2. **Note:** All seams are ½ inch wide. To make one cushion, begin by piecing together two side gussets and two end gussets end-to-end. Be sure to alternate the sides and ends; the finished assembly should look like the diagram in **Figure M.** Now align the two free ends of the assembly, right sides together. Stitch the seam, making sure the gusset is not twisted. It should now be a large rectangle.

3. Place one of the front pieces right side up on a flat surface. If you are using piping, pin a length of piping all the way around the edges of the front, as shown in **Figure N.** Note that the raw edges of the piping are placed about ¼ inch from the raw edges of the front piece and the corded edge extends in toward the center. Baste the piping in place.

4. Pin the gusset assembly to the front piece, placing right sides together and aligning one long edge of the gusset with the raw edges of the front, as shown in **Figure O.** Note that the side gussets are aligned along the long edges of the front piece and the end gussets are aligned along the ends. (If you are using piping, it will be sandwiched between the gusset and front.) Stitch the seam all the way around, as shown. (**Note:** If you included piping in step 3, use a zipper foot to stitch the seam. This will allow you to stitch as closely as possible to the cord inside the piping, making a neat seam.)

5. Repeat step 3 to baste piping to one of the back pieces.

6. Place the front-and-gusset assembly right side up on a flat surface. Place the back right side down on top and pin the free long edge of the gusset to the raw edges of the back. Stitch the seam along both long edges and one end, leaving the opposite end open. (**Note:** If you are covering purchased cushions, you'll need a larger opening than one end will provide. Leave one entire end open plus a 10- or 12-inch portion of each adjacent side seam. Again, if you are using piping, use a zipper foot to stitch as closely as possible to the corded edge of the piping.) Clip all corners and turn the cushion right side out. Press the seam allowances to the inside along the open end.

7. Fold or cut and stack one package of quilt batting to match the size of the cushion cover. (If you want more padding than this, use another package or part of one.) Insert the batting inside the cushion cover, pushing it all the way into the corners. Blindstitch the edges together along the open end.

8. (Optional) Arrange ten upholstery buttons on one side of the cushion and mark their positions. Stitch a button to BOTH sides of the cushion at each marked location.

9. Repeat steps 2 through 8 to make a second cushion.

THE CHAIR

The chair is identical to the couch, but it is not as long.

Cutting the Parts

1. Cut from pine 2 x 4 the parts listed in this step and label each one with its code letter. A cutting layout, showing how we

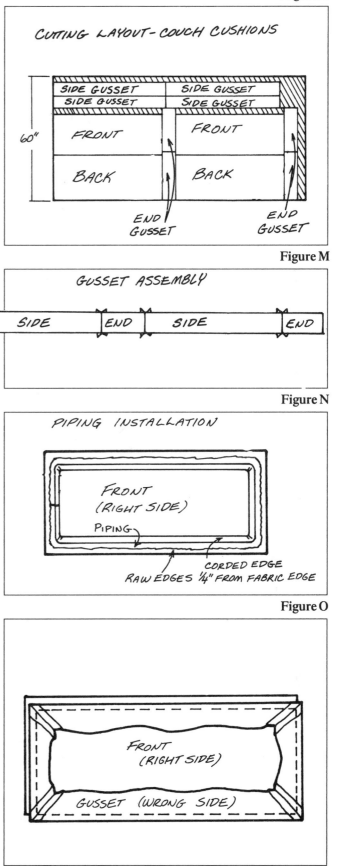

Figure L

Figure M

Figure N

Figure O

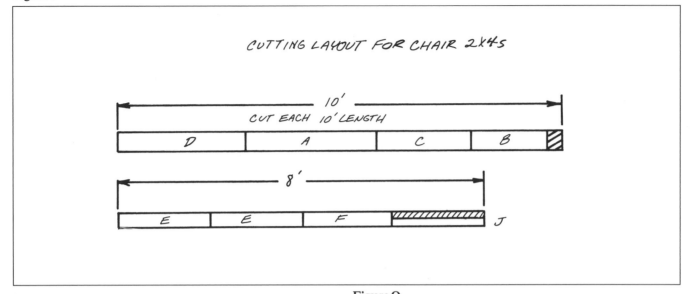

CUTTING LAYOUT FOR CHAIR 2X4s

CUT EACH 10' LENGTH

10'

| D | A | C | B |

8'

| E | E | F | | J |

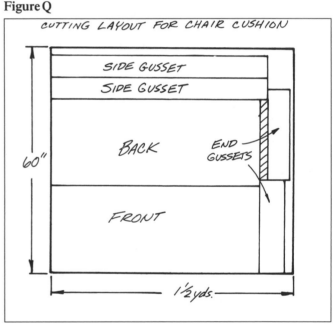

CUTTING LAYOUT FOR CHAIR CUSHION

SIDE GUSSET
SIDE GUSSET

60"

BACK

END GUSSETS

FRONT

1½ yds.

used the 2 x 4s specified in the materials list, is provided in **Figure P**. All parts are the full thickness and width of the stock (1½ x 3½ inches). Quantities are for one chair.

Code	Length	Quantity	Description
A	29⅛ inches	2	Top Rail
B	25⅜ inches	2	Bottom Rail
C	26 inches	2	Front Leg
D	38 inches	2	Back Leg
E	24 inches	2	Lower Span
F	25½ inches	1	Top Span
J	see step 2	1	Lower Support

2. Rip and cut from leftover 2 x 4 one J lower support, 1½ x 1½ x 22 inches (see **Figure P**). Label it J.

3. Refer to the instructions for the couch under the heading "Cutting the Parts," steps 2 through 7, and follow the same procedures to modify the 2 x 4 chair parts. The code letters for the chair parts are the same as those for the couch.

4. Cut from pine 1 x 2 the parts listed in this step and label them with their code letters. All parts are the full thickness and width of the stock (¾ x 1½ inches). We cut three G back slats from each of two 6-foot 1 x 2s; three H seat slats from the third 6-footer; and four H seat slats from the 8-footer.

Code	Length	Quantity	Description
G	24 inches	6	Back Slat
H	21 inches	7	Seat Slat

Assembly

As we said, the chair is identical to the couch except that it is not as long. To assemble the chair, follow the assembly instructions and diagrams provided for the couch. (Code letters for all parts are the same.) In step 4 (installing the front panel), we used only four lengths of 1 x 8, as the measurement between the front legs was only 22½ inches. Your chair may be slightly different. In step 6, you'll be using only one cushion for the chair. If you are going to make or cover a cushion, please read the instructions that follow.

Making the Cushion

To make the single cushion for the chair, please read and follow the instructions for the couch cushions, skipping step 1, which provides cutting dimensions and quantities. Cutting instructions for the chair cushion are provided here.

Cut the fabric pieces listed here and label each one. A cutting layout is provided in **Figure Q**. Quantities are for one cushion. If you are covering a purchased cushion, it may be necessary to alter the dimensions slightly. Please refer to the "**Note**" in the step 1 instructions for the couch cushions.

Description	Dimensions	Quantity
Front & Back	24 x 46 inches	2
Side Gusset	3½ x 47 inches	2
End Gusset	3½ x 25 inches	2

Bunk Beds

This easy-to-build project combines handsome styling with inexpensive materials! It's a sturdy space-saver both you and your kids will enjoy. Overall size is 79 x 76 x 44 inches.

Materials

Pine 2 x 4: seven 8-foot lengths and three 10-foot lengths
Pine 2 x 6: four 10-foot lengths
50 linear feet of pine 1 x 6, or an equivalent amount of wider or narrower standard pine 1-by stock
½-inch plywood: one full sheet and a 4 x 4-foot half-sheet
To support the mattresses, either two sheets of ½-inch plywood or five 8-foot lengths of pine 1 x 4
1-inch wooden dowel rod: four 3-foot lengths
¾-inch wooden dowel rod: one 2-foot length
Eight 2-inch plate-mount ball casters, for the drawers
Flathead wood screws in 1¼-, 1½- and 2½-inch lengths

The individual upper and lower bunks are identical. Two storage drawers fit underneath the lower bunk. Each bunk consists of identical head- and footboards joined by a 2 x 6 rail on each side (**Figure N**). The headboards are frame-and-panel assemblies (**Figure I**), divided horizontally into upper and lower openings. The upper opening contains a panel made of 1-by boards (**Figure L**). The lower opening has no panel, but you may wish to add one.

The drawer faces are also frame-and-panel assemblies (**Figures O** and **P**), which repeat the design of the headboards. The interior drawer boxes are attached to the faces, but not to the bunk bed structure itself. The drawers roll easily on ball casters, which eliminate the need for drawer guides inside the bunk frame. If you have no need of the extra storage space, you can eliminate the drawers.

Cutting the Parts

Note: In most instances, we refer to both the headboards and footboards as headboards, because they are identical.

1. Cut the lengths of pine 2 x 4 listed in this step and label each one with its code letter, for reference during assembly. All parts are the full thickness and width of the 2 x 4 stock – 1½ x 3½ inches – except for the D's and E's, which are only 2⅜ inches wide. A cutting layout showing how we used the 2 x 4s is provided in **Figure A**. For the D's and E's, rip one 10-foot and one 8-foot 2 x 4 to 2⅜ inches wide before cutting the parts to length. Save the narrow ripped strips for use in step 6.

Code	Description	Length	Quantity
Headboards:			
A	Rail	44 inches	8
B	Stile	38 inches	8
Ladder:			
C	Rail	57½ inches	2
Drawer Faces:			
D	Rail	37¾ inches	4
E	Stile	12½ inches	4

Figure A

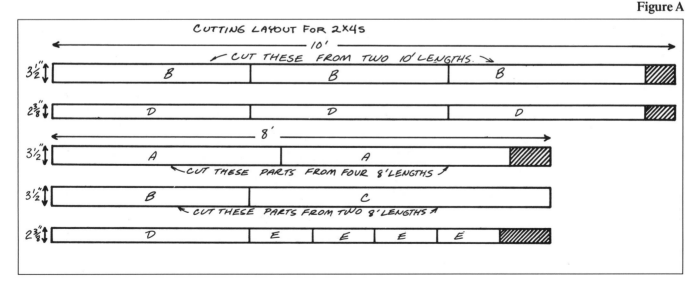

Figure B

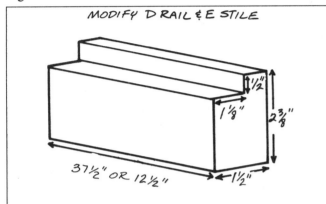

MODIFY A RAIL & B STILE

1. FLAT MITER

45°   45°

3½"

2. ALTERNATE : LAP CUTS

3½"   3½"

¾"   1½"   ¾"

¾"   ¾"

EDGE VIEW

Figure C

MODIFY D RAIL & E STILE

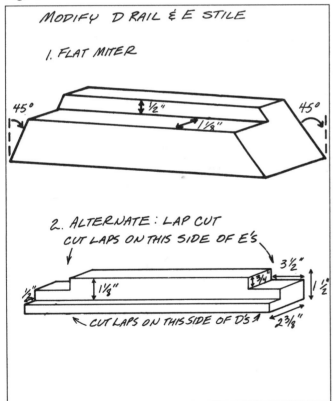

1½"

1⅛"

2⅜"

37½" OR 12½"   1½"

Figure D

MODIFY D RAIL & E STILE

1. FLAT MITER

45°   ½"   45°

1⅛"

2. ALTERNATE : LAP CUT

CUT LAPS ON THIS SIDE OF E'S

3½"

¾"

½"   1⅛"   ¾"   1½"

← CUT LAPS ON THIS SIDE OF D'S ↑   2⅜"

2. The A and B headboard rails and stiles will be assembled with either miter or lap joints (see **Figure I**). Structurally, it doesn't matter which you use, but they all should be the same. For miter joints, flat miter both ends of each A rail and B stile at a 45-degree angle toward the same edge, as shown in **Figure B**, diagram 1. For lap joints, cut a ¾ x 3½-inch half lap at each end, on the same side of the board, as shown in diagram 2.

3. The D and E drawer-face rails and stiles are rabbeted to accommodate their panels, as shown in **Figure C**. Cut or rout a ½ x 1⅛-inch rabbet along one long edge of each D and E, exactly as shown in relation to the sides and edges.

4. The D and E rails and stiles will be joined at the corners in the same manner as the headboards (see **Figure O**). We suggest that you keep to the same type joints, for continuity of style. Flat miter or lap the ends of the D's and E's (whichever you did for the A's and B's in step 2), as shown in **Figure D**. **Note:** Cut the miters toward the rabbeted edge on all D's and E's, as shown in diagram 1. Cut the laps on the rabbeted side of all four E's and on the non-rabbeted side of all four D's, as shown in diagram 2.

5. The C ladder rails are drilled to accommodate the dowel-rod rungs, as shown in **Figure E**. Draw a straight center line along one side of each C rail. Measure along the line 2½ inches from each end and mark these points. Mark 7½-inch intervals between the first points. At each marked location, drill a 1-inch-diameter socket ¾ inch deep.

6. The keepers that will hold the headboard and drawer panels in their frames are ripped and cut from the narrow strips leftover from step 1. You should have one 8-foot-long strip and one 10-foot-long strip, each 1 x 1½ inches. First, rip each strip into six separate smaller strips, each about ½ inch square and the full length of the original strip, as shown in the end-view diagram, **Figure F**. (Because of the width of the saw cuts, the smaller strips will actually measure closer to ⅜ inch, rather than ½ inch square.) Cut from the smaller strips the lengths listed in this step and label as listed.

Code	Length	Quantity
Headboard Keepers:		
F	38 inches	16
G	17 inches	16
Drawer Keepers:		
H	9 inches	4
J	34 inches	4

7. Cut from pine 2 x 6 the parts listed in this step and label, for reference during assembly. All parts are the full thickness and width of the 2 x 6 stock – 1½ x 5½ inches. We cut one of each length from each of the four 10-foot 2 x 6s. (**Note:** The L divider rails will be used in the headboard assemblies, as shown in **Figure I**. If you opted for lap joints at the corners of the headboards, you may wish to use lap joints for the divider rails as well. If so, cut the divider rails 44 inches long instead of 37 inches. You will still be able to get one K and one L from each 10-foot 2 x 6.)

Code	Description	Length	Quantity
K	Long Rail	76 inches	4
L	Divider Rail	37 inches	4

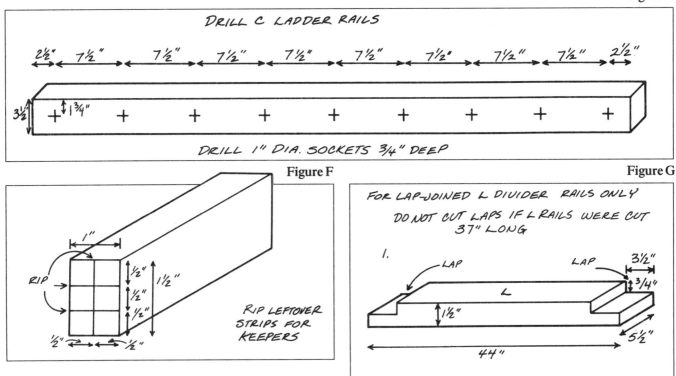

DRILL C LADDER RAILS

2½" 7½" 7½" 7½" 7½" 7½" 7½" 7½" 7½" 2½"

3½" 1¾"

DRILL 1" DIA. SOCKETS ¾" DEEP

Figure F

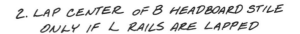

1"

½"
1½"
½"
½"

RIP

½" ½"

RIP LEFTOVER STRIPS FOR KEEPERS

Figure G

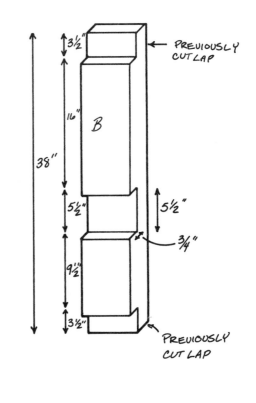

FOR LAP-JOINED L DIVIDER RAILS ONLY
DO NOT CUT LAPS IF L RAILS WERE CUT
37" LONG

1.

LAP   LAP   3½"

L   ¾"

1½"

5½"

44"

2. LAP CENTER OF B HEADBOARD STILE ONLY IF L RAILS ARE LAPPED

3½"   PREVIOUSLY CUT LAP

16"   B

38"

5½"   5½"

¾"

9½"

3½"   PREVIOUSLY CUT LAP

8. Note: Follow this step only if you cut the L divider rails 44 inches long, to accommodate lap joints. Cut a ¾ x 3½-inch lap across each end of each L divider rail, on the same side of the board, as shown in **Figure G**, diagram 1. The B headboard stiles will also need to be lapped, to accommodate the divider rails. Cut a ¾ x 5½-inch lap across the already lapped side of each B stile, where indicated in diagram 2.

9. The 1 x 6 (or other 1-by lumber you purchased) will be used for the panels in the headboards and drawer faces. The panel boards will be cut to length later, during assembly. For now, rip four ¾ x ¾ x 72-inch strips from the 1-by lumber. These will serve as anchor strips for the slats or plywood mattress supports. Label them **M**.

10. If you purchased pine 1 x 4 lumber for the slats, cut ten 40½-inch lengths (two from each 8-footer) and label them as the slats. If you purchased ½-inch plywood for solid mattress supports, cut two 40½ x 75-inch pieces.

11. Cut from the remaining sheet and half sheet of ½-inch plywood the drawer parts listed in this step. A cutting layout is provided in **Figure H**. **Note:** Measure the total height of the casters you purchased, from the bottom of the ball to the top of the mounting plate. If it is more than 3¼ inches, reduce the 9-inch width of the N drawer sides and P front/backs accordingly.

Code	Description	Dimensions	Quantity
Drawer parts:			
N	Side	9 x 42 inches	4
P	Front/Back	9 x 35 inches	4
R	Bottom	35 x 41 inches	2

12. For the ladder rungs, cut each 3-foot length of 1-inch dowel in half. You should now have eight 18-inch lengths of dowel to serve as the rungs.

Figure H

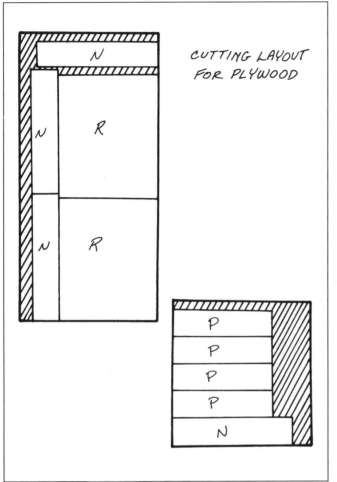

CUTTING LAYOUT
FOR PLYWOOD

Figure J

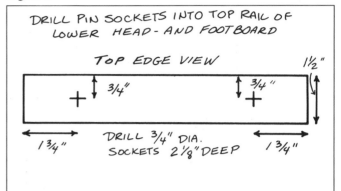

DRILL PIN SOCKETS INTO TOP RAIL OF
LOWER HEAD-AND FOOTBOARD

TOP EDGE VIEW

3/4"   3/4"   1 1/2"

DRILL 3/4" DIA.
SOCKETS 2 1/8" DEEP

1 3/4"   1 3/4"

Assembly

Note: We used screws to secure most of the joints, but you might prefer to use dowel pins. Some of the joints will require very long screws unless you drill extra long recesses, using a bit slightly larger than the screw head. If you opt for this method, be sure to mark the desired depth of the recess on your drill bit, or you could drill right into the joint before you know it. Cover all screw recesses (both normal and extra long) with plugs cut from dowel rod or matching stock.

1. The headboard frame assembly is shown in **Figure I**. If you opted for miter joints, glue together the A rails and B stiles, matching mitered corners. Secure each corner joint with screws or dowel pins inserted into the edges of the B stiles, through the stiles and into the A rails. Insert the L divider rail 16 inches below the top rail and secure with screws or pins inserted through the B stiles and into the ends of the L rail. If you opted

Figure I

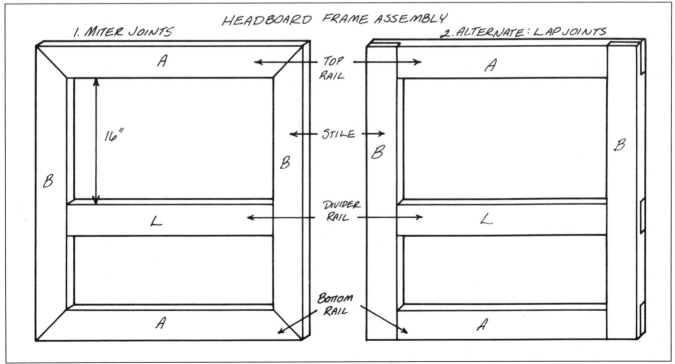

HEADBOARD FRAME ASSEMBLY

1. MITER JOINTS

2. ALTERNATE: LAP JOINTS

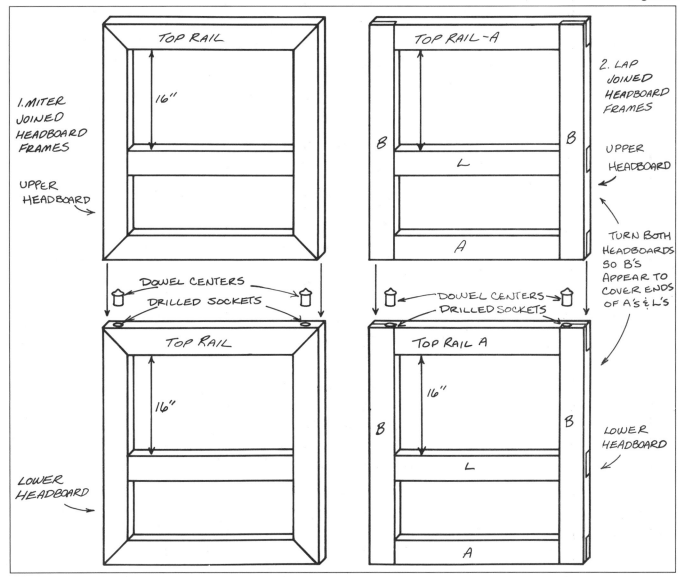

for lap joints, fit the parts together, matching lap cuts as shown in diagram 2, **Figure I**. Glue all joints and secure with screws or pins. Assemble four identical headboards in this manner.

2. When they have been completely assembled, the upper and lower bunks will be joined by four dowel-rod pins. It will be much easier to drill the dowel holes now, before the panels and connecting rails add weight to the structures. First, mark the four headboard frames according to where they will fit in the structure: upper headboard, upper footboard, lower headboard and lower footboard. On the top rail of the LOWER headboard and footboard only, mark two drilling points where indicated in **Figure J**. **Note** that the top rail is the one farther from the divider rail (see **Figure I**), so be sure you are marking the upper edge of the top rail, not the bottom rail. Mark the points 1¾ inches from each end and midway between the sides, as shown. At each marked point, drill a ¾-inch-diameter socket, 2⅛ inches deep. Use a drilling jig, if necessary, to make sure the sockets are perfectly square with the frames.

3. To be sure of perfect alignment, we used dowel centers to mark the positions of the sockets in the upper head- and footboard. Insert a dowel center into each socket in the lower headboard top rail. Place the upper headboard on top (**Figure K**), making sure it is turned right-end up. (**Note:** If you assembled the frames using lap joints, be sure both the lower and upper frames are turned with the same side facing you before you mark the socket positions. By this, we mean that when you look at the frames stacked one on top of the other, the B stiles should appear to cover the ends of the A and L rails on both frames. If one is turned with the opposite side facing you, the rails will appear to cover the ends of the stiles.) Make sure the headboards are aligned flush along the edges and sides. Press the upper headboard downward to mark the socket positions in its bottom rail. Remove the upper headboard and drill the same size sockets into the lower edge of the bottom rail, at the marked locations. Remove the dowel centers from the lower headboard, insert them into the sockets in the lower footboard and repeat

Figure L

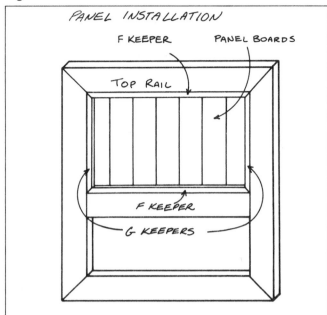

PANEL INSTALLATION

F KEEPER   PANEL BOARDS

TOP RAIL

F KEEPER

G KEEPERS

Figure M

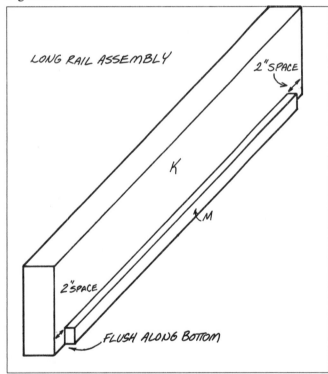

LONG RAIL ASSEMBLY

2" SPACE

K

M

2" SPACE

FLUSH ALONG BOTTOM

the procedures to mark and drill the upper footboard.

4. We fit a panel into the upper opening of each headboard and footboard, but left the lower openings empty. This helps give the bunk beds a less massive appearance. The upper opening should measure very close to 37 inches across and 16 inches vertically. To create one panel, we cut seven 16-inch lengths of 1 x 6 and aligned them edge-to-edge, measured across them and trimmed one board to make the total width 37 inches. If you

purchased wider or narrower 1-by stock, you may need to cut more or fewer than seven boards to make up the width, but the 16-inch length will still apply. Cut the 1-by boards to make up one panel, to match the width of the opening.

5. The panel is held in place by a keeper frame on each side (**Figure L**). For one keeper frame you will need two F and two G keepers. Miter both ends of each one at a 45-degree angle so they fit exactly into the upper opening of the headboard when assembled. Glue them into the opening, flush with one side of the headboard, and secure using finishing nails. Place the headboard on a flat surface with the attached keeper frame down. Place the panel boards into the opening, resting on the attached keeper frame. Miter and assemble a second keeper frame on top of the panel boards. Secure with glue and nails.

6. Repeat steps 4 and 5 to assemble and secure a panel into the upper opening of the other headboard and both footboards.

7. Attach an M anchor strip to each K long rail, as shown in **Figure M**, using glue and at least ten screws. Note that the two parts are flush along the bottom. The strip is centered between the ends of the rail.

8. Join the upper-bunk headboard and footboard, using two K long rails, as shown in **Figure N**. Note that the K rails are positioned so that they are even with the L divider rails in the head- and footboards. Note also that the K rails are turned so that the M anchor strips are at the bottom, facing center. (If you used lap joints in the head- and footboards, make sure that each one is turned the right way – on the outside, the B stiles should cover the ends of the A and L rails.) Secure the assembly by inserting screws through the head- and footboards into the ends of the K rails, countersink and cover with plugs. When you assemble the lower bunk, line up the head- and footboards next to the assembled upper bunk so you're certain the K long rails were cut exactly the same length. Otherwise, the dowel sockets will not match.

9. If you are using pine 1 x 4 for slats, place five of them across the upper bunk frame, evenly spaced and with the ends resting on the anchor strips. Secure each slat with at least one screw at each end. (We do not recommend that you leave the slats unattached, as they will tend to fall out, with unpleasant consequences, when the kids inevitably start leaping on or off the beds.) If you are using plywood mattress supports, place one inside the upper bunk frame, resting on the anchor strips, and secure with several screws along each edge. Do not install slats or a mattress support in the lower bunk frame just yet.

10. For the dowel pins, cut four 4-inch lengths of ¾-inch dowel rod. Chamfer and groove each one, as described in Tips & Techniques.

11. You'll need some help with this step. Glue a dowel pin into each socket in the headboard and footboard of the lower bunk. Tap lightly with a hammer to make sure they are seated properly. Place the upper bunk on top, fitting the pins into their sockets. Do not glue the pins into the upper bunk.

Drawer and Ladder Assembly

1. Each drawer face is a frame-and-panel assembly. **Figure O** shows the frame assembly for both miter and lap joints. Glue together one drawer-face frame, using two D's and two E's. Make sure all four frame members are turned with the rabbets

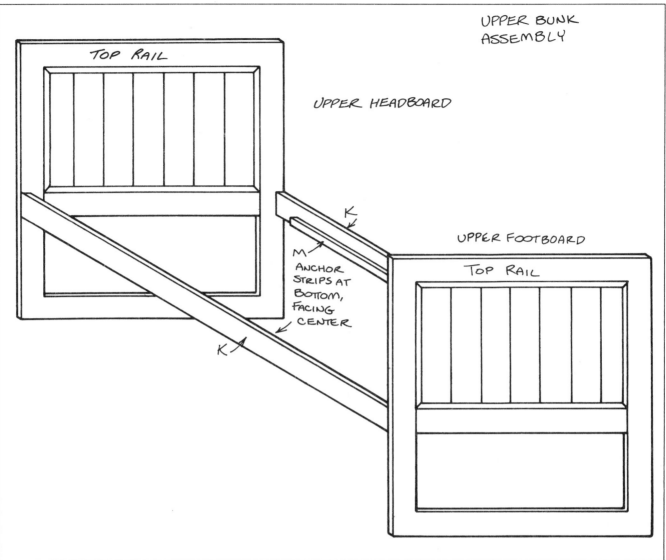

UPPER BUNK ASSEMBLY

UPPER HEADBOARD

TOP RAIL

UPPER FOOTBOARD

TOP RAIL

K

M
ANCHOR STRIPS AT BOTTOM, FACING CENTER

K

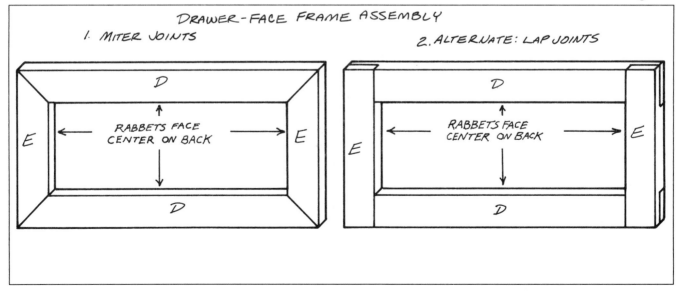

DRAWER-FACE FRAME ASSEMBLY

1. MITER JOINTS

2. ALTERNATE: LAP JOINTS

D

E

RABBETS FACE CENTER ON BACK

E

D

D

E

RABBETS FACE CENTER ON BACK

E

D

Figure P

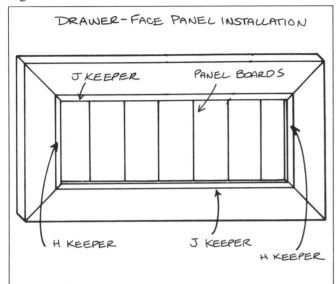

DRAWER-FACE PANEL INSTALLATION

J KEEPER   PANEL BOARDS

H KEEPER   J KEEPER

H KEEPER

Figure Q

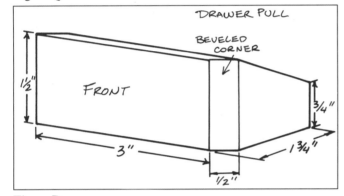

DRAWER PULL

BEVELED CORNER

FRONT

1½"

¾"

3"

1¾"

½"

Figure R

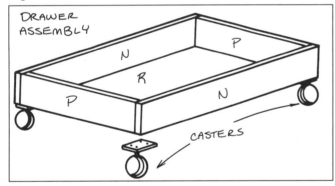

DRAWER ASSEMBLY

N   P

R

P   N

CASTERS

on the same side, facing center. Secure the joints. Assemble a second, identical drawer-face frame.

2. The panel will fit into the rabbeted side of the frame, within the rabbets. The rabbeted opening should measure very close to 8½ x 33¾ inches. To create the panel, we cut seven 8½-inch lengths of pine 1 x 6 and aligned them edge-to-edge, measured across them and trimmed one board to make the total width 33¾ inches. If you purchased wider or narrower 1-by stock, you may need to cut more or fewer than seven boards to make up the width. Cut the 1-by boards to make up one panel, to match the

height and width of the opening.

3. Place the panel boards into the rabbeted opening on the back of one drawer-face frame. The panel is held in place on the back side by a keeper frame, as shown in **Figure P**. You can miter the ends of the H and J keepers at a 45-degree angle or just trim them to butt together at the corners and fit the opening. Glue the keepers into the opening and secure with finishing nails driven through the keepers and into the frame.

4. Repeat steps 2 and 3 to install a panel and keeper frame in the second drawer-face frame.

5. We made our own drawer pulls from leftover 2 x 4 lumber, as shown in **Figure Q**. Cut and shape four drawer pulls. Attach two to each drawer face by drilling through the panel and into the back of the pull, using a bit slightly smaller than the mounting screws. We used two screws for each pull so that they wouldn't twist.

6. The drawer box assembly is shown in **Figure R**. Note that the N sides cover the ends of the P front and back members. Glue together the sides and ends around the R bottom, with all parts flush at the bottom. Secure with finishing nails. Assemble a second drawer box in the same manner.

7. Install a ball caster beneath each corner of each drawer box, as shown in **Figure R**.

8. Slide the drawer boxes underneath the lower bunk and insert the drawer faces, flush with the long rails and head- and footboard stiles. Work through the open lower bunk frame to mark the level of the top edge of the drawer box on the back of each drawer face. Remove the faces and drawers from the bunk frame. Attach a drawer box to each drawer face, centered between the ends and aligning the marked placement line with the top of the drawer box. We used screws only, inserted through the drawer front into the back of the face. Slide the drawers back under the bunk frame. (You may wish to plane or sand a little off the bottom of each drawer face if they rub against the floor.)

9. Attach the slats or plywood mattress support to the bottom bunk frame, as you did previously for the top bunk.

10. Note that you can see the drawers through the openings in the head- and footboard of the lower bunk. If you do not like the way this looks, there are a couple of options. You can make and install panels in the same manner as you did for the upper openings; you can make simpler panels from plywood; or you might consider covering the openings on the inside by stretching and stapling fabric over them.

11. To assemble the ladder, align the two C ladder rails on edge on a flat surface, with the drilled surfaces facing center. Glue a dowel-rod rung into each set of aligned sockets. Turn the ladder so it rests on one edge and tap with a hammer to make sure the rungs are seated fully and evenly in the sockets. It's not really necessary, but you may wish to secure each rung by inserting a screw through the adjacent rail into each end.

12. Place the ladder against one side of the assembled bunk beds, where indicated in **Figure S**. The lower end should be flush with the bottom of the long rail of the lower bunk. The top will extend above the long rail of the top bunk. Be sure it is square with the rails and secure with four long screws.

13. You may wish to round off the sharp corners at the top of the upper head- and footboard and at the top of the ladder.

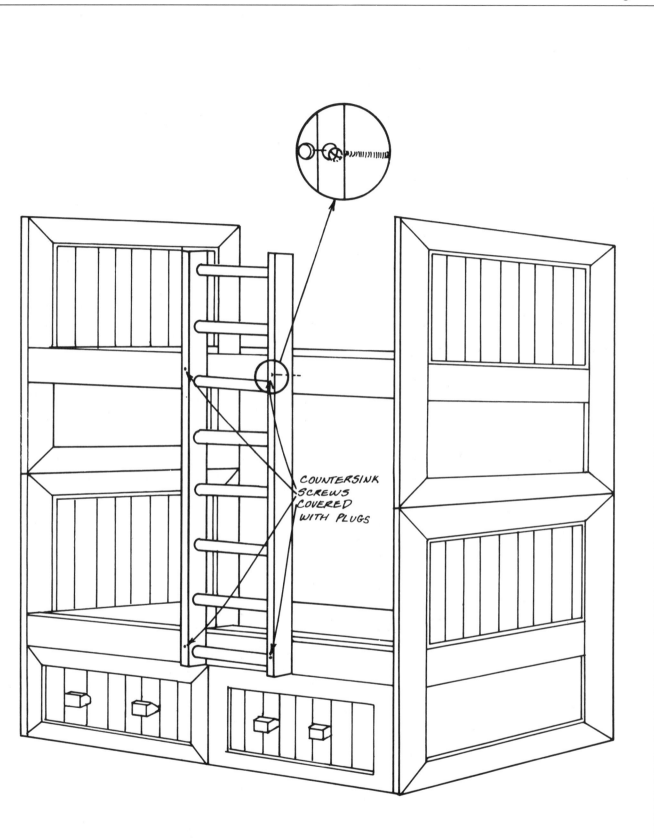

COUNTERSINK
SCREWS
COVERED
WITH PLUGS

Chopping-Block Kitchen Center

You'll be in your salad days with this convenient rolling kitchen work center! It features a removable cutting board, inset mixing bowl and swing-out bin. Overall size is 36 x 33 x 22 inches.

Materials

Pine 2 x 4: seven 10-foot lengths and three 6-foot lengths

Pine 1 x 8: one 4-foot length

½-inch plywood: 2 x 4-foot piece for the swing-out bin and a 3 x 3-foot piece for a routing jig

½-inch wooden dowel rod: 1-foot length

¼-inch wooden dowel rod: 1-foot length

Four locking swivel casters (flat plate or shank-type)

13-inch-diameter mixing bowl with a lip around the top (We used a stainless steel bowl.)

Flathead wood screws in 1½-, 2- and 2½-inch lengths

2d or ¾-inch-long finishing nails

Carpenter's wood glue; wood filler; and finishing materials of your choice

For the cutting board:

14 x 18-inch piece of better-quality ¾-inch plywood or an equivalent amount of ¾-inch-thick solid wood stock. If you can't find solid stock this wide, purchase narrower stock and spline together two or more lengths to form the 14 x 18-inch piece. **Note** that a solid-wood cutting board is almost sure to warp unless the wood was sufficiently kiln-dried. It must also be sealed thoroughly with a non-toxic finish, to prevent warpage in a kitchen atmosphere.

This easy-to-build kitchen work center has several special features that make it more handy than a standard butcher block. A removable cutting board fits into the chopping-block counter top, concealing a removable mixing bowl below. A dowel peg, which extends from one end of the counter top, serves as a hanger for the cutting board when you are using the bowl. Additional hanger pegs keep your most-used utensils and pot holders right at hand. The spacious lower storage shelf supports a swing-out

Figure A

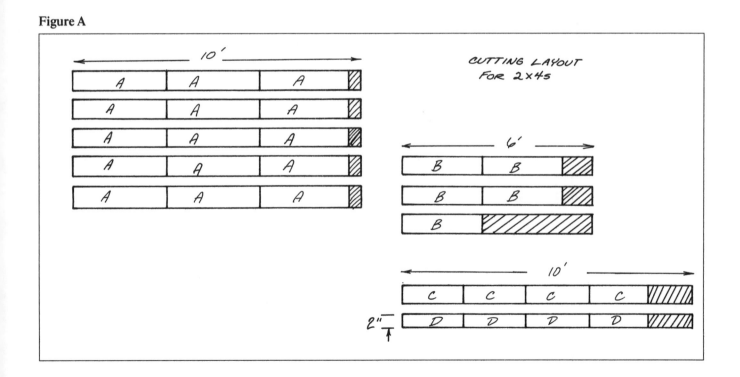

bin that can hold supplies or trash. Locking swivel casters allow you to roll the unit wherever it's needed and hold it steady when the locks are engaged.

Cutting the Parts

1. The parts listed in this step are lengths of 2 x 4. The A and B slats and the C legs are the full thickness and width of the stock (1½ x 3½ inches). For the D narrow legs, rip one of the 10-foot-long 2 x 4s to a width of 2 inches before cutting the lengths (do not alter the thickness). We have provided a cutting layout in **Figure A**, showing how we used the 2 x 4s specified in the materials list. Cut the parts and label each one with its code letter, for reference during assembly. Save the leftover pieces of 2 x 4 for use in step 3.

Code	Description	Length	Quantity
A	Counter Slat	36 inches	15
B	Shelf Slat	30¾ inches	5
C	Wide Leg	26¼ inches	4
D	Narrow Leg	26¼ inches	4

2. The C and D legs are rabbeted at the upper and lower ends, as shown in **Figure B**. Note that both rabbets are cut on the same side of the leg. Rabbet all eight legs, as shown.

3. Rip and cut from leftover 2 x 4 the parts listed in this step and label each one with its code letter.

Code	Description	Dimensions	Quantity
E	Leg Block	1 x 2¾ x 2¾ inches	8
F	Bin Handle	1½ x 1⅛ x 5 inches	1
G	Bin Foot	1½ x 1⅛ x 1¼ inches	1

4. An optional step is to rout a cove along one edge of the F bin handle, as shown **Figure C**, diagram 1. Exact dimensions are not critical – the cove will simply make it easier to grasp the handle. An alternate approach is to rout or cut a rabbet along the edge, as shown in diagram 2.

5. The G bin foot is drilled and then cut in half, as shown in **Figure D**. First, drill a ½-inch-diameter hole straight through the center length. Cut the drilled piece in half lengthwise, as shown. Label each of the resulting pieces G.

6. Cut from pine 1 x 8 the parts listed in this step and label each one with its code letter. All of the parts are the full ¾-inch thickness of the stock.

Code	Description	Dimensions	Quantity
H	Counter Support	3 x 13⅜ inches	2
J	Bin Support	¾ x 6½ inches	1
K	Bin Floor	5 x 11 inches	1
L	Filler Block	¾ x 1 inch	4
M	Bin Stop	¾ x 9¼ inches	1

7. Bevel one long edge of the K bin floor at a 30-degree angle.

8. Cut from ⅜-inch plywood the bin parts listed in this step and label each one with its code. For the two sides, enlarge the scale drawing provided in **Figure E**.

Code	Description	Dimensions	Quantity
N	Side	use pattern	2
P	Back	11 x 11 inches	1
Q	Front	13 x 14⅝ inches	1

9. Bevel one edge of the P bin back at a 30-degree angle.

Figure B

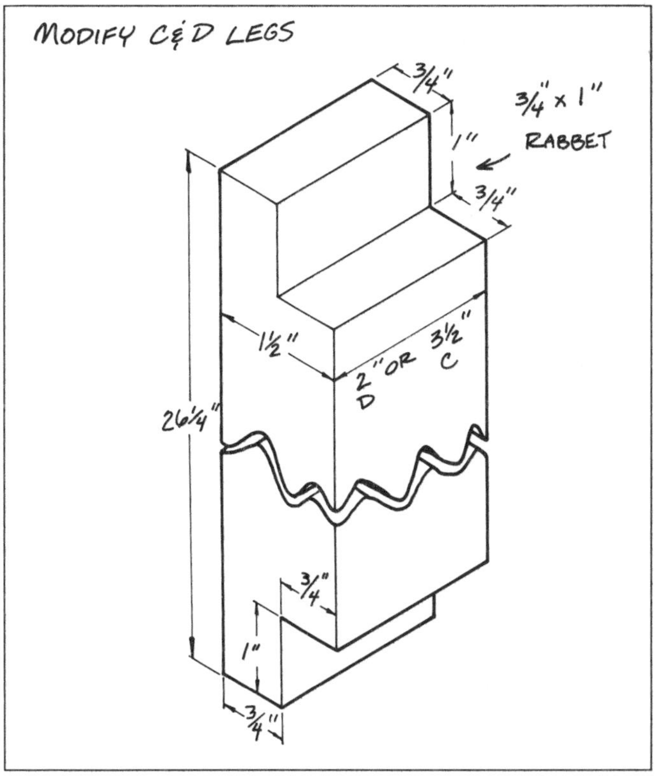
MODIFY C & D LEGS
3/4"
3/4" x 1" RABBET
1"
3/4"
1/2"
2" OR D
3 1/2" C
26 1/4"
3/4"
1"
3/4"

Figure C

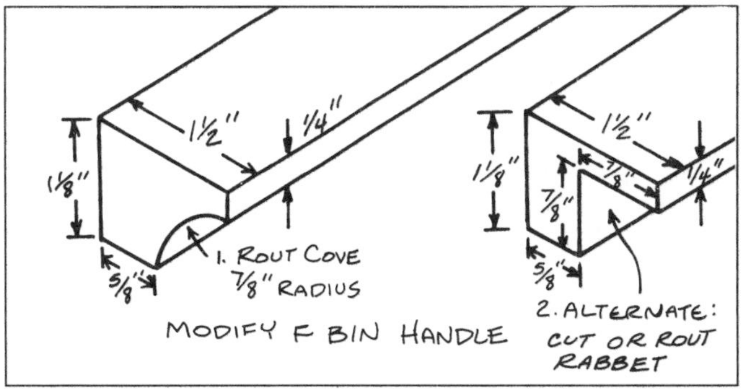
1/2"
1/4"
1 1/8"
5/8"
1. ROUT COVE 1/8" RADIUS
7/8"
2. ALTERNATE: CUT OR ROUT RABBET
MODIFY F BIN HANDLE

Figure D

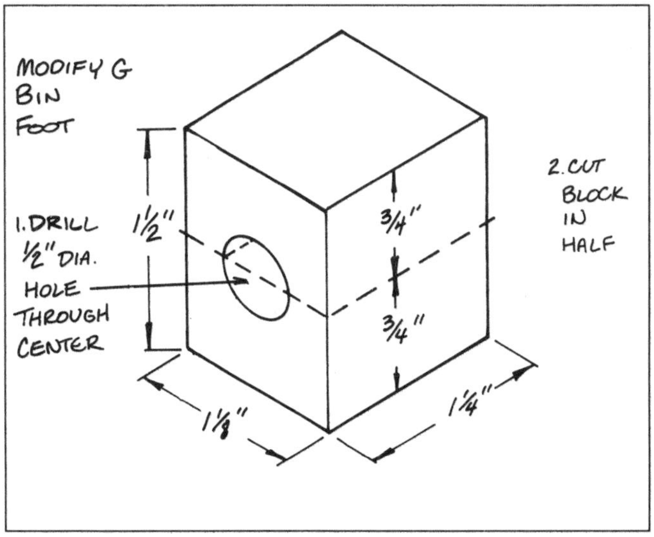
MODIFY G BIN FOOT
1. DRILL 1/2" DIA. HOLE THROUGH CENTER
1 1/2"
3/4"
3/4"
2. CUT BLOCK IN HALF
1 1/8"
1 1/4"

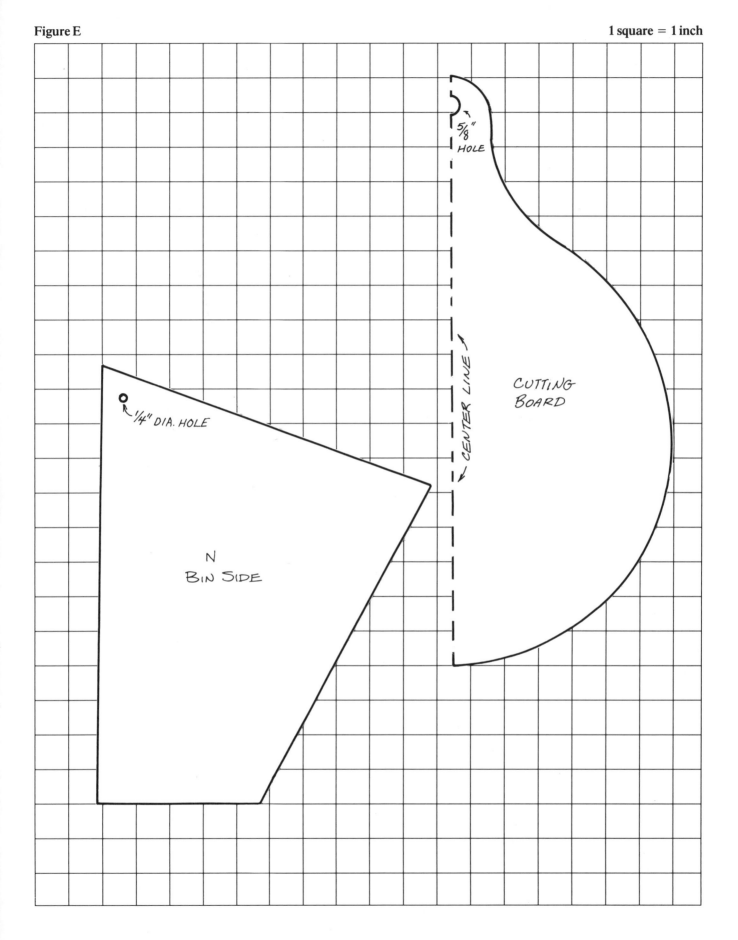

5/8"
HOLE

CENTER LINE

CUTTING
BOARD

1/4" DIA. HOLE

N
BIN SIDE

10. A scale drawing for the cutting board is provided in **Figure E**. Enlarge to full size. Cut one cutting board from better-quality ¾-inch plywood or from solid wood stock (as discussed in the materials list). If you are using plywood that is not veneer core, fill the edges with wood filler and allow to dry before sanding smooth. Sand the cutting board and drill a ⅝-inch-diameter hole through the handle, where indicated on the pattern.

Counter Top and Shelf Assembly

The basic counter top assembly is cut to accommodate the mixing bowl and cutting board (**Figures E** through **K**). Support boards are then attached to the underside (**Figure L**). The shelf assembly is shown in **Figure M**.

1. The counter top consists of the fifteen **A** slats joined side-to-side. Before they are glued, you will need to clamp them together temporarily and cut openings for the mixing bowl and cutting board. Align the **A** slats with wide sides together, even at both ends (**Figure F**). Examine each slat and turn it best edge up. Securely clamp the assembly (do not use glue). Place the cutting board on top of the slats and adjust it so that the drilled handle end extends about 1½ inches beyond the outer slat, as shown. Make sure that the cutting board is square with the slats. Use a pencil to trace the outline onto the slats. Remove the cutting board, but do not remove the clamps and do not cut the hole just yet.

2. The mixing bowl will rest in a slightly smaller hole and the cutting board will fit into a recess over the bowl, as shown in the cross section, **Figure G**. Measure the outside diameter of your mixing bowl, just underneath the lip around the top. Draw a circle of the same diameter in the center of the traced cutting-board outline, as shown in **Figure H**.

3. Now you can cut the hole for the mixing bowl, which should look like the diagram in **Figure I** when finished. For this job you can use a saber saw with a long blade, a band saw or a jigsaw. Carefully remove the clamps from the slat assembly. One at a time, remove each slat that contains a portion of the mixing-bowl outline and cut through the slat, following the mixing-bowl outline on the upper edge. DO NOT cut along the outer cutting-board outline. When the slat has been cut, you will have two lengths instead of just one (except in the case of two of the slats, which will each have just a rounded cutout); replace the two portions back in their positions among the other slats, as shown in **Figure I**.

4. Reclamp the slats and trim or sand the edge of the hole until it is reasonably smooth. Test the fit by inserting the mixing bowl down into the hole – the bulk of the bowl should fit through the hole and the lip should rest flat on top of the slats, keeping the bowl from falling through. When you have a good fit, remove the clamps and glue the slats together. Reclamp while the glue dries.

5. When the glue has dried, you're ready to cut the recess that will support the lip of the mixing bowl below the top of the counter and into which the cutting board will fit (**Figures G** and **J**). This involves routing out the area between the mixing-bowl hole and the cutting-board outline to a depth of ⅞ inch. We made a plywood pattern to guide the router. To do this, trace the cutting-board outline onto a 3 x 3-foot piece of plywood. Draw another outline outside the first one, at a distance equal

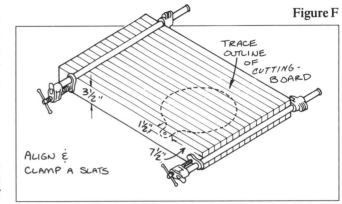

Figure F

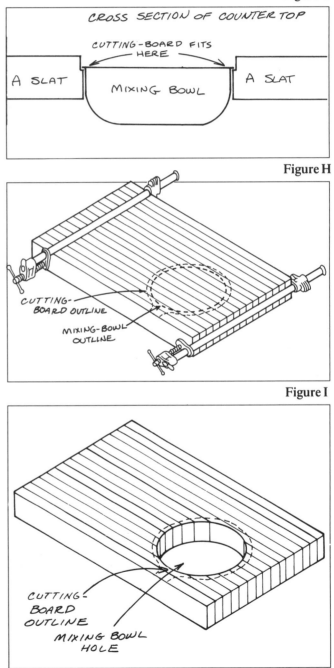

Figure G

Figure H

Figure I

Figure J

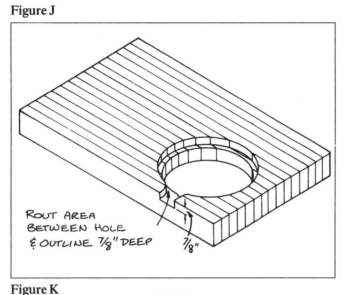

ROUT AREA BETWEEN HOLE & OUTLINE 7/8" DEEP   7/8"

Figure K

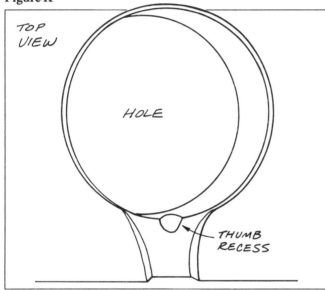

TOP VIEW

HOLE

THUMB RECESS

Figure L

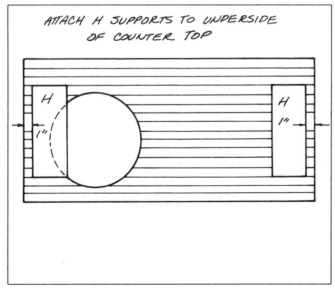

ATTACH H SUPPORTS TO UNDERSIDE OF COUNTER TOP

H   H

1"   1"

Figure M

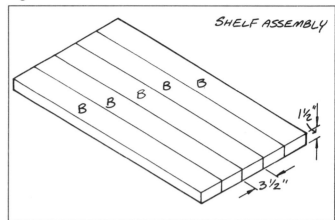

SHELF ASSEMBLY

B B B B B

1 1/2"

3 1/2"

to the radius of your router's bottom plate. Cut out the plywood within the outer line. Use the outer plywood piece, not the one shaped like the cutting board, as the pattern. Place the plywood pattern on top of the assembled slats, around the cutting-board outline, and temporarily tack it in place with thin nails. We used a ½-inch straight bit for the routing. Because the bit was not long enough to rout out the entire ⅞-inch depth in a single pass, we routed to the maximum depth of the bit and then removed the plywood pattern and went over the area again. Don't overlook the handle portion of the cutting-board area (see **Figure J**).

6. To test for fit, place the mixing bowl into the hole – the lip should now rest in the routed area, with the bulk of the bowl extending below the slats (**Figure G**). Place the cutting board into the recess on top of the bowl; it may be necessary to sand the cutting board or recess to achieve a good fit.

7. To make it easier to remove the bowl, we filed out a rounded finger notch at the edge of the hole, as shown in **Figure K**. Note that the notch is centered in the handle portion of the cutting-board recess. The easiest way to create the notch is to use a half-round file.

8. Place the two H counter supports flat against the underside of the assembled counter top, as shown in **Figure L**. Each support should be 1 inch from the adjacent end of the counter and centered between the long edges. The support nearest the end with the mixing-bowl hole will cover a portion of the hole and will be trimmed to match later. When the placement is correct, glue the supports and secure with screws. We countersunk the screws slightly but did not cover them with plugs, as they will not show.

9. Use a saber saw, jigsaw or hand keyhole saw to trim away the portion of the H counter support that extends into the mixing-bowl hole.

10. The lower shelf consists of the five B shelf slats joined edge-to-edge (**Figure M**). Edge-glue the five slats, even at both ends, and clamp while the glue dries.

Leg Assembly and Installation

The leg assembly is shown in **Figures N, O** and **P**. They are attached to the counter and shelf as shown in **Figures Q** and **R**.

1. Each leg consists of five parts: a C wide leg, a D narrow leg, two E leg blocks and an L filler block. To assemble one

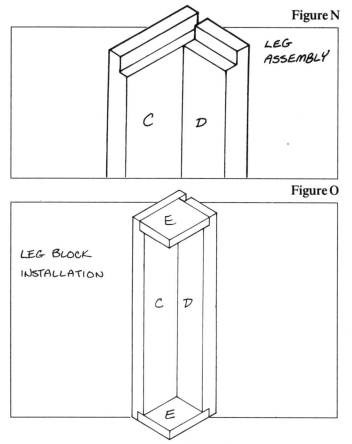

Figure N

LEG ASSEMBLY

C D

Figure O

LEG BLOCK INSTALLATION

E

C D

E

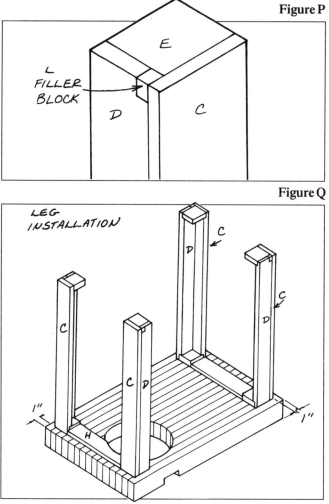

Figure P

L FILLER BLOCK

E

D C

Figure Q

LEG INSTALLATION

C

D

C

D

C

C D

1"

1"

H

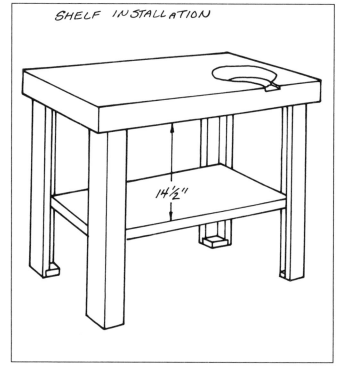

Figure R

SHELF INSTALLATION

14½"

leg, begin by glueing together a C and D leg at right angles, even at both ends, as shown in **Figure N**. Note that the C wide leg covers the adjacent edge of the D narrow leg and that both legs are turned so that the rabbets face the inside corner. Secure the joint by inserting three screws through the narrow leg into the wide leg – one near the upper end, one near the lower end and one near the center. These screws should be countersunk and covered with plugs.

2. Glue an E leg block into the rabbets at one end of the C-D leg assembly, as shown in **Figure O**. Glue a second leg block into the rabbets at the other end. To secure, insert two screws through each leg board into the block. Countersink and plug.

3. Note that there are gaps at the top and bottom of the leg assembly, between the leg block and the outer edge of the C leg. An L filler block is used to fill each gap, as shown in **Figure P**. It may be necessary to trim or sand the block to get it to fit, but it should be a tight fit. Glue a filler block into each gap.

4. Repeat the procedures described in steps 1 through 3 to assemble three more identical legs, using the remaining C, D, E and L parts.

5. The legs are attached to the underside of the counter top, as shown in **Figure Q**. Note that each leg is turned so that the C wide leg faces the adjacent end of the counter top and is flush with the outer edge of the H support. Note also that the L blocks are butted against the ends of the H supports. Glue each leg in place and secure by inserting two screws through the L block into the counter top. Countersink the screws slightly, but they need not be plugged.

6. Insert the assembled shelf into the corners formed by the legs, as shown in **Figure R**. Use a level to insure that each leg

CHOPPING-BLOCK KITCHEN CENTER

Figure S

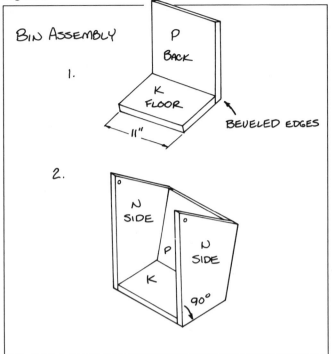

Figure T

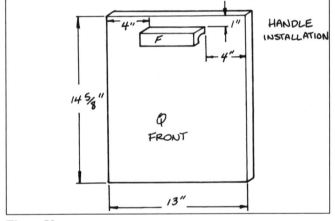

Figure U

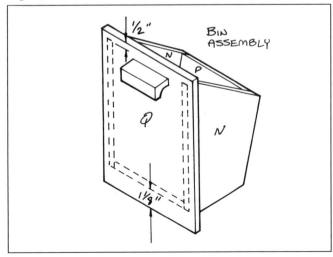

is straight and square with the others – it may be necessary to trim or sand the shelf for a good fit. **Note**: The 14½-inch distance between the underside of the counter top and the upper surface of the shelf is critical, if you want the bin to fit correctly and not fall out on your toes. Check to be sure that the shelf is level and secure it by inserting a screw through each C leg and each D leg into the shelf. Countersink and plug the screws.

Bin Assembly

The bin assembly is shown in **Figures S** through **W**.

1. The bin consists of six main parts: the Q Front, the two N sides, the P back, the K floor and the F handle. To begin, glue the back to the beveled edge of the floor, flush at the bottom, as shown in **Figure S**, diagram 1. Note that the back is turned with the beveled edge at the lower end. The side edges of the back should be flush with the ends of the floor. Secure the joint with three or four finishing nails.

2. Glue the sides to the back and floor, flush at the bottom, as shown in **Figure S**, diagram 2. Note that each side is turned so that the square lower corner is at the front. The sides cover the edges of the back and the ends of the floor. Secure with finishing nails.

3. It will be easier to attach the F handle to the Q bin front before the front is attached to the partially assembled bin. Placement of the handle is shown in **Figure T**. Note that it is turned with the routed cove (or rabbet) at the bottom, facing the bin front. Glue the handle in place and secure by inserting two screws through the front into the handle.

4. Glue the front to the bin sides and floor, as shown in **Figure U**. Note that the front should extend ½ inch above the upper ends of the sides and 1⅛ inch below the floor and lower ends of the sides. It should extend equally beyond the outer surfaces of the two sides. Secure with finishing nails.

5. Cut two ⅞-inch lengths of ¼-inch dowel and taper one end of each length, as shown in **Figure V**. These dowel pegs will be used to hold a small garbage bag in place in the bin. They are tapered so that they can be removed when you wish to change the bag. For the time being, insert the tapered end of a peg into the hole at the top front corner of one of the bin sides (from the outside in). Push it in until it is wedged securely in place. Wedge the other peg into the opposite bin side in the same manner. After the bin has been finished, just insert a plastic bag, wrap the top of the bag over the tops of the side and back walls and use the pegs to secure the bag.

6. The two grooved G bin feet are attached to the underside of the floor, as shown in **Figure W**. Note that each foot rests flat on the underside of the floor, butted against the back surface of the bin front. The 6½-inch space between the feet is critical for fit. Glue the two feet to the floor and front. Secure each one by driving two finishing nails through the foot and into the front, as shown, placing the nails below the level of the groove.

Final Assembly

There are only a few things left to do: install the bin supports (**Figure X**), install the hanger pegs, attach the casters and finish the unit.

1. The bin is held in place between the counter top and shelf by means of the M bin stop at the top and the J bin support and

Figure V   Figure W

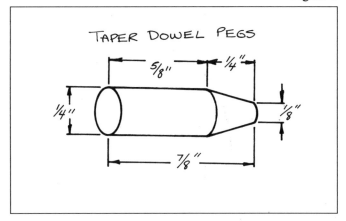

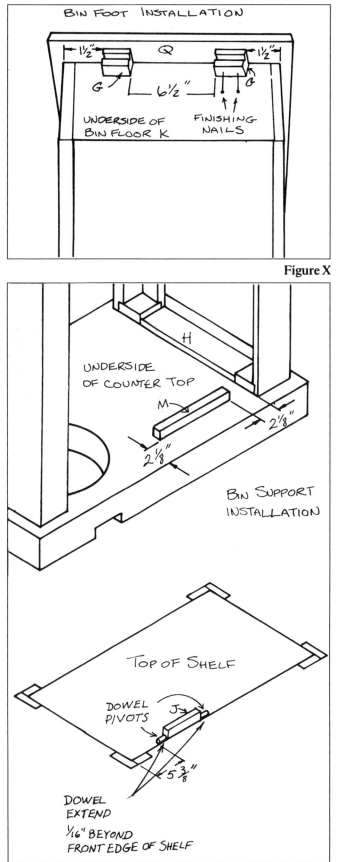

dowel pivots at the bottom (**Figure X**). Glue the **M** stop to the underside of the counter top, placing it 2⅛ inches from the edge, as shown. Be sure that it is parallel to the counter edge and secure with a few finishing nails.

2. Glue the **J** support to the top surface of the shelf, placing it as shown in the second diagram, **Figure X**. (It will be directly below the **M** Stop.) Note that the support is flush with the front edge of the shelf and 5⅜ inches from the closest end. Secure with finishing nails.

3. For the pivot dowels, cut two 1¼-inch lengths of ½-inch dowel. Glue them to the shelf and **J** support, as shown in **Figure X**. **Note** that each pivot dowel extends ¹⁄₁₆ inch beyond the front edges of the support and shelf. Secure each dowel with a couple of finishing nails.

4. To insert the bin, place it between the shelf and counter top and lower it until the grooved feet rest on the pivot dowels. Now grasp the handle and pull outward – the bin should pivot outward until the back hits the top stop. Push it back inward and it should come to rest in an upright position when the front hits the top stop.

5. The dowel hanger for the cutting board is attached to the end of the counter top closest to the cutting-board recess. Drill a ½-inch-diameter socket into the center of the counter-top end, at a slight downward angle so the dowel will slant upward, keeping the board from sliding off. The socket should be about 1 inch deep. Cut a 2½-inch length of ½-inch dowel for the hanger peg. Cut one end of the peg at a slight angle. Glue the peg into the socket.

6. If you wish to have additional hanger pegs for utensils, pot holders and other kitchen paraphernalia, follow the procedures described in step 5 to cut the dowels, drill the sockets and install them. You can use leftover ½-inch or ¼-inch dowel for these pegs, depending on the weight of the items to be suspended from them.

7. Turn the unit upside down to install the casters. If you purchased shank-type casters, you will need to drill a hole through the lower block of each leg, to accommodate the caster shank. Follow the manufacturer's instructions to install the shank-type casters. If you purchased flat-plate casters, drill pilot holes into the lower leg blocks, to accommodate the mounting screws.

8. Sand and finish the unit as you like.

CHOPPING-BLOCK KITCHEN CENTER

Microwave Cart

This handsome and convenient kitchen helper couldn't be simpler to build. Size is 29 x 31 x 20 inches.

Materials

Pine 2 x 4: two 8-foot lengths
Pine 1 x 8: three 10-foot lengths
½-inch wooden dowel rod: one 2-foot length
Flathead wood screws in 1¼- and 2-inch lengths
Four locking swivel casters, shank or flat-plate type
Carpenter's wood glue; and Danish oil or other finishing materials of your choice

This handy cart can be used for many purposes. It consists of a top frame that contains the counter-top slats (**Figures F** and **G**), a bottom frame (**Figure H**) and slat-style walls and shelves (**Figures I** and **J**).

Cutting the Parts

1. Cut from 2 x 4 lumber the parts listed in this step and label each one with its code letter. All parts are the full thickness and width of the stock (1½ x 3½ inches). A cutting diagram is provided in **Figure A**, showing how we used the 2 x 4s.

Code	Description	Length	Quantity
Top Frame:			
A	Side	28¾ inches	2
B	End	17 inches	2
Bottom Frame:			
C	End	17 inches	2
D	Side	26½ inches	2

2. Cut or rout a ¾ x ¾-inch rabbet along one edge of one **A** frame side, as shown in **Figure B**. Note that the rabbet is stopped ¾ inch from one end and 3 inches from the other. Drill a ½ x ½-inch socket into the rabbeted side of the board, where indicated in **Figure B**. When you rabbet and drill the second **A**, be sure to make it a mirror image of the first one.

3. Cut or rout a ¾ x ¾-inch rabbet along both edges on one side of each **B** frame end, as shown in **Figure C**.

4. Cut or rout a ¾ x 2¾-inch rabbet along one edge of each **C** frame end, as shown in **Figure D**.

5. Cut from 1 x 8 lumber the parts listed in this step and label each one. A cutting diagram·is provided in **Figure E**, showing how we used the lengths of 1 x 8. All parts are the full ¾-inch thickness of the stock.

Code	Description	Dimensions	Quantity
E	Top Slat	7¼ x 25 inches	2
F	Top Slat	4 x 25 inches	1
G	Wall Slat	3 x 28 inches	1
H	Shelf Slat	3 x 23⅝ inches	10
J	Shelf Support	¾ x 16 inches	4

6. Cut an 18-inch length of ½-inch dowel rod. This will serve as the towel bar.

Assembly

1. Begin by assembling the top frame, as shown in **Figure F**. Note that all four boards are turned so that the rabbets face

Figure A

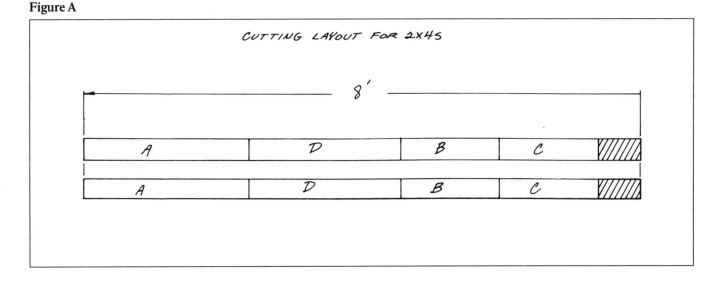

center and the A's are turned with the rabbets at the top. Note also that the B's fit between the A's; the rabbets all match up around the top edge, forming a lip that will support the counter-top boards. The ends of the dowel-rod towel bar fit into the sockets in the A's, as shown. Glue the joints and insert screws through the A's into the ends of the B's. Countersink the screws and cover with plugs.

2. The E and F slats form the counter top. Spline them to-gether edge-to-edge and even at both ends, but there's no need to glue the spline joints. (See Tips & Techniques, if necessary.) Assemble the slats and splines and glue them into the rabbeted lip in the assembled top frame (**Figure G**) – it may be necessary to plane or sand the edges or ends of the assembled slats to get them to fit. To secure, insert screws down through the slats into the A's and B's. Countersink and cover with plugs.

3. Assemble the C's and D's to form the bottom frame, as

Figure C

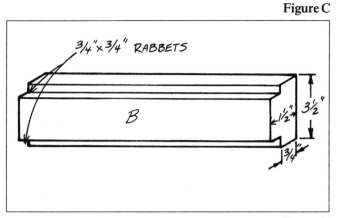

Figure D

Figure B

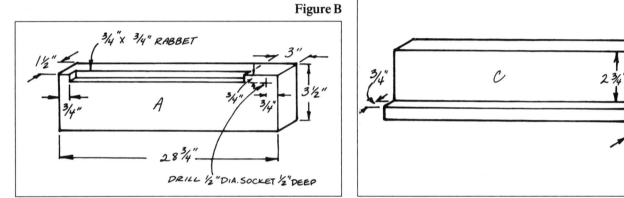

Figure E

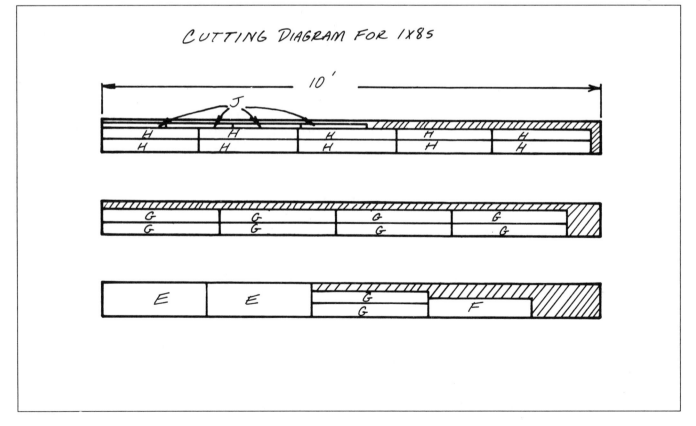

CUTTING DIAGRAM FOR 1X8S

Figure F

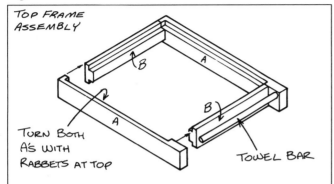

TOP FRAME ASSEMBLY

TURN BOTH A'S WITH RABBETS AT TOP

TOWEL BAR

Figure G

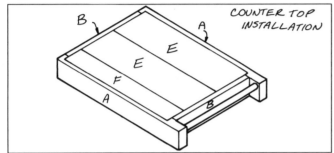

COUNTER TOP INSTALLATION

Figure H

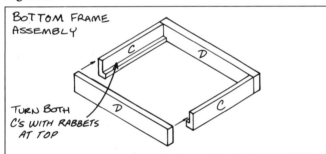

BOTTOM FRAME ASSEMBLY

TURN BOTH C'S WITH RABBETS AT TOP

Figure I

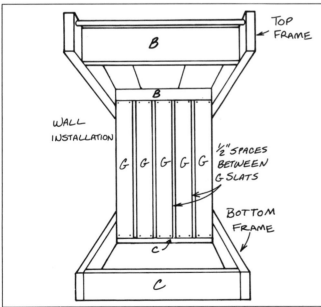

TOP FRAME

WALL INSTALLATION

½" SPACES BETWEEN G SLATS

BOTTOM FRAME

Figure J

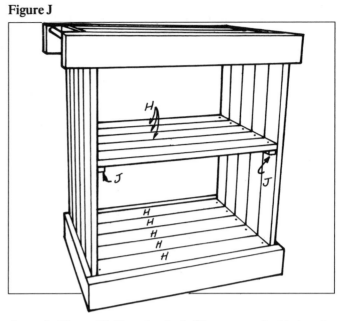

shown in **Figure H**. Note that both C's are turned with the rabbets at the top, facing center. The C's fit between the D's, flush at the ends, as shown. Glue the joints and insert screws through the D's into the ends of the C's. Countersink the screws and cover with plugs.

4. The top and bottom frames are connected by a slat-style wall at each end. One wall is shown in **Figure I**. Glue five G slats between the frames, as shown. Note that the upper ends fit flush into the rabbet along the lower edge of the top-frame B. The lower ends fit flush into the rabbet along the upper edge of the bottom-frame C. There should be a space of about ½ inch between each two slats. Insert two screws through the top of each slat into the B frame. Insert two more through the bottom of each slat into the C frame. Countersink the screws slightly. We did not cover them with plugs, but you may wish to.

5. Use the five remaining G slats to assemble the opposite wall in the same manner.

6. The two shelves are also made up of slats. They are supported by the J shelf supports, which are attached to the walls (**Figure J**). For the upper shelf, glue a J shelf support to the inside of each wall, making sure they are level and even with each other. We placed them about 12 inches below the upper ends of the wall slats. Secure each support with three screws and countersink slightly. For the lower shelf, place the J supports ¾ inch below the upper edge of the bottom frame.

7. For the upper shelf, glue five H slats to the two J supports, aligning them with the wall slats, allowing a space of about ½ inch between each two. Secure with one screw near each end of each slat, inserted down into the support. Again, we countersunk the screws slightly, but did not cover them with plugs. You may wish to.

8. Repeat to install the five lower-shelf H slats.

9. Turn the unit upside down. For shank-type casters, drill a socket into each corner of the lower frame, to accommodate the caster shank. If you are using flat-plate casters, mark and drill pilot holes for the mounting screws. Install the casters.

10. Sand and finish as you like.

Table & Chairs

This table and chairs make a terrific dinette, especially if you're just setting up housekeeping. The table top measures 41 x 30 inches and stands 29 inches tall. The chairs measure 19 x 19 x 34 inches.

Materials

For the table:

2 x 4 pine: two 10-foot lengths, one 8-foot length and one 6-foot length

1 x 8 pine: two 6-foot lengths and one 4-foot length

For one chair:

1 x 8 pine: two 6-foot lengths and one 8-foot length

20 x 20-inch piece of ¼-inch (or thicker) plywood, for the seat

24 x 24-inch piece of upholstery fabric, for the seat

Several 24 x 24-inch pieces of quilt batting, for the seat

Miscellaneous:

Flathead wood screws in 1¼-, 1½- and 2½-inch lengths

Staple gun and staples

Carpenter's wood glue; and Danish oil or other finishing materials of your choice

We hope you'll enjoy building the table and chairs as much as we did. The set makes a great game table, paper-work station or dinette for a small family. The size of the table top can be altered quite easily.

THE TABLE

Cutting the Parts

1. Cut from pine 2 x 4 the parts listed in this step and label each one with its code letter. Each part is the full thickness and width of the stock (1½ x 3½ inches), except for the C supports, which are only 3 inches wide. Refer to **Figure A** for a cutting diagram, showing how we used the lengths of 2 x 4 specified in the materials list. Rip the 6-foot 2 x 4 to 3 inches wide before cutting the C supports. (Save the leftover narrow strip for use in step 1 of the assembly.)

Code	Description	Length	Quantity
A	Frame Side	40 inches	2
B	Frame End	30 inches	2
C	Support	27 inches	2
D	Block	7½ inches	2
E	Leg	28¼ inches	2
F	Foot	27½ inches	4

Figure A

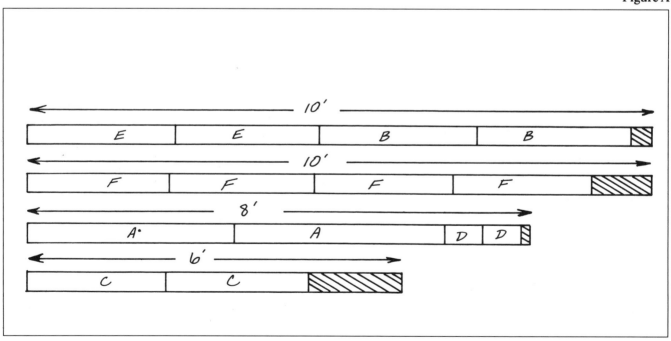

Figure B

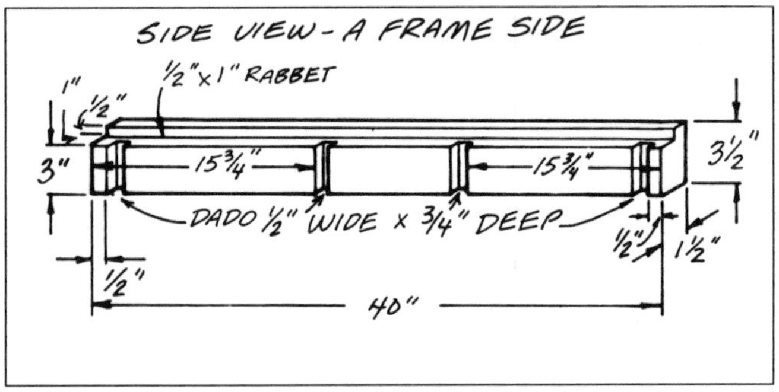
SIDE VIEW - A FRAME SIDE
½"x1" RABBET
1"
½"
3"
15¾"
15¾"
3½"
DADO ½" WIDE x ¾" DEEP
½"
1½"
½"
40"

Figure C

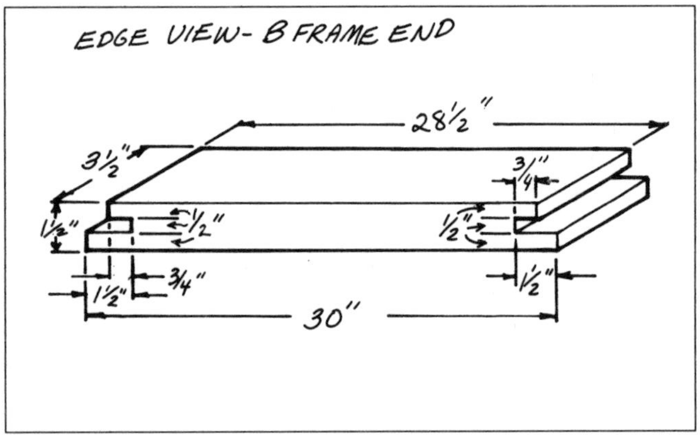
EDGE VIEW - B FRAME END
28½"
3½"
¾"
1½"
½"
½"
1½"
¾"
½"
30"

Figure D

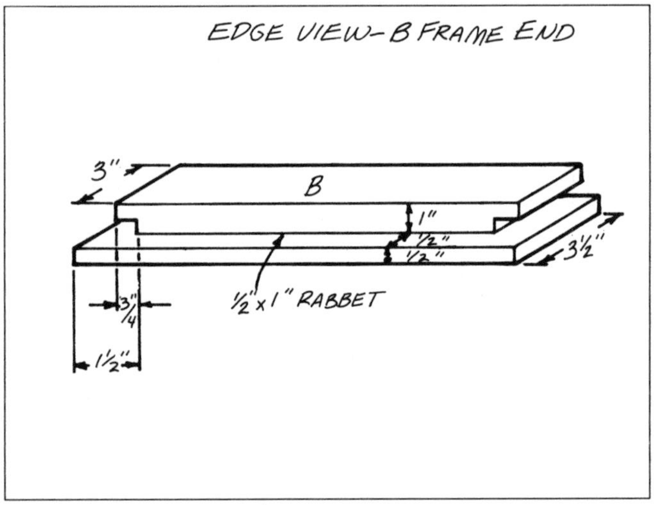
EDGE VIEW - B FRAME END
3"
B
1"
½"
½"
3½"
½"x1" RABBET
¾"
1½"

Figure E

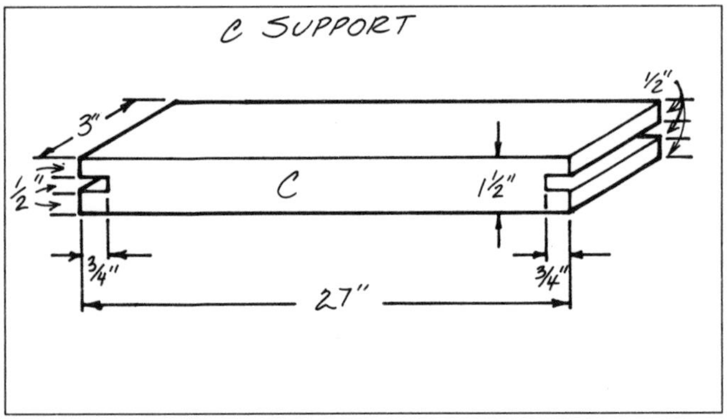
C SUPPORT
½"
3"
½"
C
1½"
¾"
¾"
27"

Figure F

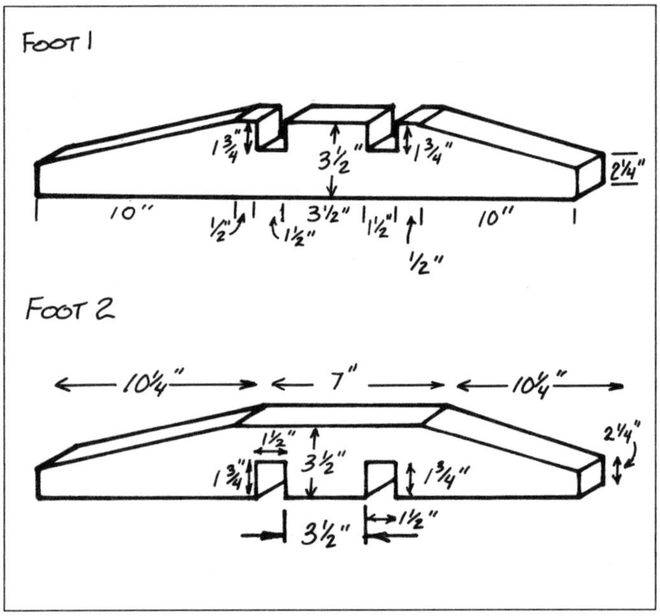
FOOT 1
1¾"
3½"
1¾"
2¼"
10"
½"
1½"
3½"
1½"
10"
½"
FOOT 2
10¼"
7"
10¼"
2¼"
1½"
3½"
1¾"
1¾"
3½"
1½"

2. Both A frame sides are dadoed and rabbeted, as shown in **Figure B**. First, cut or rout four dadoes across one side of the board: one ½ inch from each end and another 15¾ inches from each end, as shown. Each dado should be ½ inch wide by ¾ inch deep. On the same side of the board, cut or rout a ½ x 1-inch rabbet along one long edge, as shown.

3. Both B frame ends are dadoed to form interlocking joints with the A sides. Refer to **Figure C** and cut or rout a ½ x 1½-inch dado along the center of each end. Trim both extensions on one side of the board to ¾ inch long, as shown, leaving the extensions on the other side the full 1½ inches long.

4. Now cut or rout a ½ x 1-inch rabbet along one long edge of each B frame end, on the side with the shorter extensions, as shown in **Figure D**.

5. Each C support is dadoed to accommodate two splines. Cut or rout a ½ x ¾-inch dado along the center of each end, as shown in **Figure E**.

6. Rip both D blocks to 3 inches wide.

7. The F feet are mitered and dadoed, as shown in **Figure F**. Modify two F's as shown for Foot 1. Modify the other two F's as shown for Foot 2.

8. Cut from pine 1 x 8 the parts listed in this step and label each one with its code letter. **Figure G** shows how we used the lengths of 1 x 8 specified in the materials list.

Code	Description	Dimensions	Quantity
G	Slat	7¼ x 35 inches	3
H	Slat	3⅝ x 35 inches	2
J	End Trim	2½ x 29 inches	2
K	Spacer	⅞ x 28¼ inches	2
L	Spline	1½ x 3 inches	4

9. Plane or rip the two K spacers to a thickness of ½ inch so that each one measures ½ x ⅞ x 28¼ inches. Plane the four L splines to a thickness of ½ inch so that each one measures ½ x 1½ x 3 inches.

Figure I

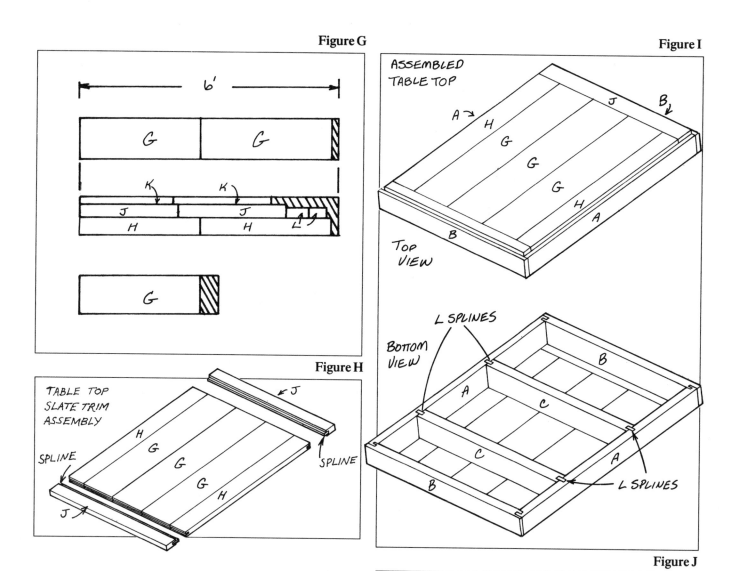

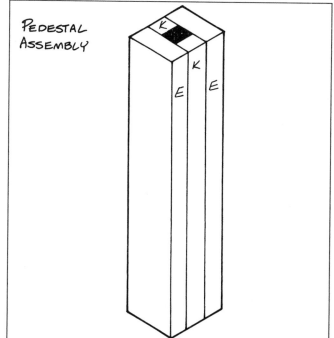

Assembly

The table top consists of splined 1 x 8 boards within a 2 x 4 frame (**Figures H** and **I**). It is supported by a pedestal and base (**Figures J** through **M**).

1. The G and H slats and the J end trims are splined together, as shown in **Figure H**. None of the ends or edges of the assembly will show, because the slats will be contained within the 2 x 4 frame, so you needn't make blind splines. (The short L splines that you cut in step 8 above should not be used for this assembly – rip and cut ¼-inch-thick splines from leftover 2 x 4. Refer to Tips & Techniques, if necessary.) Spline together the G and H slats, as shown, and spline a J Trim to each end of the slat assembly. There's no need to use glue.

2. Assemble the A and B frames around the slat assembly, as shown in **Figure I**. Note that the frames are turned with the rabbeted edges at the top, facing center. The slats should rest in the rabbets and will extend about ¼ inch above the frames. Add the crosswise C supports on the underside, as shown, using the short L splines to secure the C-to-A joints. The C supports should rest against the underside of the slat assembly and the A's, B's and C's should be flush along the lower edges. Glue and clamp the frame joints.

Figure K

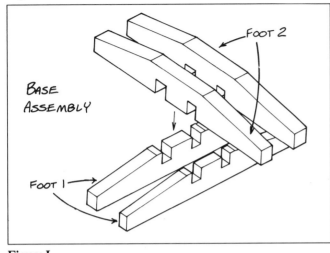

Figure L

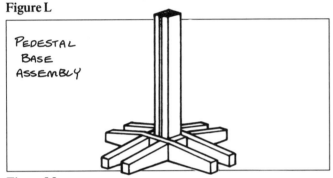

Figure M

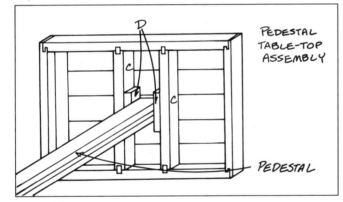

Figure N

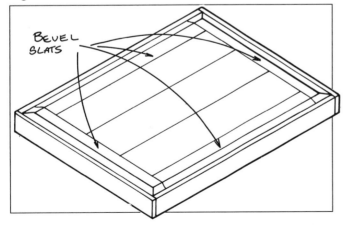

3. Secure each B-to-A corner frame joint with two countersunk wood screws. Cover the heads with plugs. Secure each A-to-C joint in the same manner.

4. The pedestal assembly is shown in **Figure J**. Glue the two K spacers between the two E legs, flush along the outside edges, as shown. Secure with several countersunk screws and cover with plugs.

5. The base assembly is shown in **Figure K**. Interlock the four F feet, as shown, glueing the dado joints. You may need to sand or plane the dadoes slightly to get a good fit – when the feet are pushed together all the way, all upper and lower edges should be flush.

6. Insert and glue the pedestal into the assembled base (**Figure L**), flush at the bottom. Insert a screw through each F foot into the pedestal. Countersink and cover with plugs.

7. The pedestal is attached to the underside of the assembled table top, as shown in **Figure M**, using the two D blocks as spacers. Glue the blocks to the pedestal, flush at the top, and secure each one with two screws. Insert the assembly between the two table-top C supports, as shown. It should be a tight fit – you may have to plane the D blocks if it is too tight or add a thin shim if it is not tight enough. Be sure the pedestal is inserted as far as it will go – the upper edges of the blocks and the top of the pedestal should be butted against the underside of the table-top slats. Secure by inserting two screws through each C support into the adjacent D block. Countersink the screws, but don't bother to cover them with plugs.

8. For a finishing touch, we beveled the table-top slats along the edges and ends (**Figure N**). This will even them up with the 2 x 4 frames. We started with a plane, to remove most of the material and get the correct general angle, and then finished up with a sander.

9. Sand and finish as you like.

THE ARMCHAIR

Cutting the Parts

1. Cut from 1 x 8 lumber the parts listed in this step and label each one with its code letter. Refer to **Figure O** for a cutting diagram, showing how we used the lengths of 1 x 8 specified in the materials list.

Code	Dimensions	Quantity
A	2¼ x 17 inches	8
B	2¼ x 26 inches	2
C	2¼ x 9 inches	4
D	2¼ x 16 inches	2
E	4½ x 17⅝ inches	2
F	4½ x 4½ inches	4
G	2¼ x 18⅜ inches	2
H	2¼ x 14¾ inches	2
J	2¼ x 14½ inches	6
K	2¼ x 16¾ inches	2
M	2¼ x 19 inches	2
N	2¼ x 34 inches	2

2. The eight A's will be used in several different assemblies on the chair. Cutting diagrams are provided in **Figure P**, showing how the A's should be notched and labeled. Cut two notches

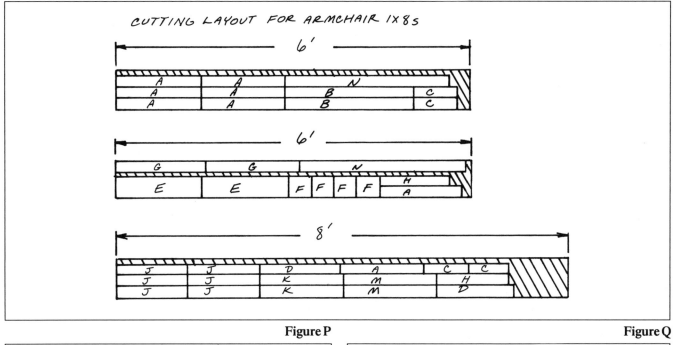

CUTTING LAYOUT FOR ARMCHAIR 1X8s

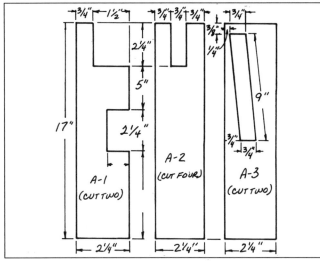

A-1 (CUT TWO)

A-2 (CUT FOUR)

A-3 (CUT TWO)

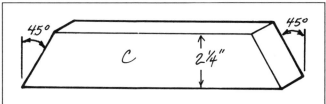

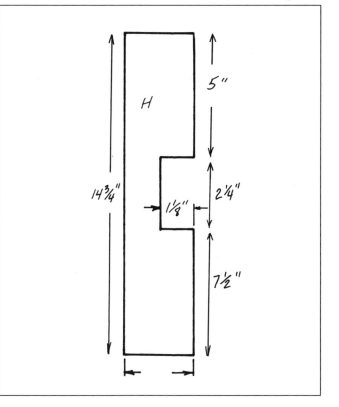

into each of two A's and label these A-1, as shown in the left-hand diagram. Cut a single notch at one end of each of four A's and label these A-2, as shown in the middle diagram. Cut or rout a ¾ x 9-inch mortise into each of the two remaining A's and label these A-3, as shown in the right-hand diagram.

3. Flat miter both ends of each C board at a 45-degree angle, as shown in **Figure Q**.

4. Cut a 1⅛ x 2¼-inch notch into one long edge of each H board, 5 inches from one end, as shown in **Figure R**.

5. Cut from plywood one seat, following the cutting diagram provided in **Figure S**.

Assembly

The armchair assembly is shown in **Figures T** through **AA**.

1. Each front leg consists of one A-2, one A-1 and one B.

Figure S

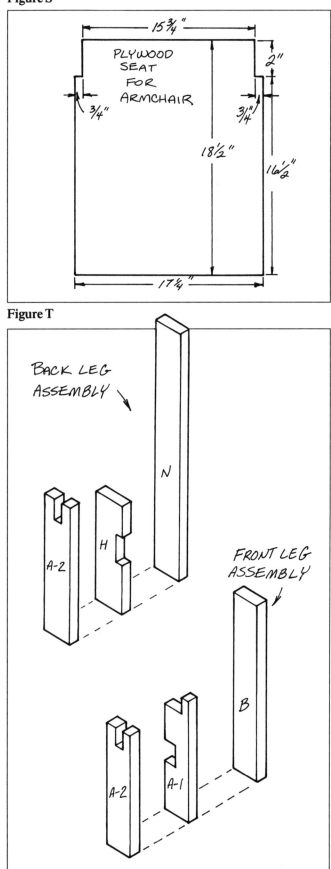

PLYWOOD SEAT FOR ARMCHAIR

15¾"

2"

¾"

3¾"

18½"

16½"

17¾"

Figure T

BACK LEG ASSEMBLY

N

A-2

H

FRONT LEG ASSEMBLY

A-2

A-1

B

Figure U

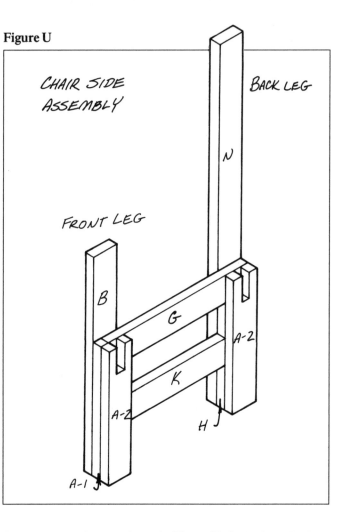

CHAIR SIDE ASSEMBLY

BACK LEG

N

FRONT LEG

B

G

A-2

K

A-2

H

A-1

Glue them together, as shown in **Figure T**, flush along the long edges and at the lower end. For the second front leg, reverse the order so that it is a mirror image (see **Figure V**).

2. Each back leg consists of one **N**, one **H** and one **A-2**. Glue them together, as shown in **Figure U**, flush along the long edges and at the lower end. For the second back leg, reverse the order so that it is a mirror image (see **Figure V**).

3. The diagram in **Figure U** shows one back leg and one front leg joined by upper and lower side rails. (You are looking at the side that will face the center of the chair.) Join one back and one front leg as shown, inserting the ends of the **K** lower side rail into the facing notches in the back-leg **H** and front-leg **A-1** boards. Be sure the **K** rail is pushed into the notches as far as possible. The front end of the **G** upper rail should fit into the notch at the top of the front-leg **A-1** board; the back end should sit on top of the back-leg **H**, flush with the back long edge of the **N** board.

4. Join the remaining front and back legs in the same manner so the assembly is a mirror image of the first one.

5. The next steps are shown in **Figure V**. First, use a **D** rail at the front and another at the back to join the two front-back leg assemblies, inserting the ends into the notches at the tops of the **A-2**'s, as shown. On each side of the chair, glue an **M** armrest across the outside of the front and back legs, flush with the top of the front leg. (Make sure the **M** armrest is level.) Glue

Figure V

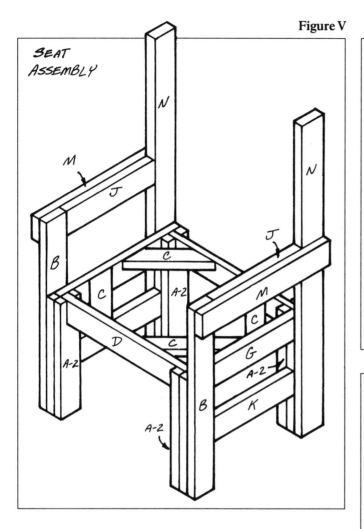

SEAT ASSEMBLY

Figure W

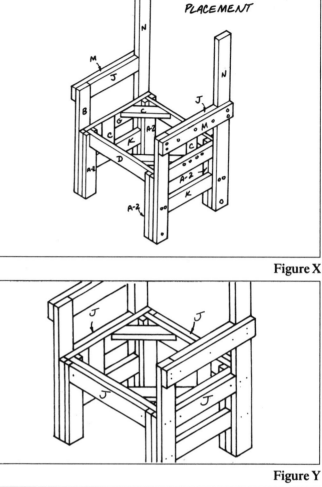

SCREW PLACEMENT

Figure X

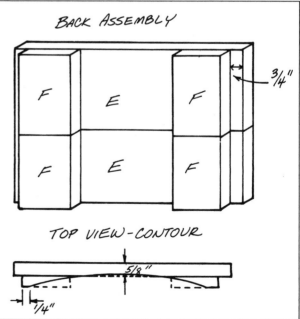

Figure Y

BACK ASSEMBLY

F E F
F E F

3/4"

TOP VIEW - CONTOUR

5/8"

1/4"

a **J** inner armrest to the inside surface of each **M**, between the front and back legs. Glue the four mitered **C** braces to the inside corners of the seat, flush at the top.

6. We used countersunk screws covered with plugs to secure the assembly. Placement is shown for one side in **Figure W**.

7. To complete the seat portion of the chair, glue a **J** rail to the outside surface of each inner seat rail (front, back and sides), as shown in **Figure X**. Secure with countersunk screws covered with plugs.

8. The back is assembled separately, as shown in **Figure Y**. First, glue two **F** blocks to each **E** seat back, ¾ inch from each end, as shown in diagram 1. Glue together the two seat backs edge-to-edge, as shown. When the glue has dried thoroughly, shape the assembly as shown in the top view, diagram 2. (We used a band saw followed by a belt sander, but you can use a wood gouge to get the initial shape.)

9. The final assembly is shown in **Figure Z**. Glue the ends of the **E** seat backs into the mortises in the two **A-3** boards. Note that the **A-3**'s are turned so that the top of the seat back slants backward. Glue this assembly between the two **N** back legs of the chair, as shown. The lower ends of the **A-3**'s should rest on the seat frame and the upper ends should be flush with the tops of the **N**'s. Secure with screws inserted through the back legs and cover with plugs.

Figure Z

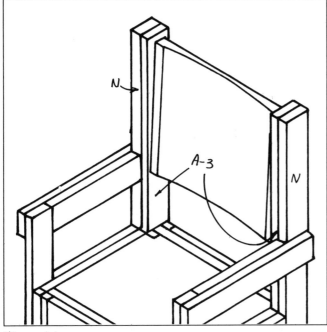

Figure CC

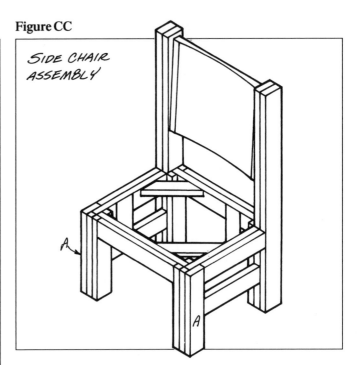

SIDE CHAIR ASSEMBLY

Figure AA

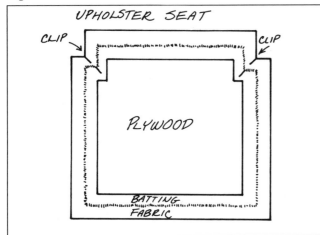

UPHOLSTER SEAT

CLIP

CLIP

PLYWOOD

BATTING
FABRIC

Figure BB

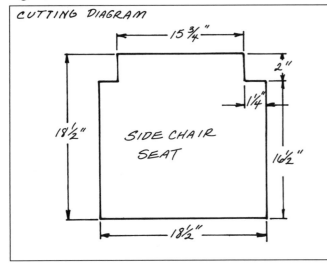

CUTTING DIAGRAM

15 ¾"

2"

1¼"

18½"

SIDE CHAIR
SEAT

16½"

18½"

10. To upholster the plywood seat, cut one or more layers of batting, about 2 inches larger than the plywood all the way around. Cut a fabric piece slightly larger than the batting and press a ½-inch hem to the wrong side along each edge. (Clip the fabric at the inside corners to get it to lie flat.)

11. Place the fabric wrong side up on a flat surface and center the batting layers and plywood on top (**Figure AA**). Clip the batting and fabric at the inside back corners. Fold the edges of the batting and fabric to the top of the plywood and staple in place; start with a single staple at the center of each edge and work out to the corners, alternating edges every few staples, so the fabric will not be pulled off center or distorted on the front. Turn right side up and insert the seat into the chair.

THE SIDE CHAIR

We made a couple of armchairs and a couple of side chairs (with no arms). If you wish to make any side chairs, follow the cutting and assembly instructions for the armchairs, but note these exceptions:

1. Refer to the parts list in step 1, "Cutting the Parts." Note the following differences:

    a. Cut ten instead of eight A's.

    b. Do not cut any B's.

    c. Cut four instead of six J's.

    d. Do not cut any M's.

2. Refer to step 2, "Cutting the Parts." Notch and label eight of the A's as described; leave the two remaining A's unnotched and labeled simply as A.

3. Refer to step 5, "Cutting the Parts." Follow the diagram provided in **Figure BB** to cut the plywood seat.

4. The assembly procedures are basically the same, except that there are no arms. An assembly diagram for the side chair is provided in **Figure DD**. Note that the outer board on each front leg is the unnotched A. All other parts are the same.

Television Stand

Anyone can build this easy, handsome rolling TV stand! The lower shelf provides convenient storage space for your VCR, weekly program listing and other accessories. Overall size is 29 x 16 x 15 inches. It can be altered very easily.

Materials

Pine 2 x 2: three 8-foot lengths
30 x 30-inch piece of ½-inch interior plywood
Four shank-type swivel casters
2½-inch-long flathead wood screws
Carpenter's wood glue; and Danish oil or other finishing materials of your choice

The television stand consists of two identical end sections (**Figure B**) and four connecting rails (**Figure C**). The rails are rabbeted to accommodate the plywood shelves (**Figure D**). That's all there is to it!

Size Alterations

The upper shelf, on which your television must fit, is 26 x 15 inches. Unless you place the unit flat against a wall, you won't have to worry about the 15-inch depth, because the back of the television can extend out beyond the back of the shelf.

The 26-inch width has no leeway, because the end sections extend above the top of the shelf (see **Figure D**). The end sections also limit the width of the lower shelf. If you need extra width (or wish to decrease it), refer to step 2 under "Cutting the Parts" and make a note to alter the length of the **C** long rails.

If you alter the length of the long rails, you will also have to alter the specified 25⅞-inch length of the plywood shelves (refer to step 1 under "Cutting the Parts"). Cut the shelves ⅛ inch shorter than the long rails.

In our unit, there is a vertical space of 8 inches between the upper and lower shelves. If you want more space, cut the **D** legs longer than 16 inches (see step 2, "Cutting the Parts").

Cutting the Parts

1. Cut from plywood two shelves, each 12⅞ x 25⅞ inches.
2. Cut the lengths of pine 2 x 2 listed in this step and label each part with its code letter. All parts are the full thickness and width of the stock – 1½ x 1½ inches. A cutting layout, showing how we used the lengths of 2 x 2 specified in the materials list, is provided in **Figure A**.

Code	Description	Length	Quantity
A	Top Rail	15 inches	2
B	Short Rail	12 inches	4
C	Long Rail	26 inches	4
D	Leg	16 inches	4

Figure A

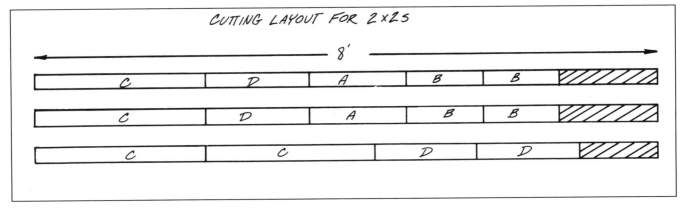

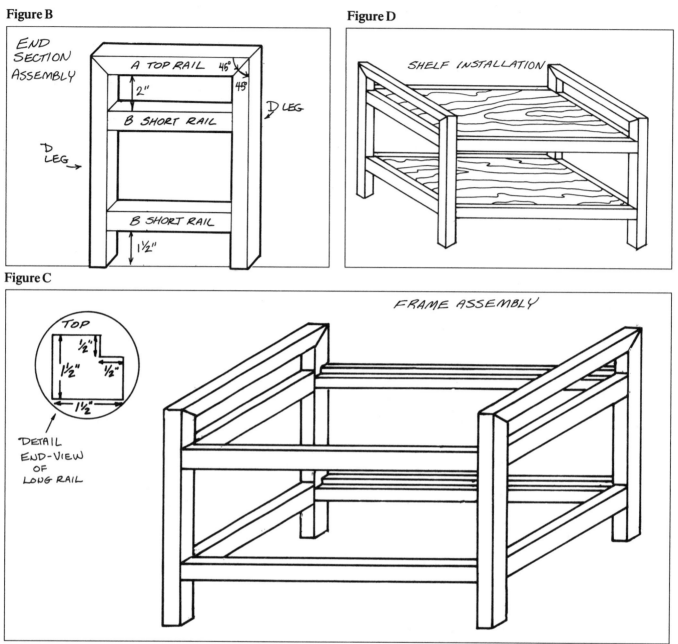

Figure B

END SECTION ASSEMBLY

A TOP RAIL 45°
2"
B SHORT RAIL
D LEG
D LEG
B SHORT RAIL
1½"

Figure D

SHELF INSTALLATION

Figure C

TOP
½"
1½" ½"
1½"

DETAIL END-VIEW OF LONG RAIL

FRAME ASSEMBLY

3. Miter both ends of each **A** top rail and one end of each **D** leg at a 45-degree angle, as shown in the assembly diagram, **Figure B**.

4. The shelves will fit into rabbets cut into the **C** long rails, as shown in **Figure C**. The detail diagram in **Figure C** shows a cross section of one long rail, providing a detail view of how the rabbet should be cut. Cut or rout a ½ x ½- inch rabbet along one edge of each long rail, as shown.

Assembly

1. One end section is shown fully assembled in **Figure B**. Glue an **A** top rail and two **B** short rails between two **D** legs, matching the miters at the top corners, as shown. Secure each joint with two countersunk screws and cover with filler or plugs.

2. Assemble a second, identical end section.

3. Glue the four **C** long rails between the two end sections, as shown in **Figure C**. Note that the long rails are even with the short rails in the end sections. **Note** also that each long rail should be turned so that the rabbet is at the top, facing center. Secure each joint with countersunk and plugged screws.

4. Place the plywood shelves into the rabbets, as shown in **Figure D**. It may be necessary to sand the edges slightly, to get a good fit. The shelves may be glued in place and secured with finishing nails or they may be left unglued.

5. Sand and finish as you like. Turn the unit upside down and mark the lower end of each leg for socket placement to accommodate the caster shank. Drill the sockets and insert the casters.

Table & Chairs
(page 55)

Armchair
(Table & Chairs, page 55)

Side Chair
(Table & Chairs, page 55)

Television Stand
(page 63)

Night Stand
(page 65)

Night Stand

This handsome night stand provides easily accessible storage space for all of your bedside necessities. The clean lines and contemporary style compliment any decorating theme. Dimensions of the top surface are 17 x 31 inches. Each of the lower shelves is slightly smaller. The stand is 22 inches tall.

Materials

Pine 2 x 2: three 8-foot lengths
Pine 1 x 6: one 6-foot length
¼-inch interior plywood: 3 x 4-foot piece
Flathead wood screws in 2½- and 1¼-inch lengths
2d finishing nails
Carpenter's wood glue; and Danish oil or other finishing materials of your choice

If you have already built the television stand featured in this book, the night stand will be a real snap. The basic structures are identical, although the night stand is a bit taller and includes a frame-and-panel top.

Cutting the Parts

1. Cut the lengths of pine 2 x 2 listed in this step and label each one with its code letter. All parts are the full thickness and width of the stock – 1½ x 1½ inches. A cutting layout is provided in **Figure A**, showing how we used the lengths of 2 x 2 specified in the materials list.

Code	Description	Length	Quantity
A	Top Rail	15½ inches	2
B	Short Rail	12½ inches	4
C	Long Rail	26 inches	4
D	Leg	21 inches	4

2. Cut from pine 1 x 6 the parts listed in this step. All parts are the full ¾-inch thickness of the stock. A cutting layout is provided in **Figure B**. Label each part with its code letter.

Code	Description	Dimensions	Quantity
E	Short Support	¾ x 16½ inches	2
F	Long Support	¾ x 29 inches	2
G	Short Trim	1½ x 18 inches	2
H	Long Trim	1½ x 32 inches	2

Figure A

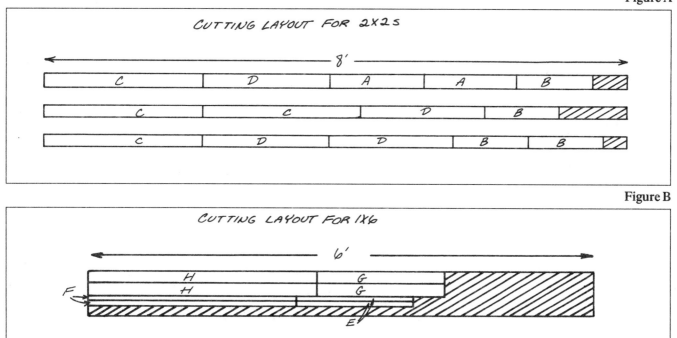

Figure B

Figure C

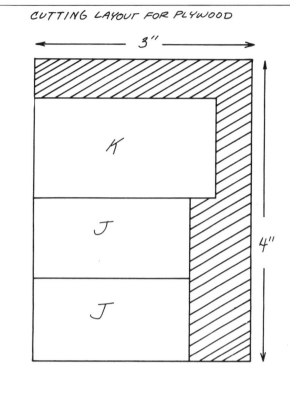

CUTTING LAYOUT FOR PLYWOOD

Figure D

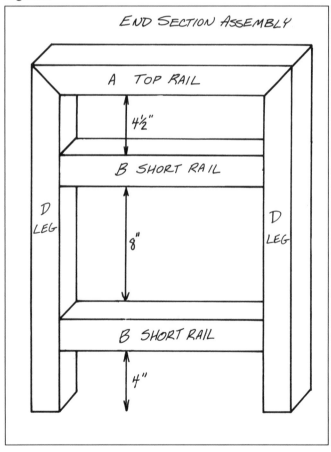

END SECTION ASSEMBLY

Figure E

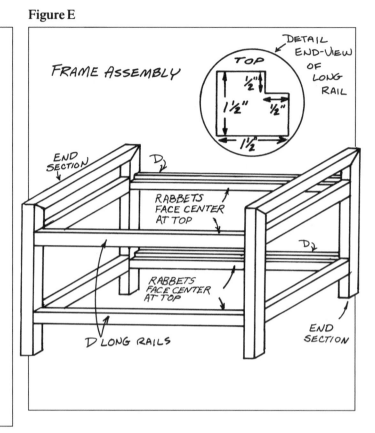

FRAME ASSEMBLY

3. Cut from ¼-inch plywood the parts listed in this step. A cutting layout is provided in **Figure C**.

Code	Description	Dimensions	Quantity
J	Shelf	13⅜ x 25⅞ inches	2
K	Top	16 x 30 inches	1

4. Miter one end of each D leg and both ends of each A top rail at a 45-degree angle (refer to the assembly diagram, **Figure D**). Note that for the A top rail, both miters are cut toward the same edge. Cut the miters so that you do not reduce the overall length along the resulting longest side.

5. The shelves will fit into rabbets cut into the C long rails. A detail cross-section view of a rabbeted long rail is provided in the assembly diagram, **Figure E**. Cut or rout a ¼ x ½-inch rabbet along one edge of each C long rail, as shown.

Assembly

1. One assembled end section is shown in **Figure D**. Glue an A top rail and two B short rails between two D legs, as shown. The vertical distances between the rails are provided as a guide; you may wish to alter them to create more or less space between the upper and lower shelves or between the upper shelf and the top assembly (see **Figure I**). Secure each joint.

2. Assemble a second, identical end section.

3. Glue the four C long rails between the two end sections, as shown in **Figure E**. Note that the long rails are even with the short rails in the end sections. **Note** also that each long rail should be turned so that the rabbet is at the top, facing center, exactly as shown in the detail inset. Secure the joints.

2 X 4 FURNITURE

Figure F

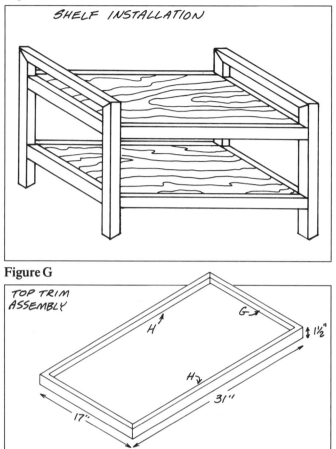

SHELF INSTALLATION

Figure G

TOP TRIM ASSEMBLY

H

G

1½"

H

31"

17"

Figure H

SUPPORT INSTALLATION

E & F SUPPORTS ARE ¾" BELOW TOP OF OUTER FRAME

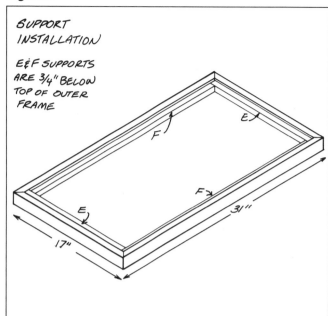

F

E

F

E

31"

17"

Figure I

K TOP

TRIM FRAME

4. Place the plywood J shelves into the rabbets, as shown in **Figure F**. It may be necessary to sand the edges slightly, to get a good fit. The shelves may be glued in place and secured with finishing nails or they may be left unglued.

5. The G and H trim pieces must be edge-mitered to fit around the top of the assembled base, as shown in **Figures G** through **I**. The trims were cut longer than necessary, to allow for any differences in finished dimensions of the base. Measure around the outside of the base, at the top. Edge-miter the G and H trims at a 45-degree angle so that they will fit around it, as shown. Glue them together, flush along upper and lower edges and matching miters at the corners. Secure with finishing nails.

6. The E and F supports must be trimmed to fit inside the assembled frame, as shown in **Figure H**. (The supports, like the trims, were cut longer than necessary.) Trim the supports to fit, as shown. Glue them to the inside surfaces of the trim frame members, ¼ inch below the top edges of the frame. Secure the supports with screws.

7. The plywood K top fits inside the frame, resting on the supports. It was cut slightly larger than necessary. Trim and sand the edges of the top so that it fits tightly into the frame (**Figure I**). It can be left as is, or you may prefer to secure it with glue and screws or nails.

8. Place the assembled top over the base (**Figures H** and **I**). It can be left as is, or you may prefer to attach the frame to the top rails of the base, using screws.

9. Sand and finish the unit.

Outdoor Conversation Pit

This versatile bench-and-table combination makes a comfortable, convenient, cozy conversation area for your patio, porch or yard. It can be butted up against the walls or made as a freestanding unit of any size.

Materials

We used 2 x 4 pine for the inner frames, 1 x 6 redwood for the slats that cover the frames and 1 x 2 pine for a contrasting trim. You can use all pine or any combination of redwood, pine, cedar, fir or just about any other lumber you like. If 1 x 6 lumber is not available, substitute 1 x 4 or 1 x 8. Be sure to use rust-resistant hardware.

For one 19 x 21 x 90-inch bench that is not butted against another bench or wall at either end or side, you'll need the amounts of dimensional lumber listed below. We suggest that you read through the instructions and decide where and how large you want your conversation pit to be. Then you can either work out a detailed materials list for your project or estimate what you'll need, based on the list below. If you estimate, be aware that the amount of 1 x 6 required will vary greatly, depending on whether each bench is butted against any walls or other benches.

Pine 2 x 4: four 10-foot lengths
Redwood 1 x 6: 90 linear feet
Pine 1 x 2: 50 linear feet

For one 16-inch-tall table with a 4-foot-square top, you'll need the following amounts of lumber:

Pine 2 x 4: four 8-foot lengths
Redwood 1 x 6: 80 linear feet
Pine 1 x 2: 40 linear feet

Miscellaneous:

8d and 3d common nails, either galvanized or made of brass, bronze or stainless steel

Wood preservative (optional); and stain and sealer, exterior paint or other finishing materials of your choice

Figure A

```
CUTTING LAYOUT FOR 2X4s

|←————————— 10' —————————→|

[        A        ][ B ][ B ][///]
[        A        ][ B ][ B ][///]
[        A        ][ C ][ C ][ C ][/]
[        A        ][ C ][ C ][ C ][/]
```

These easy projects are also very versatile. You can adjust the dimensions to fit just about any area where you want outdoor seating. Our benches are 21 inches deep by 90 long by 19 tall. The table is 16 inches tall with a 4-foot-square top.

Building the Benches

Each bench consists of a rectangular frame made of 2 x 4s, which is covered by slats cut from 1 x 6. The 1 x 2 lumber serves as trim. You can join two benches together to form a right angle, as shown in the illustration, use individual benches or join several to form any other convenient shape. Where two or more benches join together, or where one butts against a wall, you will not need to cover the concealed portion with 1 x 6 slats.

If you wish to alter the size of the bench, please refer to the assembly diagrams (**Figures B** through **E**) and to the cutting instructions in step 1. Note the differences to the lengths of the 2 x 4 frame members.

1. Cut from 2 x 4 lumber the parts listed in this step and label each one with its code letter. Each part is the full thickness and width of the stock – 1½ x 3½ inches. We have provided a cutting diagram in **Figure A**, showing how we used the four 10-foot 2 x 4s. (**Note:** To make a longer or shorter bench, alter the length of the A frames. To make a deeper or shallower bench, alter the length of the B frames. To make a taller or shorter bench, alter the length of the C frames.)

Code	Length	Quantity
A	85 inches	4
B	13 inches	4
C	11 inches	6

2. The bench frame consists of two identical side sections joined by four crossbars. To build one side section, assemble two A's and three C's, as shown in **Figure B**. The middle C should be equally distant from the ends of the long A's. Toenail to secure each joint, using two 8d nails. Assemble a second, identical side section, using the remaining A's and C's.

3. Nail the four B crossbars between the two side sections, flush at the ends, as shown in **Figure C**. Note that the side sections cover the ends of the crossbars and the A's and B's are flush at the top and bottom.

4. If you are making two or more benches that will be connected, align the frames in the desired configuration and nail them together.

5. If your bench or benches will be butted against a wall, put them in place before proceeding. The 1 x 6 slats are now added, as shown in the top-view diagram, **Figure D**. We covered each end and then each side of the frame, allowing the outer slats on each side to lap over the edges of the adjacent slats on the ends – you may prefer to start at one corner and work your way around. Cut enough slats to cover the entire frame, or only the sides and ends that are not butted against another bench or wall. The slats should not extend beyond the top or bottom of the frame – if you made the frame the same size as we did, cut the slats 18 inches long. You'll probably have to rip the last slat on each end and side to come out flush at the corners. Use 3d nails to secure each slat: two near the top and two near the bottom.

6. The top is also covered with slats (**Figure E**). We cut them 2 inches longer than the depth of the slat-covered frame. They

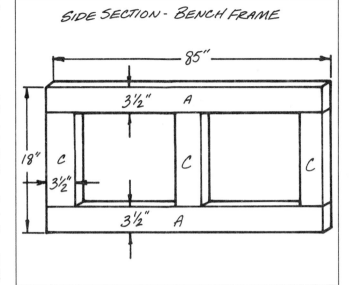

Figure C

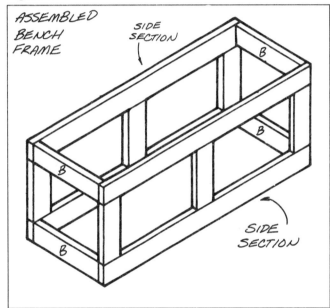

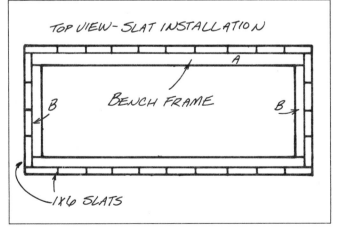

Figure E

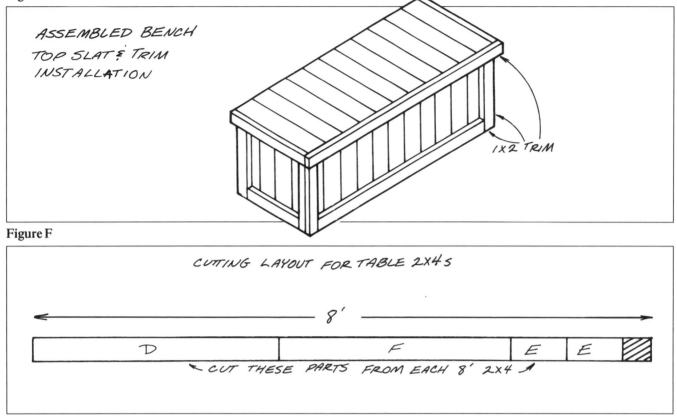

ASSEMBLED BENCH
TOP SLAT § TRIM
INSTALLATION

1X2 TRIM

Figure F

CUTTING LAYOUT FOR TABLE 2X4s

8'

D   F   E   E

← CUT THESE PARTS FROM EACH 8' 2X4 →

extend 2 inches beyond the front and are flush with the back, which is butted against a wall. If your bench is not butted against anything, cut the top slats about 4 inches longer. They will extend 2 inches beyond both the front and back. Cut enough 1 x 6 slats to cover the top, allowing them to extend over the ends as well as the front and back (if your bench is not butted against anything at the ends). Again, secure each slat with four 3d nails.

7. Cut lengths of 1 x 2 lumber for the trim, as shown in **Figure E**. We added trim around the bottom of the base, along each vertical corner and along the edges and ends of the top slats. Again, you need not attach trim to any side or end that will be butted against something else. Where two trim strips meet at a corner, either edge miter or allow one to lap flush over the other. Secure the trim with glue and 3d common or finishing nails.

Building the Table

The table is very much like the bench. Its square frame is made in exactly the same manner and is covered by slats. The top slats are quite a bit longer than the frame, extending about 4 inches beyond it on each side. Our slat-covered frame measures 40 x 40 inches and is 15½ inches tall. The top slats form a 4-foot-square table top.

If you want a larger table top, you need not alter the size of the frame. A smaller table top may required a smaller frame, as the top should extend at least a few inches beyond each side. If you want to make any changes, refer to the cutting instructions in step 1 and the assembly diagrams in **Figures G** through **I**. Note any differences you will have to account for.

1. Cut from 2 x 4 lumber the parts listed in this step and label each one with its code letter. Each part is the full thickness and width of the stock (1½ x 3½ inches). **Figure F** shows how we used each 8-foot 2 x 4. (**Note:** Refer to **Figure H**. To make a wider or narrower frame, alter the length of the D's and F's. To make a taller or shorter frame, alter the length of the E's.)

Code	Length	Quantity
D	38½ inches	4
E	8½ inches	4
F	35½ inches	4

2. The table frame consists of two identical sections joined by four crossbars. To build one frame section, assemble two D's and two E's, as shown in **Figure G**. Toenail each joint, using two 8d nails. Assemble a second, identical frame section.

3. Nail the four F crossbars between the two frame sections, flush at the ends, as shown in **Figure H**. Note that the frame sections cover the ends of the crossbars. The D's and F's are flush at the top and bottom.

4. The 1 x 6 slats are now added, as shown in the top-view diagram, **Figure I**. Cut enough 15½-inch-long slats to cover the entire frame, lapping the end slat on each successive side over the adjacent slat on the previous side. You'll probably have to rip the last slat on each side to come out flush at the corners. Use four 3d nails to secure each slat: two near the top and two near the bottom.

5. The top slats are also lengths of 1 x 6. We cut them 46½ inches long, which will make a 48-inch length when the trim

is added. Cut enough slats to cover the width of the frame plus another 3 inches on each side. (The slats should extend equally beyond all four sides of the base.) Again, secure each slat with four 3d nails.

6. Cut lengths of 1 x 2 lumber for the trim, as you did for the bench. We added trim around the bottom of the base, along each vertical corner and along the edges and ends of the top slats. Where two trim strips meet at a corner, either edge miter or allow one to lap flush over the other. Secure the trim with glue and 3d common or finishing nails.

Figure H

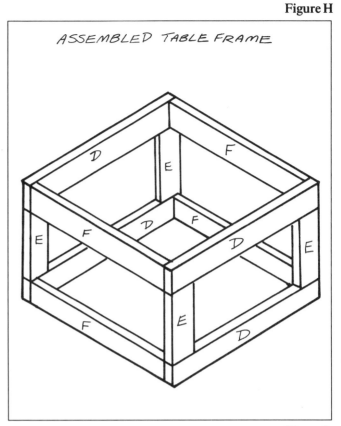

ASSEMBLED TABLE FRAME

Figure G

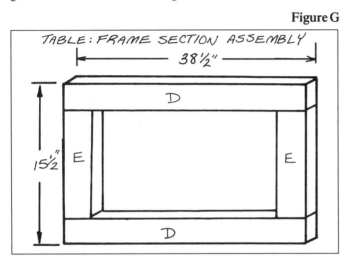

TABLE: FRAME SECTION ASSEMBLY

Figure I

TABLE TOP VIEW DETAIL—SLAT INSTALLATION

1X6 SLATS

FINISHED VIEW

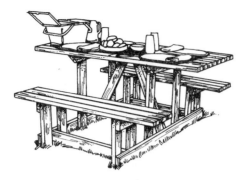

Picnic Table

This picnic table is so easy to build, you'll probably want to make more than one and give them as gifts! The table top measures 32 x 72 inches and stands 32 inches tall. The two benches measure 12 x 60 x 17 inches. Bolted joints mean you can disassemble the structure for storage or transport.

Materials

Notes: We used redwood for this project, because it's an especially good wood for outdoor furniture (see Tips & Techniques). You may wish to substitute pine, which is less expensive but requires paint or preservative for outdoor longevity; or use another type of lumber of your choice. Be sure to use rust-resistant hardware (see Tips & Techniques).

2 x 4 lumber: fourteen 10-foot lengths
¼ x 3½-inch carriage bolts, each with a flat washer and nut to fit (You'll need about fifty.)
2½-inch-long flathead wood screws
6d common nails
Finishing materials of your choice (optional)

The picnic table assembly is very simple. It consists of a basic frame structure that supports the bench and table-top slats. The support structure is shown in **Figures D** through **F** and the final assembly is shown in **Figure G**.

Cutting the Parts

1. Cut the lengths of 2 x 4 lumber listed here and label each one with its code letter. All parts are the full thickness and width of the stock – 1½ x 3½ inches. A cutting layout is provided in **Figure A**, showing how we used the fourteen 10-foot 2 x 4s specified in the materials list.

Figure A

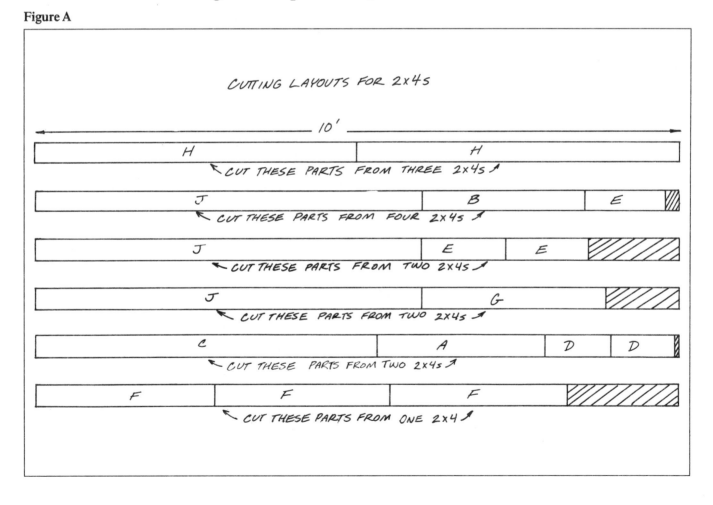

CUTTING LAYOUTS FOR 2x4s

— 10' —

| H | H |

← CUT THESE PARTS FROM THREE 2x4s →

| J | B | E |

← CUT THESE PARTS FROM FOUR 2x4s →

| J | E | E |

← CUT THESE PARTS FROM TWO 2x4s →

| J | G |

← CUT THESE PARTS FROM TWO 2x4s →

| C | A | D | D |

← CUT THESE PARTS FROM TWO 2x4s →

| F | F | F |

← CUT THESE PARTS FROM ONE 2x4 →

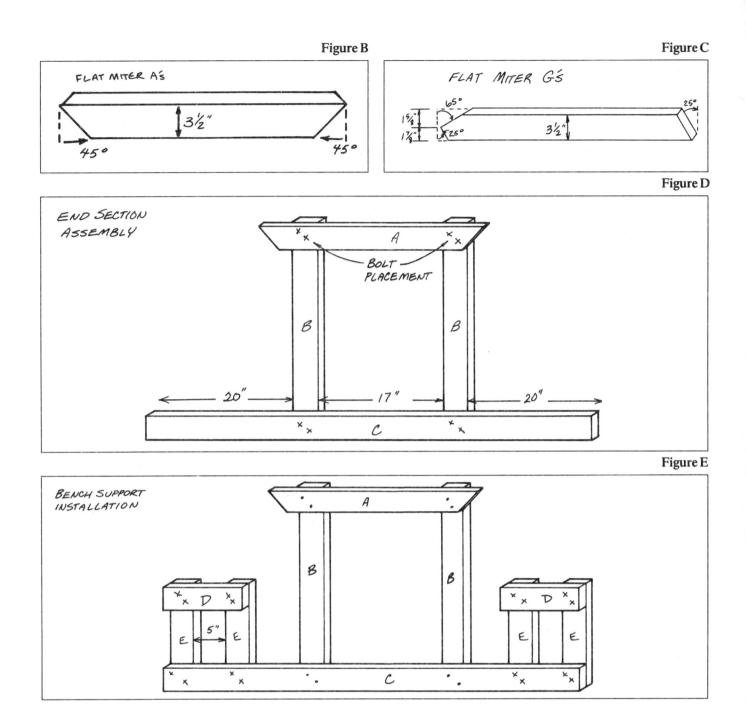

Figure B

FLAT MITER A's

3½"

45°   45°

Figure C

FLAT MITER G's

65°
1⅝"
1⅞"   25°   3½"   25°

Figure D

END SECTION ASSEMBLY

A

BOLT PLACEMENT

B   B

20"   17"   20"

C

Figure E

BENCH SUPPORT INSTALLATION

A

B   B

D   D

E   5"   E   E   E

C

Code	Description	Length	Quantity
A	Top Support	31 inches	2
B	Table Leg	30 inches	4
C	Connector	64 inches	2
D	Bench Support	12 inches	4
E	Bench Leg	15½ inches	8
F	Connector	33 inches	3
G	Brace	34 inches	2
H	Bench Slat	60 inches	6
J	Top Slat	72 inches	8

2. Flat miter both ends of each A support at a 45-degree angle, as shown in **Figure B**.

3. The two G braces are mitered at the ends, as shown in **Figure C**. Be sure to cut the double-mitered end correctly, in relation to the single miter at the opposite end.

Assembly

1. One end section is shown in **Figure D**. Use 6d temporary holding nails for the initial assembly; do not drive the nails in all the way, as you will have to pull them out again in step 2. Note the spacing indicated in the diagram. The A support and C connector should each extend equally beyond the two B's. Note that the A and B's are flush at the top. The C and B's should be flush at the bottom.

Figure F

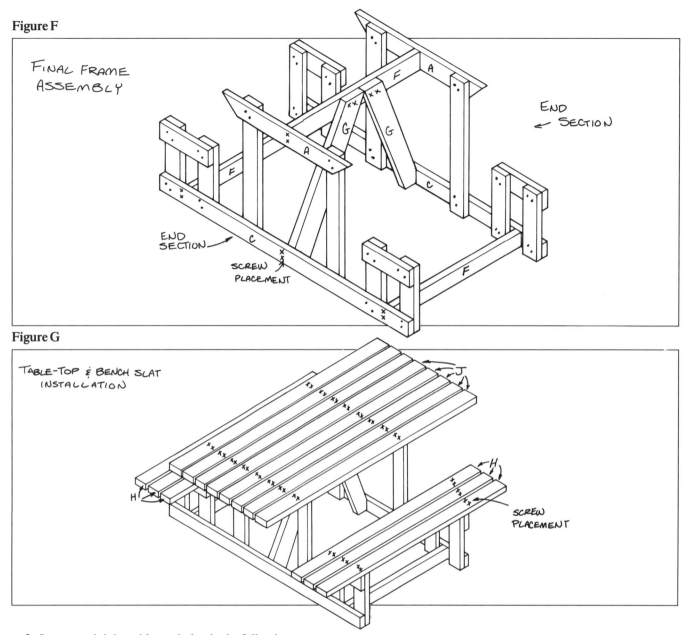

FINAL FRAME ASSEMBLY

END SECTION

END SECTION

SCREW PLACEMENT

Figure G

TABLE-TOP & BENCH SLAT INSTALLATION

SCREW PLACEMENT

2. Secure each joint with two bolts, in the following manner: Drill a ¼-inch hole through the joint for the first bolt. Insert the bolt and secure with a flat washer and nut. Remove the holding nail and drill the second bolt hole where the nail was, so there will not be an extra hole in the wood. Insert the second bolt and secure on the same side of the assembly with a washer and nut.

3. The E bench legs and D bench supports are now added to the end section, as shown in **Figure E**. Note that the outer E's are flush with the ends of the C connector. The two E's at each end are flush with the ends and top of the D support, as shown. The C and E's are flush at the bottom. Proceed as you did in step 1, performing the initial assembly with temporary holding nails; then secure each joint with two bolts, as described in step 2. All bolts should be inserted from the same side.

4. Repeat steps 1 through 3 to build a second, identical end section, using the remaining A through E parts.

5. The two end sections are now joined, as shown in **Figure F**. Align the sections about 3 feet apart. (Make sure that each one is turned with the bolt heads facing outward and the nuts facing center.) Install the three F connectors where indicated, flush with the C's and A's along the top and bottom. Secure with two screws at each end, as shown.

6. Install the two G braces where indicated in **Figure F**. Secure each one with two screws inserted into the F connector and two through the C connector into the G.

7. The final assembly is shown in **Figure G**. Place the eight J top slats across the support assembly, extending equally at each end and with a space of about ½ inch between slats. Secure each slat with four screws: two near each end, as shown. Recess these screws slightly; they should be flush with or slightly lower than the surface of the table top.

8. Place three H bench slats across the support structure on one side of the table (**Figure G**), extending equally at each end. Allow about ¾ inch of space between slats. Secure with screws, as you did the top slats. Install the three remaining H slats across the bench supports on the opposite side of the table.

Rubbish Rickshas

These handy trash-can carts are especially helpful if neighborhood pets get into the garbage on collection days. They are also a big help with yard work and they're very easy to build! We've included instructions for one- and two-can sizes.

Materials

For a single-can cart:
Construction-grade 2 x 4: three 10-foot lengths

For a double-can cart:
Construction-grade 2 x 4: four 10-foot lengths
Construction-grade 2 x 8: one 4-foot length

For either size:
Two 8-inch-diameter lawn mower wheels.
28-inch length of ½-inch-diameter metal rod, for the axle
Two cotter pins, about 1½ inches long
Six flat metal washers with ½-inch center hole
1¼- and 2½-inch-long flathead wood screws
Exterior paint

The final assembly for the single-can ricksha is shown in **Figures L** and **M**. See **Figure T** for the double ricksha. Each one consists of a top frame and a bottom frame, which are connected by four legs.

SINGLE-CAN RICKSHA

Cutting the Parts

1. Cut the lengths of 2 x 4 lumber listed in this step and label each part with its code letter, for reference during assembly. All parts are the full thickness and width of the stock – 1½ x 3½ inches. A cutting layout, showing how we used the lengths of 2 x 4 specified in the materials list, is provided in **Figure A**.

Code	Length	Quantity
A	20 inches	4
B	23 inches	4
C	23 inches	1
D	25 inches	2
E	28 inches	2
F	16 inches	2

Figure A

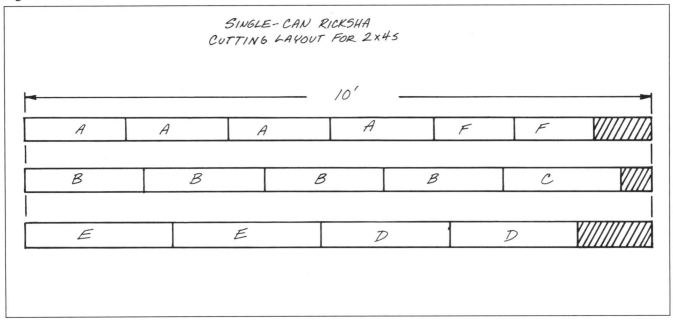

Figure B

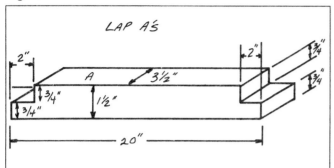

LAP A'S

Figure C

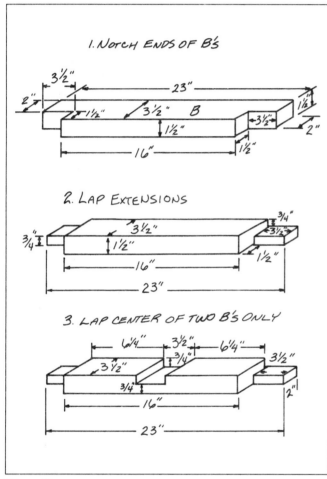

1. NOTCH ENDS OF B'S

2. LAP EXTENSIONS

3. LAP CENTER OF TWO B'S ONLY

Figure D

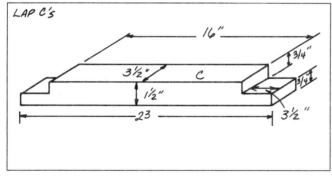

LAP C'S

Figure E

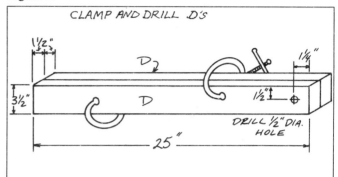

CLAMP AND DRILL D'S

DRILL ½" DIA. HOLE

Figure F

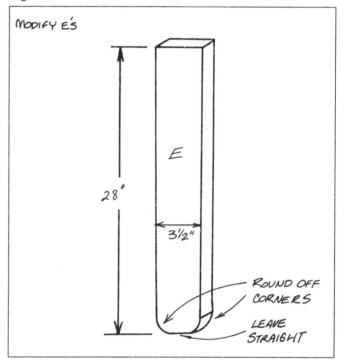

MODIFY E'S

ROUND OFF CORNERS

LEAVE STRAIGHT

2. The A's are lap-cut at the ends, as shown in **Figure B**. Modify all four of the A's. Note that both laps are cut on the same side of the board and both are ¾ x 2 inches.

3. The B's are notched and then lapped at the ends, as shown in **Figure C**. Modify all four of the B's, as shown in diagrams 1 and 2. First, cut a 1½ x 3½-inch notch from each end, into the same edge of the board, as shown in diagram 1. Then trim the thickness of the extension at each end to create a lap, as shown in diagram 2. Leave two of the B's as they are and label them B-Top. The remaining two B's must be lap-cut across the center, as shown in diagram 3. Note that the lap is made on the same side of the board as the laps at the ends. The center lap is ¾ inch deep by 3½ inches wide. Modify two of the B's, as shown, and label them B-Bottom.

4. The C board is lap-cut at the ends, as shown in **Figure D**. Note that both laps are cut on the same side of the board. Both are ¾ x 3½ inches.

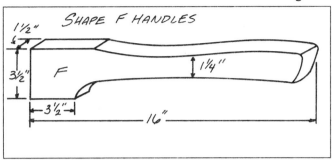

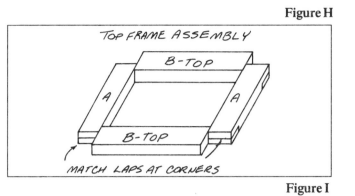

Figure I

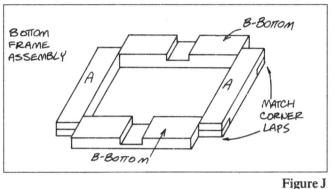

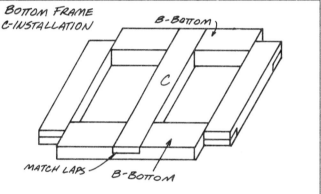

5. The two D boards will serve as the front legs and are drilled to accommodate the metal axle rod. It's important that the holes line up exactly. We suggest that you temporarily clamp or nail together the two D's and drill the holes simultaneously, as shown in **Figure E**. Mark the drilling point midway between the long edges and 1¼ inches from one end, as shown. Drill a ½-inch-diameter hole through both boards.

6. Slightly round off the corners at one end of each E back leg, as shown in **Figure F**. Be careful not to shorten the overall length of the board and be sure to leave a flat surface at the rounded end. This will be the lower end of the back leg.

7. The two F boards will serve as the handles and are shaped as shown in **Figure G**. You can make the initial cuts to achieve the approximate shape, using a saber saw; then smooth out the contours with a sander or wood rasp. Shape both F boards in this manner.

Assembly

Note: We suggest that you countersink all screws slightly, to prevent scratches caused by protruding screw heads.

1. The top frame is assembled first. Assemble two A's and the two B-Tops, matching laps at the corners, as shown in **Figure H**. There will be a 1½ x 3½-inch space at each corner, which will accommodate a leg. Glue the lap joints and secure each one with two of the shorter wood screws.

2. Now assemble the bottom frame (**Figure I**). Glue together the remaining two A's and the two B-Bottoms, matching laps at the corners. Again, there will be a space at each corner, to accommodate the legs. Secure each joint with two of the shorter wood screws.

3. Fit the C brace across the center of the bottom frame, matching lap cuts, as shown in **Figure J**. Glue the lap joints and secure each one with two of the shorter screws.

4. To join the two frames, fit the D front legs and E back legs into the openings at the corners, as shown in **Figure K**. Be sure that each front leg is turned with the axle hole near the lower end. Each back leg must be turned with the rounded corners at the bottom. All four legs should be flush with the top frame. The back legs will extend farther below the bottom frame than the front legs. Glue the legs to the frames and secure to each frame with two of the longer screws.

5. Fit the F handles against the inside surfaces of the two back legs, as shown in **Figure L**, butted against the underside of the top frame. Glue in place and secure each one with three of the longer screws.

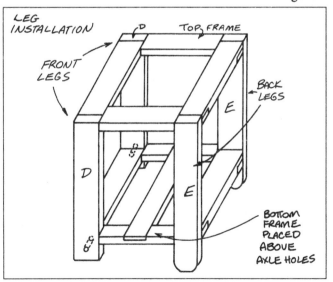

Figure L

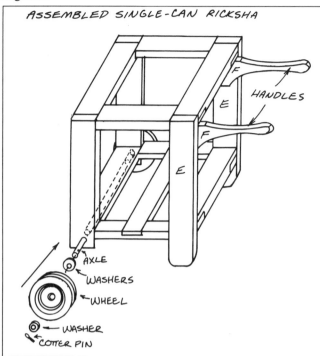

ASSEMBLED SINGLE-CAN RICKSHA

HANDLES

AXLE
WASHERS
WHEEL
WASHER
COTTER PIN

Figure M

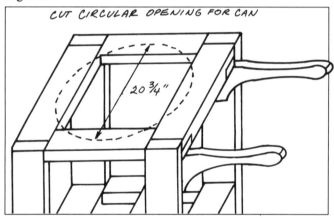

CUT CIRCULAR OPENING FOR CAN

20 3/4"

6. Insert the axle rod through the aligned holes in the two front legs, leaving equal extensions at each end, as shown in **Figure L**. At each end, install two washers, a wheel and another washer. (If the axle extends more than about ¼ inch beyond each wheel, you may wish to trim the length.) At each end, drill a hole through the axle just outside of the outer washer, using a bit that will accommodate a cotter pin. Install the cotter pins to hold the wheels on the axle, as shown.

7. Draw the outline of a 20¾-inch-diameter circle on the top frame, as shown in **Figure M**. Use a saber saw to cut the top-frame boards along the outline, to create a round opening for the trash can.

8. Sand to eliminate the worst splinters and rough spots. Paint, being careful to avoid the axle and wheels.

DOUBLE-CAN RICKSHA

Cutting the Parts

1. Cut the lengths of 2 x 4 and 2 x 8 lumber listed in this step and label each part with its code letter. All parts are the full thickness and width of the stock – 1½ x 3½ inches or 1½ x 7¼ inches. A cutting layout showing how we used the lengths of 2 x 4 specified in the materials list is provided in **Figure N**.

Code	Length	Quantity
Cut from 2 x 4:		
A	20 inches	4
B	46¼ inches	4
C	23 inches	2
D	25 inches	2
E	28 inches	2
F	16 inches	2
Cut from 2 x 8:		
G	23 inches	2

2. The A's are lap-cut at the ends, just as the A's for the single-can ricksha were (see **Figure B**). Modify all four of the A's as shown. Note that both laps are cut on the same side of the board and both are ¾ x 2 inches.

3. The B's are notched and then lapped at the ends, as shown

Figure N

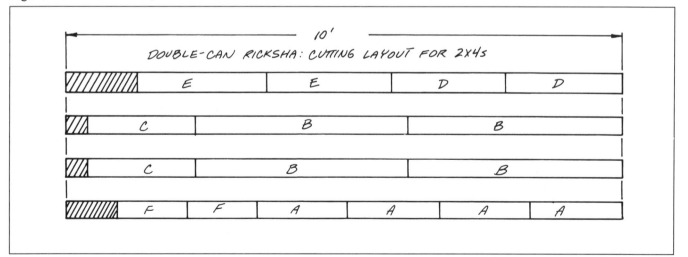

10'

DOUBLE-CAN RICKSHA: CUTTING LAYOUT FOR 2X4s

E	E	D	D
C	B	B
C	B	B
F	F	A	A	A	A

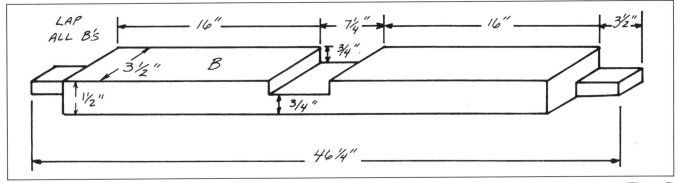

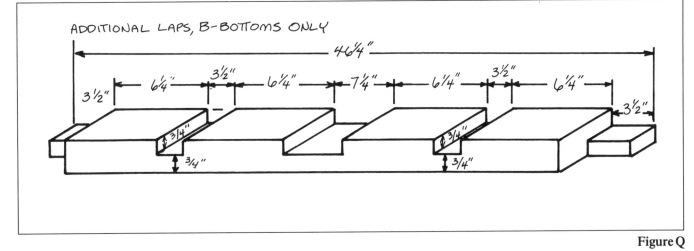

for the single cart B's in diagrams 1 and 2, **Figure C**. The only difference is that the B's for the double cart are much longer, but the procedures shown in diagrams 1 and 2 are the same. Modify all four of the B's: First, cut a 1½ x 3½-inch notch from each end, into the same edge of the board, as shown in diagram 1. Then trim the thickness of the extension at each end to create a lap, as shown in diagram 2. Label two of them B-Top and the other two B-Bottom.

4. All four of the B's are lapped across the center, as shown in **Figure O**. Note that the lap cut is made on the same side of the board as the lap cuts at the ends and that it is ¾ inch deep by 7¼ inches wide.

5. Two additional lap cuts are made across the same side of each B-Bottom, as shown in **Figure P**. DO NOT cut these laps in the two B-Tops. Note that these laps are made on the same side of the board as the center and end laps and that they are each ¾ inch deep by 3½ inches wide.

6. Each C brace is lapped at the ends, as shown for the single-ricksha C brace in **Figure D**. Note that both laps are cut on the same side of the board and both are ¾ x 3½ inches.

7. The two D boards will serve as the front legs and are drilled to accommodate the metal axle rod. It's important that the holes line up exactly. We suggest that you temporarily clamp or nail together the two D's and drill the holes simultaneously, as shown for the single ricksha in **Figure E**. Mark the drilling point

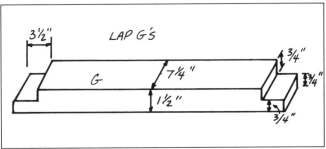

midway between the long edges and 1¼ inches from one end, as shown. Drill a ½-inch-diameter hole through both boards.

8. Slightly round off the corners at one end of each E back leg, as shown for the single ricksha in **Figure F**. Be careful not to shorten the overall length of the board and be sure to leave a flat surface at the end. This will be the lower end.

9. The two F boards will serve as the handles. They are shaped as shown for the single ricksha in **Figure G**. You can make the initial cuts to achieve the approximate shape, using a saber saw; then smooth out the contours, using a sander or wood rasp. Shape both F boards in this manner.

10. The two G boards are lapped at each end, as shown in **Figure Q**. Note that both laps are cut across the same side of the board and each is ¾ inch deep by 3½ inches wide. Modify both G's as shown.

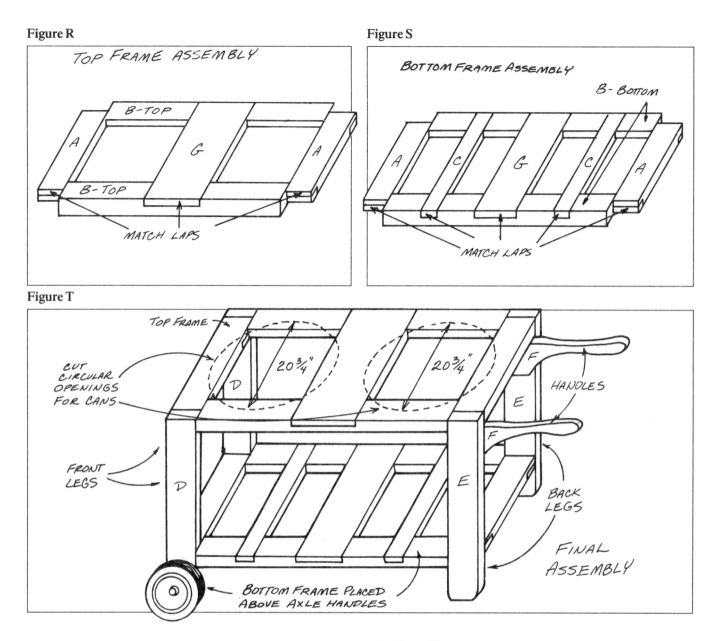

Figure R

TOP FRAME ASSEMBLY

B-TOP

A

G

A

B-TOP

MATCH LAPS

Figure S

BOTTOM FRAME ASSEMBLY

B-BOTTOM

A C G C A

MATCH LAPS

Figure T

TOP FRAME

CUT CIRCULAR OPENINGS FOR CANS

20¾"   20¾"

D

FRONT LEGS

D

E

F

F

E

HANDLES

BACK LEGS

FINAL ASSEMBLY

BOTTOM FRAME PLACED ABOVE AXLE HANDLES

Assembly

Note: Countersink all screws slightly.

1. The top frame is assembled first (**Figure R**). Be sure to use the two B-Top boards and not the ones marked B-Bottom. Match the lap cuts to join the A's and B's at the corners and to join the G center brace to the two B's. Glue all joints and secure each one with two or three of the shorter screws.

2. Assemble the bottom frame in the same manner, adding the two C cross braces, as shown in **Figure S**.

3. To join the two frames, fit the D front legs and E back legs into the openings at the corners, as shown in **Figure T**. Be sure that each front leg is turned with the axle hole near the lower end and that each back leg is turned with the rounded corners at the bottom. All four legs should be flush with the top frame. Secure each leg with glue and two of the longer screws inserted into each frame.

4. Fit the F handles against the inside surfaces of the two back legs, as shown in **Figure T**. They should butt against the underside of the top frame. Glue in place and secure each one with three of the longer screws.

5. Insert the axle rod through the aligned holes in the two front legs, leaving equal extensions at each end, as shown in **Figure T**. At each end, install two washers, a wheel and another washer. (If the axle extends more than about ¼ inch beyond each wheel, you may wish to trim it). Drill a hole through the axle just outside of the outer washer at each end, using a bit that will accommodate a cotter pin. Install the cotter pins to hold the wheels on the axle, as shown.

6. Draw the outline of a 20¾-inch-diameter circle on each section of the top frame, as shown in **Figure T**. Use a saber saw to cut the top-frame boards along each outline, to create round openings for the trash cans.

7. Sand to eliminate the worst splinters and rough spots. Paint in your choice of colors.

Rubbish Ricksha
(page 75)

Hammock Stand
(page 81)

Patio Lounger
(page 84)

Patio Bench
(page 90)

Patio Table
(page 93)

Easy Chair & Hassock
(page 96)

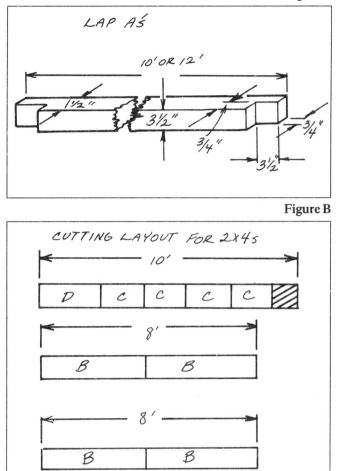

Figure B

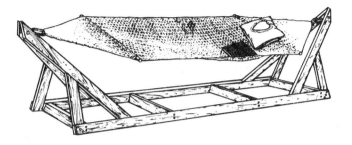

Hammock Stand

If the only reason you don't have a hammock is a lack of properly spaced trees, here's the solution! This incredibly simple and sturdy hammock stand can be built in just a few hours. The size can be altered to fit any hammock. This version is 3½ x 12 x 3 feet. It can be partially disassembled for storage or transport.

Materials

Pine 2 x 4: three 10-foot lengths and three 8-foot lengths (Note: If your hammock is a very stretchy one, purchase only one 10-foot length and two 12-foot lengths in place of the three 10-footers.)

½-inch wooden dowel rod: three 3-foot lengths

Two ⅜ x 5-inch carriage bolts, each with a flat washer and nut to fit

Twelve ⁵⁄₁₆ x 2-inch carriage bolts, each with a flat washer and nut to fit

Sixteen ¼ x 4-inch lag screws

Flathead wood screws in 2- and 2½-inch lengths

Two short lengths of chain or rope for hanging the hammock

Exterior finishing materials of your choice

There are only fourteen parts to this very easy hammock stand. We used No. 2 common pine 2 x 4s to create a very inexpensive project, which has become an extremely popular one. Be sure to use rust-resistant hardware.

Cutting the Parts

1. There are two main parts that determine the overall length of the hammock stand. We used a 10-foot-long 2 x 4 for each of these parts, but if your hammock is very stretchy you probably will want to use a 12-footer for each one. On each of two 10- or 12-foot 2 x 4s, cut a ¾ x 3½-inch half lap at each end, on the same side of the board, as shown in **Figure A**. Label these two boards A, for reference during assembly.

2. From the remaining 2 x 4s, cut the lengths listed in this step and label each part with its code letter, for reference during assembly. We have provided a cutting diagram in **Figure B**, showing how we used the 2 x 4s. All parts are the full thickness and width of the stock (1½ x 3½ inches).

Code	Description	Length	Quantity
B	Hammock Support	48 inches	4
C	Upright	20¼ inches	4
D	Center Brace	30 inches	4

Figure C

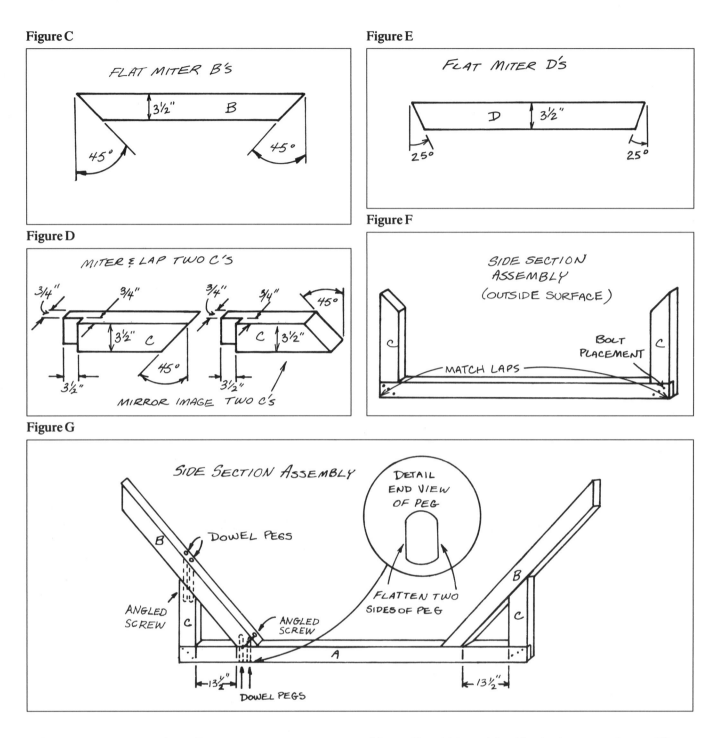

FLAT MITER B'S

3½"   B

45°   45°

Figure D

MITER & LAP TWO C'S

¾"   ¾"   ¾"   ¾"

45°

3½"   C   C   3½"

45°

3½"   3½"

MIRROR IMAGE TWO C'S

Figure E

FLAT MITER D'S

D   3½"

25°   25°

Figure F

SIDE SECTION ASSEMBLY
(OUTSIDE SURFACE)

C   C

BOLT PLACEMENT

MATCH LAPS

Figure G

SIDE SECTION ASSEMBLY

DETAIL END VIEW OF PEG

B   DOWEL PEGS

ANGLED SCREW

C   ANGLED SCREW

FLATTEN TWO SIDES OF PEG

B

C

A

13½"   13½"

DOWEL PEGS

3. Flat miter both ends of each B support at a 45-degree angle, as shown in **Figure C**.

4. The C uprights are flat mitered at one end and lapped at the other, as shown in **Figure D**. Note that two C's should be mirror images of the other two, as shown.

5. Flat miter both ends of each D brace at a 25-degree angle, as shown in **Figure E**.

Assembly

The hammock stand consists of two identical side assemblies (**Figure G**), which are joined by the four center braces (**Figure H**). A bolt at each end serves as a hanger for the hammock rope or chain (**Figure I**).

1. To assemble one side section, attach a C upright to each end of an A base, matching lap cuts, as shown in **Figure F**. We used three ⁵⁄₁₆ x 2-inch carriage bolts for each joint. The easiest way to make the joint is to clamp the boards together, matching laps, and drill the holes for the bolts. You will need to use two C's that are mirror images of each other, as you want the mitered top ends to be turned as shown. Secure each bolt on the inside with a flat washer and nut.

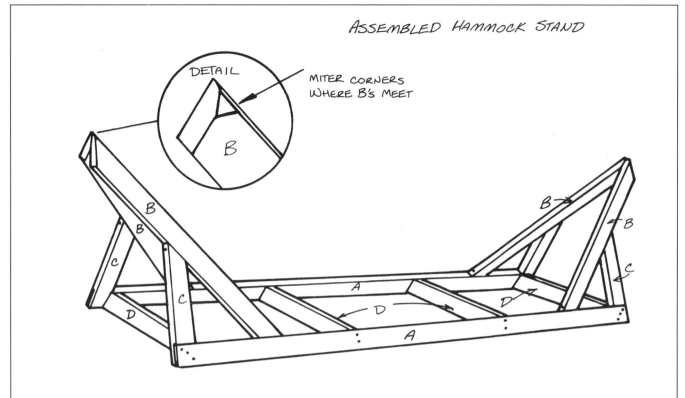

ASSEMBLED HAMMOCK STAND

DETAIL

MITER CORNERS
WHERE B'S MEET

Figure I

2. The B supports are added next, as shown in **Figure G**. There should be about 13½ inches of space between the C and B, as shown. Clamp the boards together and drill ½-inch sockets into each joint, where indicated, to accommodate dowel pegs. The sockets should be about 7 inches deep. Cut 7-inch lengths of ½-inch dowel for the pegs. Sand or trim two flat sides on each one (see detail diagram). Glue the dowels in place. Angle a 2- or 2½-inch screw into each joint, as shown.

3. Assemble a second, identical side section.

4. The four D braces are used to join the two side sections, as shown in **Figure H**. Place one D flush with each end of the aligned side sections and space the remaining two D's evenly along the length. Because the ends of the D's are mitered, the side sections will lean in toward the center. At each end of the hammock stand, you will have to miter the corners of the two B supports where they meet, as shown in the detail diagram. Secure each D brace with two lag screws inserted through the A base into each end, as shown.

5. To secure each mitered B support joint, we used a ⅜ x 5-inch carriage bolt, which also serves as a hanger bolt for the hammock rope or chain. Clamp together the B's at one end of the stand and drill a ⁷⁄₁₆-inch-diameter hole through them, as shown in **Figure I**. Insert a bolt through the hole and secure with a washer and nut. Tie the hammock rope around the bolt or temporarily remove the bolt and slip it through a link of the chain before resecuring it. Repeat these procedures at the other end of the hammock stand.

6. Stain and seal or otherwise finish your hammock stand.

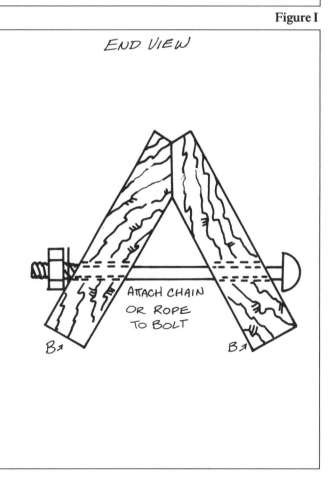

END VIEW

ATTACH CHAIN
OR ROPE
TO BOLT

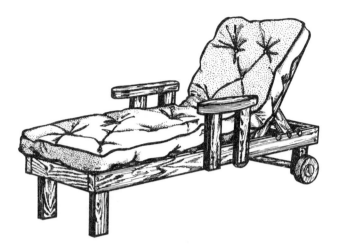

Patio Lounger

This is the life! You'll be thrilled at how easy it is to build this sturdy, comfortable patio lounger. It takes a standard-size lounge cushion and will last for years and years. Overall size is 28 x 66 x 33 inches.

Materials

Notes: We used redwood for the lounger, but you can use pine or any other lumber you prefer. Refer to Tips & Techniques for a discussion of the types of lumber best suited to outdoor use. Be sure to use rust-resistant hardware.

1 x 2 lumber: two 10-foot lengths
2 x 2 lumber: one 6-foot length
2 x 4 lumber: three 10-foot lengths
2 x 6 lumber: 4-foot length
2 x 8 lumber: 2-foot length
1-inch wooden dowel rod: one 4-foot length
Flathead wood screws in ¾-, 1½- and 2½-inch lengths
Four ¼ x 3½-inch carriage bolts, each with a flat washer and nut to fit
Two 2-inch flat metal washers with 1⅛-inch center hole
Standard patio lounge cushion
Carpenter's or waterproof glue; and exterior finishing materials of your choice

The lounger consists of a long, rectangular frame, which includes the front and back legs and axle assembly; an adjustable back support structure, which fits into grooves in the long frame; and two armrest assemblies.

Cutting the Parts

1. Cut from 2 x 4 lumber the parts listed in this step and label each one with its code letter. All parts are the full thickness and width of the stock – 1½ x 3½ inches – except for the K's, which

Figure A

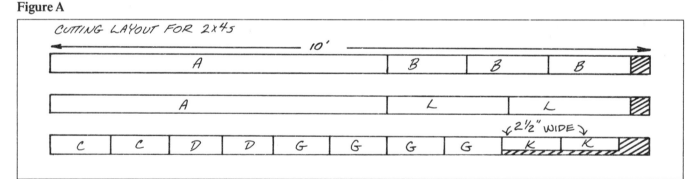

Figure B

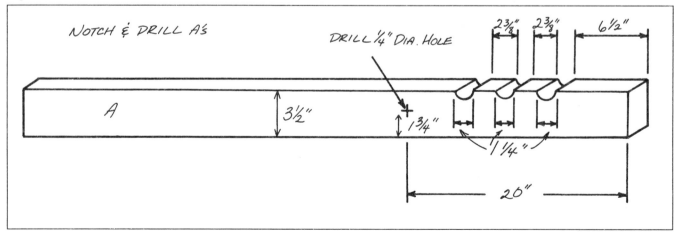

are only 2½ inches wide. A cutting layout, showing how we used the lengths of 2 x 4 specified in the materials list, is provided in **Figure A**.

Code	Description	Length	Quantity
A	Frame Side	68 inches	2
B	Cross Frame	16 inches	3
C	Front Leg	12 inches	2
D	Back Leg	10½ inches	2
G	Arm Support	11½ inches	4
K	Back Support	11½ inches	2
L	Back Frame	24 inches	2

2. Cut the lengths of 1 x 2 lumber listed in this step and label them with their code letters. Cut two of each length from one 10-foot 1 x 2 and cut the seven additional F's from the second 10-footer.

Code	Description	Length	Quantity
E	Slat Support	39⅜ inches	2
F	Seat Slat	16 inches	9

3. Cut from the specified materials the additional parts listed in this step. All parts are the full thickness and width of the stock from which they are cut. Label all parts.

Code	Description	Length	Quantity
Cut from 2 x 6:			
H	Armrest	18 inches	2
Cut from 2 x 2:			
J	Back Slat	16 inches	4

4. The A's are notched to support the back assembly at various angles, as shown in **Figure B**. Cut or drill three rounded notches across one long edge of one A where indicated. Note the size of and distance between the notches and the distance to the ends of the board. Drill a ¼-inch-diameter bolt hole where indicated. In order to make the two A's identical, use the modified A as a guide to notch and drill the second one.

5. The D's are drilled to accommodate the axle. Refer to **Figure C**. Drill a 1-inch-diameter hole through one D, midway between the long edges and 1½ inches from one end, as shown. This will be the lower end of the leg. Use the drilled D as a guide to drill the second one.

6. The K's are drilled to accommodate a bolt and a dowel rod, as shown in **Figure D**. They are also rounded at the ends. Drill and then round off the ends of one K, referring to **Figure D** for specifications. Use the modified K as a guide to modify the second one.

7. The L's are notched to accommodate the back slats and drilled to accommodate two bolts, as shown in **Figure E**. They are also rounded at the ends. Drill, notch and then round off the ends of one L, referring to **Figure E** for specifications. Use the modified L as a guide to modify the second one.

8. A scale drawing for the contoured H armrest is provided in **Figure F**. The armrests are contoured for looks and comfort, not for exact fit; you may prefer to use the scale drawing as a general guide rather than go to the trouble of enlarging it to full size. Contour the two H's that you cut in step 3, according to the scale drawing.

 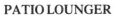
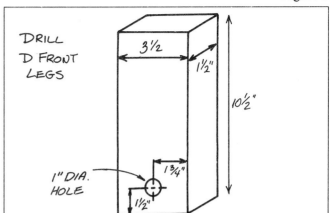

Figure C

DRILL D FRONT LEGS

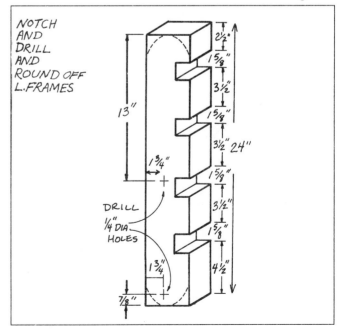

Figure D

Figure E

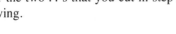

Figure F

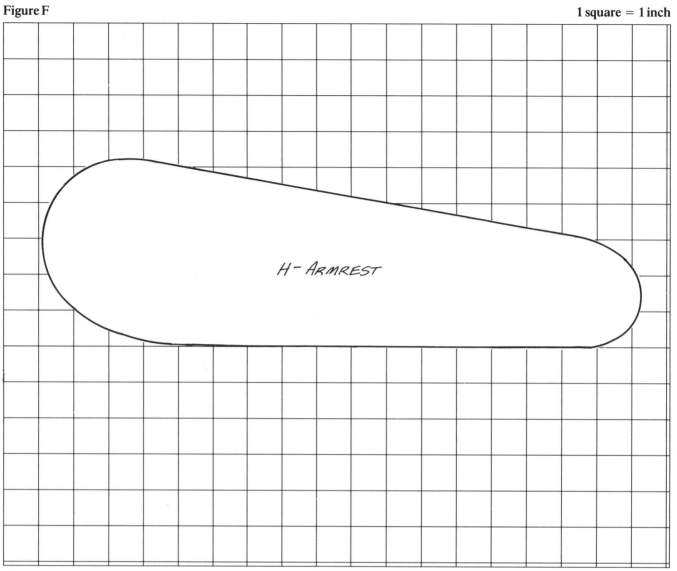

H - ARMREST

Figure G

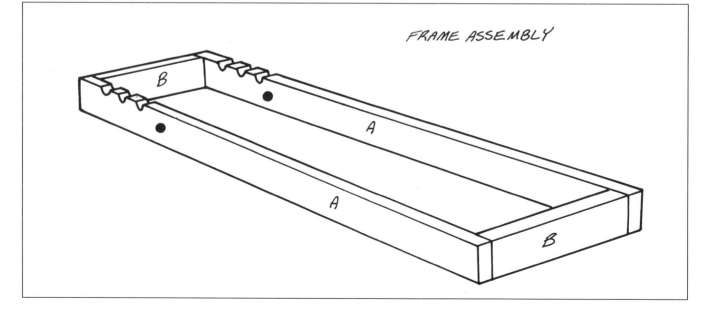

FRAME ASSEMBLY

2 X 4 FURNITURE

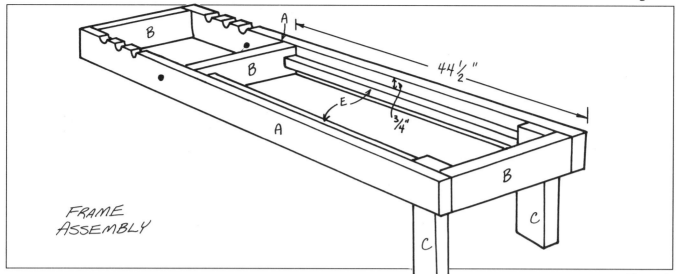

FRAME
ASSEMBLY

44½"

¾"

Figure I

9. Cut two 6-inch-diameter wheels from the 2 x 8 lumber. Drill a 1⅛-inch-diameter axle hole through the center of each.

10. To secure the wheels, we cut circular covers for the axle ends. Rip some of the leftover lumber to ⅛ or ¼ inch thick and cut two 2¼-inch-diameter circles.

Frame Assembly

1. The basic frame assembly is shown in **Figure G**. Be sure that both A's are turned the same way and that they cover the ends of the B's. Glue each joint and secure with two screws.

2. For this step, refer to **Figure H**. Install the third B between the A's, 44½ inches from the front end of the frame, as shown. Secure with glue and screws, as before. Glue the C front legs into the front corners of the frame, flush at the top, as shown. Note that the legs are turned with wide sides against the A frames. Secure with glue and screws.

3. Glue an E slat support to the inside surface of one A frame (**Figure H**), between the front leg and center B cross frame. It should be turned with a ¾-inch-wide edge against the A, ¾ inch below the top of the frame, as shown. Secure with at least four screws. Install the second E against the opposite A frame.

4. Installation of the nine F seat slats is shown in **Figure I**. Place them flat across the frame, resting on the E slat supports. Butt the front slat against the front legs and allow about 3 inches of space between slats. The last slat will be about 1¼ inches from the center B frame member. Each slat should be turned with a wide side down, so it does not extend above the A frame members. Secure each end of each slat with glue and a single screw inserted down into the E support.

5. Installation of the back legs, axle and wheels is shown in **Figure J**. For the axle, cut a 20-inch length of 1-inch dowel rod. At the back end of the frame, install a D back leg in each corner, flush at the top, as shown. Be sure that both legs are turned with the axle hole near the lower end. You may wish to insert the axle through the holes before securing the legs, to be sure the holes line up properly. Secure each leg with glue and screws. Glue the axle in place, extending equally beyond each leg.

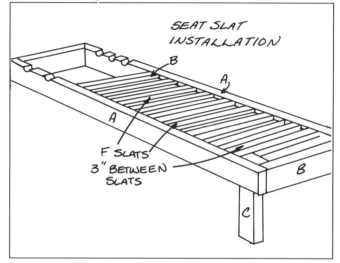

SEAT SLAT
INSTALLATION

F SLATS
3" BETWEEN
SLATS

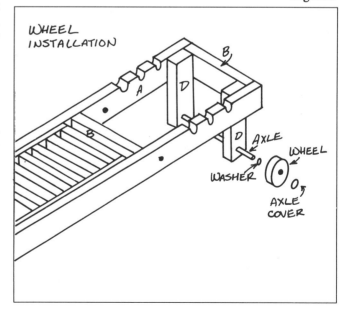

WHEEL
INSTALLATION

AXLE

WHEEL

WASHER

AXLE
COVER

Figure K

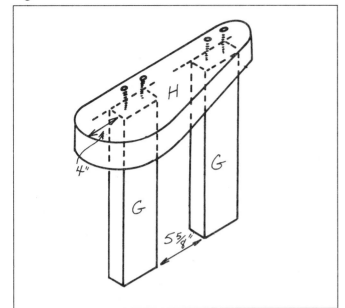

Figure L

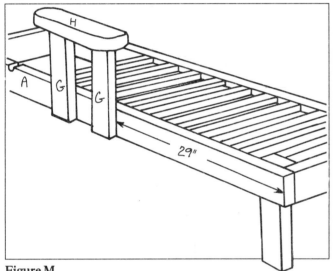

Figure M

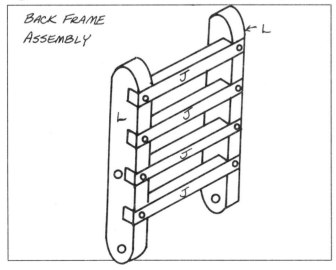

Figure N

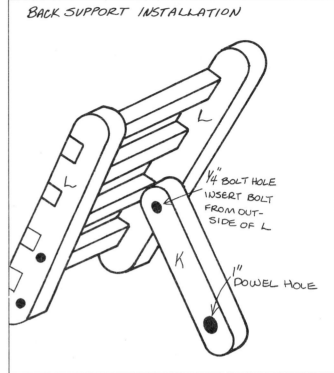

BACK SUPPORT INSTALLATION

¼" BOLT HOLE INSERT BOLT FROM OUT-SIDE OF L

1" DOWEL HOLE

6. Lubricate the center hole of each wheel, using beeswax or hard soap. At each end of the axle, install a metal washer and wheel, as shown in **Figure J**. Glue an axle cover to the end of the axle, using a short screw to secure.

7. The arm assembly is shown in **Figure K**. The G supports should be flush with the straight edge of the H armrest, as shown. Allow 5⅝ inches between the supports and 4 inches between the front support and the front end of the armrest. Glue the joints and secure with long screws inserted down through the armrest into the supports, as shown. When you build the second arm assembly, make it a mirror image of the first one (see **Figure O**).

8. The arm installation is shown in **Figure L**. Be sure the arm assembly is turned correctly, with the straight edge of the H armrest facing the center of the frame and the front end of the armrest facing the front of the frame. The G supports and A frame member should be flush at the bottom. Note the distance between the front end of the frame and the front G support. Glue the G's to the A and insert two long screws through each support into the frame. Attach the second arm assembly to the other side of the frame, directly opposite the first one.

Back Assembly

1. The back frame assembly is shown in **Figure M**. Place the two L frames on their uncut long edges, about 16 inches apart. Glue the four J slats into the aligned notches, flush with the outer surfaces of the L's, as shown. Insert a long screw through each end of each slat.

2. Installation of the K supports is shown in **Figure N**. DO NOT glue the K's to the L's, as they must be free to pivot. Place

ASSEMBLED LOUNGER

FIT DOWEL
SUPPORT INTO
ALIGNED NOTCHES

a K support against the inside of one L, aligning bolt holes, as shown. Insert the bolt from the outside and secure with a washer and nut. The support should swivel fairly easily. Install the second K against the inside of the opposite L frame.

3. For the lower support, cut a 19-inch length of 1-inch dowel. Insert it through the holes at the lower ends of the K supports, extending equally beyond each one. Glue in place.

4. Final assembly is shown in **Figure O**. DO NOT glue the back assembly to the seat frame, as it must be free to pivot. To

install the back assembly, slide the lower drilled ends of the L's down inside the seat frame, just behind the center B member. Align the bolt holes in the L's with those in the A's. On each side, insert a bolt from the outside of the A and secure loosely with a washer and nut on the inside of the L.

5. Pivot the back assembly toward the back end of the frame, fitting the extending ends of the dowel rod into a set of notches in the seat frame, as shown in **Figure O**. Place the cushion on the frame and you're in the lounging business!

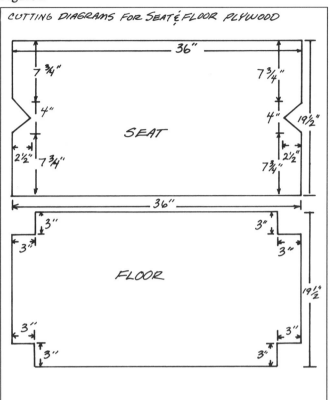

CUTTING DIAGRAMS FOR SEAT & FLOOR PLYWOOD

SEAT

FLOOR

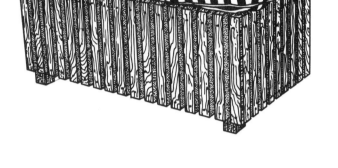

Patio Bench

Form and function get equal billing with this very easy to build outdoor bench. It takes a standard-size patio chair cushion, providing seating space for two. Inside, there's ample storage space for barbecue accessories, sporting equipment or yard tools. Overall size is 38 x 21 x 16 inches.

Materials

Notes: We used redwood for the bench, but you can use pine or any other lumber you prefer. Refer to Tips & Techniques for a discussion of the types of lumber best suited to outdoor use. Be sure to use rust-resistant hardware.

2 x 2 lumber: two 8-foot lengths and one 10-foot length
1 x 2 lumber: six 10-foot lengths and one 6-foot length
¾-inch exterior plywood: 4 x 4-foot half-sheet
6d common nails
Standard patio chair cushion

Figure A

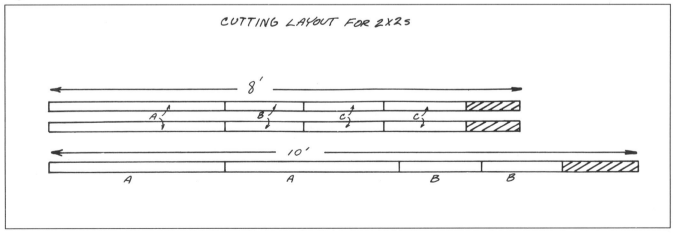

CUTTING LAYOUT FOR 2X2s

This bench couldn't be easier to build. The inside frame is made of lengths of 2 x 2 lumber (**Figure D**). It is covered by 1 x 2 slats around the sides and ends. The plywood floor and seat support rest on the frame.

Cutting the Parts

1. Cut the lengths of 2 x 2 lumber listed in this step and label each one with its code letter. All parts are the full thickness and width of the stock – 1½ x 1½ inches. A cutting layout is provided in **Figure A**, showing how we used the lengths of 2 x 2 specified in the materials list.

Code	Description	Length	Quantity
A	Connector	36 inches	4
B	Frame End	16½ inches	4
C	Leg	16 inches	4

2. Cut the floor and seat from plywood, following the cutting diagrams provided in **Figure B**. The triangular cutouts at the ends of the seat are to provide a handhold when you wish to remove the seat from the bench; dimensions of these cutouts are not critical. The corner cutouts in the floor should be made exactly as shown, as the floor must fit around the legs.

3. The slats are 14-inch lengths of 1 x 2 lumber. Cut a total of fifty-two slats: eight from each 10-foot length of 1 x 2 and four from the 6-foot length.

Assembly

1. The frame consists of two identical end sections and four long connectors. One end section is shown in **Figure C**. Nail together two B's and two C's, spacing them as shown. Note that the C's are flush with the ends of the B's and the upper B is flush with the tops of the C's. Make sure both B's are level. Assemble a second, identical end section.

2. The two end sections are joined by the four A's, as shown in **Figures D** and **E**. The plywood floor must be inserted after the lower A's are installed, but before the upper A's are installed. Be sure that both end sections are turned with the B's on the outside. Nail the two lower A's in place, flush with the lower B's and overlapping them.

3. Place the plywood floor inside the frame, as shown in **Figure E**. It may be necessary to sand the corner cutouts slightly. Nail the floor in place.

4. Nail the two upper A's in place, flush with the upper B's and overlapping them, as shown in **Figure E**.

5. The slat installation is shown in **Figure F**. Nail nine slats to each end of the frame, placing the outer slats flush with the outer edges of the A's and allowing ¾ inch between slats. **Note** that the slats should be flush with the lower A frames at the bottom and will extend ¾ inch above the upper A's. Be sure each slat is vertically straight.

6. Nail seventeen slats to each side of the frame, overlapping the outer slats on the ends, as shown in the top-view diagram, **Figure F**. Like the end slats, the side slats should be flush with the lower A's at the bottom and will extend ¾ inch above the upper A's.

7. Place the plywood seat on top of the frame, inside the extending upper ends of the slats. Place the cushion on top.

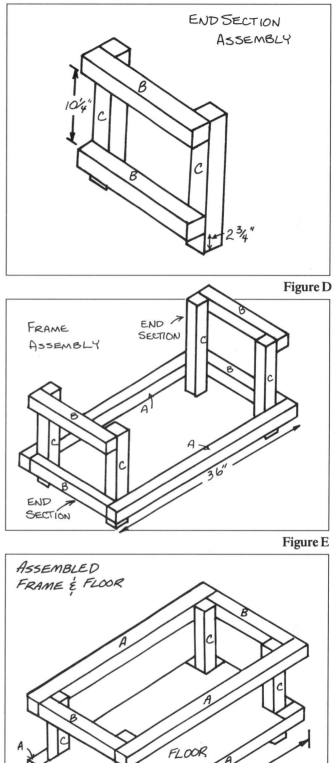

Figure C

END SECTION ASSEMBLY

10¼"

2¾"

Figure D

FRAME ASSEMBLY

END SECTION

END SECTION

36"

Figure E

ASSEMBLED FRAME & FLOOR

FLOOR

36"

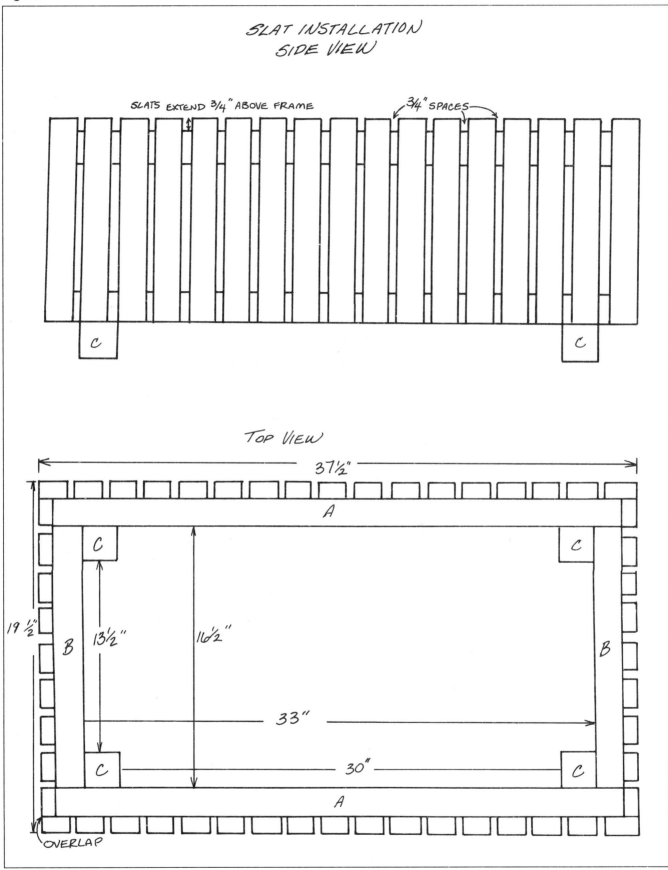

SLAT INSTALLATION
SIDE VIEW

SLATS EXTEND 3/4" ABOVE FRAME

3/4" SPACES

C   C

TOP VIEW

37½"

A

C   C

19 ½"

B   B

13½"   16½"

33"

C   C

30"

A

OVERLAP

2 X 4 FURNITURE

Patio Serving Table

This handy little serving table makes patio entertaining a breeze. The wheels make it easily movable to different locations and the 32-inch-diameter circular top provides plenty of space.

Materials

Notes: We used redwood for the table, but you can use pine or any other lumber you prefer. Refer to Tips & Techniques for a discussion of the types of lumber best suited to outdoor use. Be sure to use rust-resistant hardware.

2 x 4 lumber: one 10-foot length and one 8-foot length
2 x 6 lumber: two 8-foot lengths
2 x 8 lumber: one 3-foot length
1-inch wooden dowel rod: one 2-foot length

Flathead wood screws in 2½- and 1-inch lengths
6d common nails
Two flat metal washers with 1-inch center hole

This round-topped table is as easy to build as it is enjoyable to use. Just cut the parts to length, round off and miter a few and you're in business.

Cutting the Parts

1. Cut the lengths of 2 x 6 lumber listed in this step and label each one with its code letter. All parts are the full thickness and width of the stock – 1½ x 5½ inches. A cutting layout is provided in **Figure A**, showing how we used the lengths of 2 x 6 specified in the materials list.

Code	Description	Length	Quantity
A	Top Slat	34 inches	2
B	Top Slat	32 inches	2
C	Top Slat	26 inches	2

2. Cut the lengths of 2 x 4 lumber listed in this step and label each one with its code letter. All parts are the full thickness and width of the stock – 1½ x 3½ inches. A cutting layout is provided in **Figure B**, showing how we used the lengths of 2 x 4 specified in the materials list.

Code	Description	Length	Quantity
D	Cross Brace	26 inches	2
E	Leg	21 inches	4
F	Center Brace	15 inches	1
G	Leg Brace	22 inches	2

3. Cut two 6-inch-diameter circular wheels from the length of 2 x 8 lumber. Drill a 1⅛-inch-diameter hole through the center of each wheel.

4. The A, B and C top slats are joined edge-to-edge and contoured to form the table top, as shown in **Figure C**. Align the

Figure A

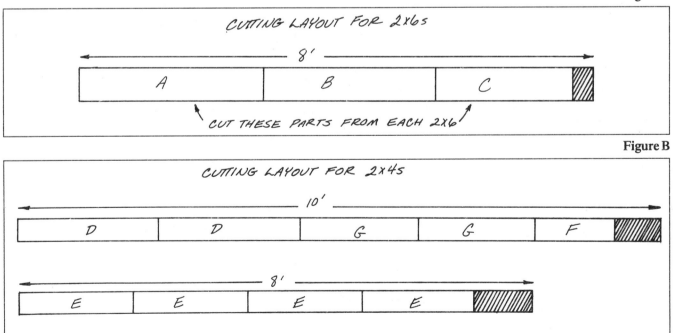

CUTTING LAYOUT FOR 2x6s

8'

| A | B | C | |

CUT THESE PARTS FROM EACH 2X6

Figure B

CUTTING LAYOUT FOR 2x4s

10'

| D | D | G | G | F | |

8'

| E | E | E | E | |

Figure C

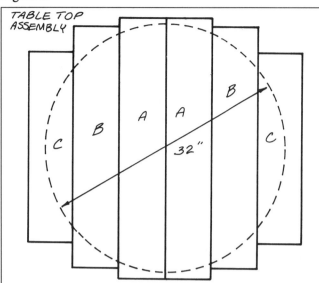

TABLE TOP ASSEMBLY

C B A A B C

32"

Figure D

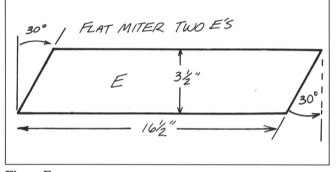

30° FLAT MITER TWO E'S

E 3½"

30°

16½"

Figure E

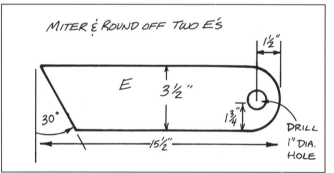

MITER & ROUND OFF TWO E'S

1½"

E 3½"

30°

1¾"

DRILL 1" DIA. HOLE

15½"

Figure F

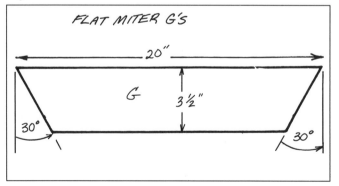

FLAT MITER G'S

20"

G 3½"

30° 30°

slats on a flat surface, in the order shown, with best sides down. Edge glue and clamp until the glue dries. Measure and find the midpoint between the ends of the center A slats; draw the outline of a 32-inch-diameter circle, using this point as the center. Cut the boards along the circular outline.

5. The E's are modified to serve as front and back legs, as shown in **Figures D** and **E**. Measure and flat miter two E's at each end, as shown in **Figure D**. To modify a third E, flat miter one end, as shown in **Figure E**. Measure the overall length and round off the opposite end, as shown. Drill a 1-inch-diameter hole centered 1½ inches from the rounded end, as shown. Use this E leg as a guide to modify the remaining E; they should be exact duplicates of each other.

6. The G leg braces are flat mitered at both ends, as shown in **Figure F**. Measure and miter each one, as shown.

7. We used wooden axle covers to hold the wheels in place. Rip some of the leftover lumber to ¼ or ⅜ inch thick. Cut two circular axle covers, each 2¼ inches in diameter.

Assembly

Note: All assemblies should be temporarily secured with 6d common nails. When you're sure of the fit, remove the nails and replace them with screws. Countersink all screws slightly. If you like, cover those that will show with wooden plugs.

1. Place the table top on a flat surface, best side down. Place the two D braces across the slats, as shown in **Figure G**. Note the 9-inch distance between the braces and note that they are equally distant from the center of the table top. Temporarily secure with a few nails. (When the table is completely assembled with nails and you're sure of the fit, secure the braces by inserting two screws into each table-top slat, as shown.)

2. Nail one mitered and one rounded E leg to the edge of one D brace, as shown in **Figure H**. Note the distance between the legs and between each leg and the center line of the table top. Nail the other two legs to the outer edge of the opposite D brace in the same manner; insert the length of dowel rod through the holes in the two rounded legs, to insure proper alignment.

3. The center brace assembly is shown isolated in **Figure I** and in place in **Figure J**. Before you temporarily assemble the center brace, measure the distance between the legs; it will probably be necessary to trim the length of the center F brace. Nail together the F and G's, as shown in **Figure I**, and nail this assembly to the legs, as shown in **Figure J**. Note the 3-inch distance between the table top and the closest edge of the G brace. Note also that the ends of the G's should be flush with the edges of the legs.

4. Remove the temporary holding nails, one at a time, and replace with screws. Refer to the assembly diagrams for placement of the screws.

5. Adjust the dowel-rod axle so that it extends equally beyond each leg and glue in place. At each end, install a metal washer and a wheel. (The wheels will turn more smoothly around the axle if you will lubricate the center holes with beeswax or hard soap.) If necessary, trim the axle end so that it extends only about ⅛ inch beyond the wheel. Center one of the wooden axle covers over the end of the axle and glue in place. Secure with a short screw.

6. Sand the table where necessary. If you wish, apply your chosen finishing materials.

Figure G

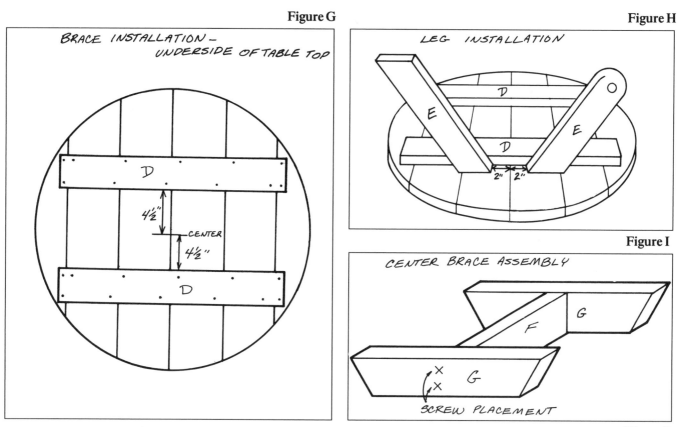

BRACE INSTALLATION —
UNDERSIDE OF TABLE TOP

D

4½"

CENTER

4½"

D

Figure H

LEG INSTALLATION

E   D   E

D

2" 2"

Figure I

CENTER BRACE ASSEMBLY

F   G

G

X
X

SCREW PLACEMENT

Figure J

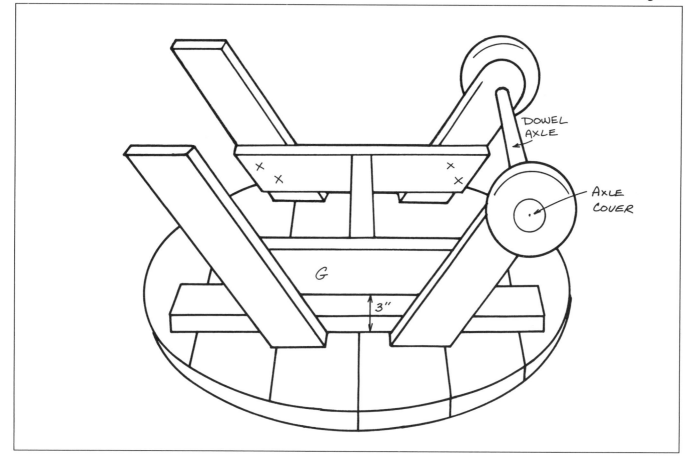

DOWEL AXLE

AXLE COVER

X
X

X
X

G

3"

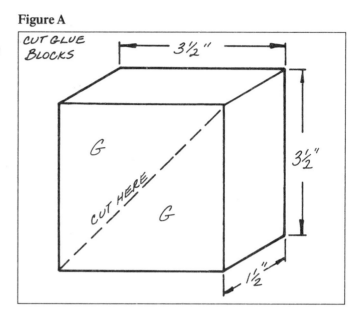

CUT GLUE BLOCKS

G

CUT HERE

G

3½"

3½"

1½"

Easy Chair & Hassock

Easy to build, easy to love! This easy chair is as comfortable as it is attractive. The hassock is open on one side, so you can store magazines and other items inside. With the opening turned toward the chair, no one can see the clutter!

Materials

Pine 2 x 4: four 10-foot lengths and one 8-foot length

Pine 1 x 6: three 10-foot lengths and one 6-foot length

½ x ¾-inch cove molding: three 10-foot lengths, one 8-foot length and one 6-foot length

Flathead wood screws in 1-, 1½- and 2¼-inch lengths

¾-inch-long wire brads

Eight cushion-glide casters, about 1¼ inches in diameter

Carpenter's wood glue; and Danish oil or other finishing materials of your choice

For the cushions:

3 yards of 60-inch-wide upholstery fabric

Upholstery thread to match the fabric

4-inch-thick foam rubber: one 24 x 25-inch piece, one 24 x 27-inch piece and one 24 x 14-inch piece

Thick quilt batting: one 30 x 60-inch piece, one 30 x 64-inch piece and one 30 x 38-inch piece

Both the chair and hassock are composed of standard frame-and-panel assemblies. We used countersunk screws covered with matching wooden plugs for the joints that would show on the finished assemblies; you may wish to secure the joints with dowel pegs instead (see Tips & Techniques).

Cutting the Parts

1. Cut a 3½-inch length from one 10-foot-long 2 x 4. (This should give you a 1½ x 3½ x 3½-inch block of wood.) Cut the block in half diagonally, as shown in **Figure A**. These triangular pieces will serve as glue blocks. Label them G, for reference during assembly.

2. All of the main frame parts for the chair and hassock are lengths of 2 x 4 lumber that have been reduced to 2 inches wide. Rip all of the 2 x 4s to 2 inches wide, but do not reduce the thickness. Each 2 x 4 should now measure 1½ inches thick by 2 inches wide by 8 or 10 feet long. Save the leftover narrow ripped strips for use in step 4.

3. Cut from the ripped 1½ x 2-inch lumber the lengths listed in this step and label them with their code letters. A cutting diagram is provided in **Figure B**, showing how we used the 8- and 10-foot lengths of stock.

Code	Description	Length	Quantity
Chair:			
A	Top Rail	30 inches	2
B	Leg	26 inches	4
C	Lower Rail	26 inches	2
D	Back Rail	24 inches	2
E	Back Stile	32 inches	2
F	Front Span	24 inches	1
Hassock:			
H	Leg	13 inches	4
J	Front Rail	20 inches	2
K	End Rail	10 inches	4
L	Back Span	20 inches	2

Butcher Block
(page 107)

Porch Swing
(page 113)

Rolling File Organizer
(page 119)

Modular Bookcase
(page 125)

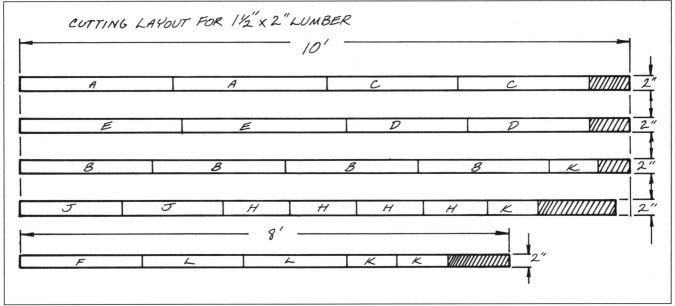

CUTTING LAYOUT FOR 1½" x 2" LUMBER

Figure C

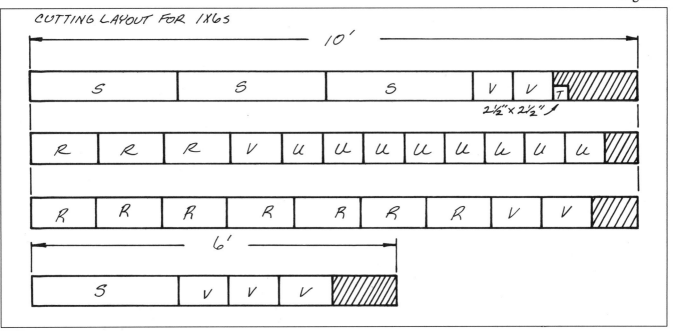

CUTTING LAYOUT FOR 1X6s

4. The parts listed in this step are cut from the narrow strips that were left over when you ripped the 2 x 4s in step 2. Rip and cut the parts and label them as listed.

Code	Dimensions	Quantity
Chair:		
M	¾ x 1½ x 24 inches	8
N	¾ x ¾ x 21½ inches	2
Hassock:		
P	½ x ¾ x 19 inches	4
Q	½ x ¾ x 10 inches	4

5. Cut from 1 x 6 lumber the parts listed in this step and label them with their code letters. All parts are the full thickness and width of the stock – ¾ x 5½ inches – except for the T's (refer to the instructions in step 6). A cutting layout is provided in **Figure C**, showing how we used the lengths of 1 x 6 specified in the materials list.

Code	Description	Length	Quantity
Chair:			
R	Side Panel	13 inches	10
S	Back Panel	29 inches	4
T	Glue Block	see step 6	1
Hassock:			
U	Panel	8 inches	8
V	Top & Floor	10 inches	8

Figure D

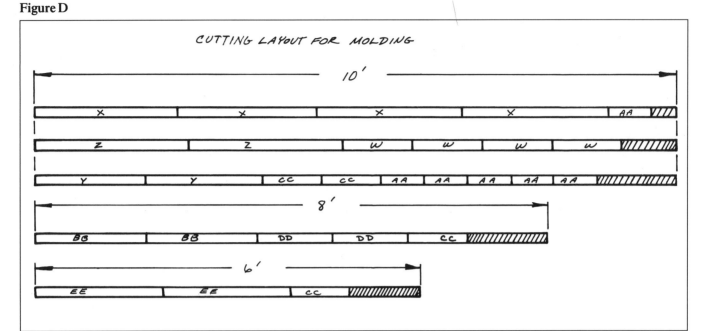

Figure E

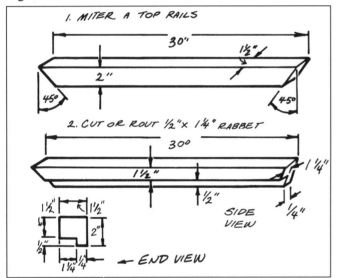

1. MITER A TOP RAILS
30"
1½"
2"
45°
45°

2. CUT OR ROUT ½" x 1¼" RABBET
30°
1½"
½"
¼"
1¼"
½"
SIDE VIEW

1½" 1½"
2"
½"
1¼" ¼"
← END VIEW

6. The T block listed in step 5 should be ¾ x 2½ x 2½ inches. Cut it in half diagonally, as you did the larger block in step 1, so that you have two triangular blocks. Label each one T.

7. Cut from cove molding the lengths listed in this step and label them with their code letters. A cutting layout is provided in **Figure D**, showing how we used the lengths of molding specified in the materials list.

Code	Length	Quantity
Chair:		
W	13 inches	4
X	27 inches	4
Y	21 inches	2
Z	29 inches	2

(Continued next column)

Code	Length	Quantity
Hassock:		
AA	8 inches	6
BB	20 inches	2
CC	10 inches	4
DD	14 inches	2
EE	24 inches	2

Assembly of Chair Sections

The chair contains three frame-and-panel sections: two identical sides (**Figure I**) and the back (**Figure J**). The overall assembly is shown in **Figures L** through **N**.

1. The side sections are assembled first, but the frame members must be modified. For the frames, you will need the **A** top rails, the **B** legs and the **C** lower rails. They are assembled with miter joints at the top corners and must be rabbeted to accommodate the panel boards (see **Figure H**). Refer to **Figure E**, which shows detail views of the **A** top rail. Flat miter both ends of each **A** top rail at a 45-degree angle toward the same edge, as shown in diagram 1. Make sure that you do not reduce the overall length when you cut the miters. Next, cut or rout a ½ x 1¼-inch rabbet along the shorter of the two long edges, exactly as shown in diagram 2.

2. Refer to **Figure F**, which shows detail views of the **B** legs. Modify one **B** completely before doing any work on the others. First, flat miter one end at a 45-degree angle, as shown in diagram 1, being careful not to reduce the overall length of the board. Next, cut or rout a ½ x 1¼ x 13-inch rabbet along the shorter of the two long edges, starting at the mitered end, as shown in diagram 2. Modify a second **B** in the same manner. Modify the remaining two **B**'s in the same manner, but make them mirror images of the first two by cutting the rabbet on the opposite side, as shown in diagram 3.

3. Cut or rout a ½ x 1¼-inch rabbet along one long edge of each **C** lower rail, as shown in **Figure G**.

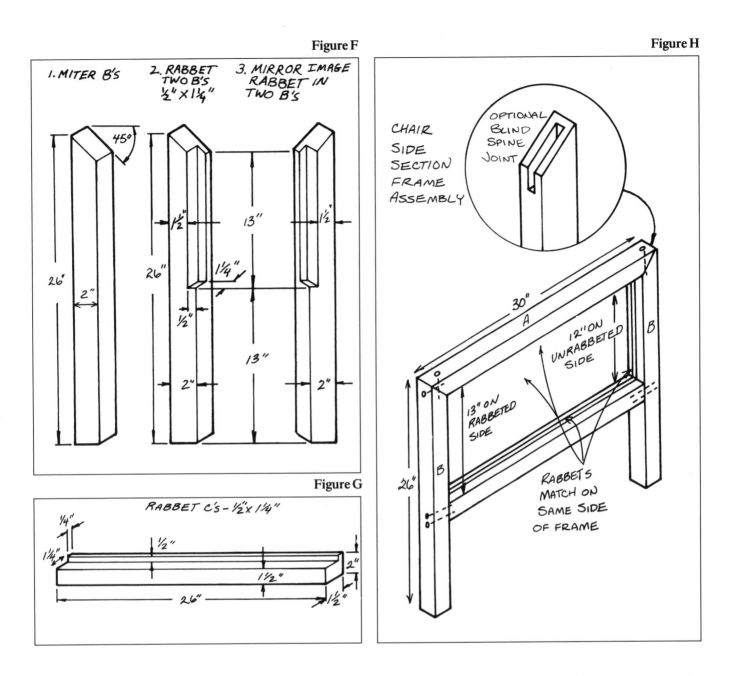

Figure G

4. Refer to **Figure H**, which shows the assembled frame for one side section. You may wish to spline the miter joints for extra strength, as shown in the detail diagram (see Tips & Techniques, if necessary). Glue together the **A** and **B**'s, using two mirror-image **B**'s and making sure all parts are turned with the rabbets on the same side of the frame. Insert a **C** lower rail between the legs, with the rabbet on the same side as the others. Note the distance between the top and lower rails: 12 inches on the unrabbeted side and 13 inches on the rabbeted side. This should make the rabbet in the **C** rail match the lower ends of the rabbets in the two **B** legs. Secure each joint with two countersunk screws and cover with plugs.

5. Refer to **Figure I**, which shows the panel installed in the frame. The panel consists of five **R** boards aligned edge-to-edge in the rabbeted opening of the frame. They are held in place by a keeper frame composed of mitered **W** and **X** molding strips.

You will have to trim the width of one **R** panel board to make the panel fit the opening, but it should be a tight fit. For a tongue-in-groove look, we used a hand plane to cut a slight bevel along all four long corner edges of each **R** board, as shown in the end-view detail diagram. Don't cut too deeply, as you do not want to remove too much material. Align the prepared panel boards in the rabbeted opening; there's no need to use glue.

6. Carefully miter both ends of two **W** and two **X** molding lengths at a 45-degree angle, to form a keeper frame that will fit precisely into the rabbeted opening, on top of the panel (**Figure I**). Be sure to cut the miters in the proper direction on all four keepers – the coved edges should match and face center, as shown in the cut-away detail diagram. Use wire brads to install the keeper frame. Recess the brads and cover with wood filler. (Note: If you do not use glue, you can more easily remove the keepers and panel, should you ever want to remodel the

Figure I

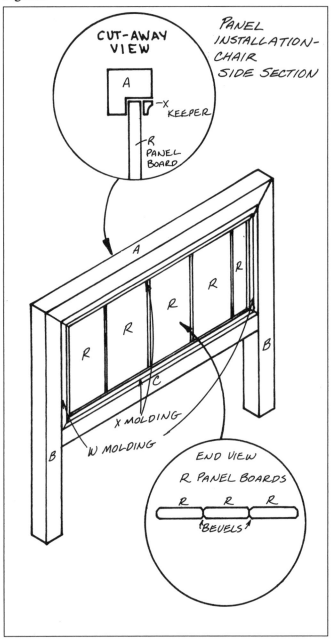

Figure J

CHAIR BACK SECTION

D
Y MOLDING
32" E S   S   S E
Z MOLDING
Y MOLDING
D
24"

Figure K

CHAIR SIDE SECTION

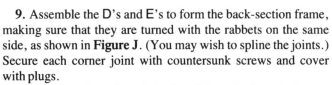

1¼"
N SUPPORT PLACEMENT
BACK SECTION PLACEMENT

chair. The overall look can be changed dramatically simply by altering the panels.)

7. Repeat steps 4 through 6 to assemble a second, identical side section.

8. The back section is shown assembled in **Figure J**. It is a frame-and-panel assembly, like the side sections, but the E stiles do not extend below the lower rail. To prepare the D rails and E stiles, flat miter both ends of each one at a 45-degree angle toward the same edge, exactly as shown for the side-section A rails in **Figure E**, diagram 1. Be careful not to reduce the overall length when you cut the miters. Next, cut or rout a ½ x 1¼-inch rabbet along the shorter of the two long edges, as shown for the A rails in **Figure E**, diagram 2.

9. Assemble the D's and E's to form the back-section frame, making sure that they are turned with the rabbets on the same side, as shown in **Figure J**. (You may wish to spline the joints.) Secure each corner joint with countersunk screws and cover with plugs.

10. The panel consists of the four S boards aligned edge-to-edge in the rabbeted opening (**Figure J**). Trim the width of one S to fit. If you beveled the side-section panel boards for a tongue-in-groove look, do the same on the back-section panel boards. Place the boards in the rabbeted opening.

11. Carefully miter the ends of the Y and Z molding lengths to form the keeper frame (**Figure J**). Install the keepers with wire brads.

Final Chair Assembly

1. Refer to **Figures K** and **L**. The first shows placement of a support strip and the back section on the inside surface of one chair side section. (The inside surface is the one that does not contain the keeper frame around the panel.) Glue an **N** support strip to the inside surface of each side section lower rail, where indicated, making sure the placement is aligned between the two sections. Secure with several screws.

2. Join the two side sections by glueing the **F** span between them, even with the side-section lower rails, as shown in **Figure L**. Use a triangular **T** glue block to reinforce each corner joint, as shown, and secure with screws.

3. Refer to **Figure M**. Place the eight **M** seat slats across the chair frame, with their ends resting on the **N** supports. Adjust them to even up the spacing. Secure each one to the **N** supports with a screw at each end.

4. Glue the back section between the two sides, as indicated by dotted lines in **Figure M**. Secure it with countersunk screws inserted through the side sections and covered with plugs.

5. The back section is reinforced with the two large **G** glue

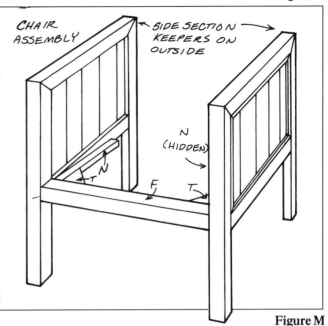

Figure L

Figure M

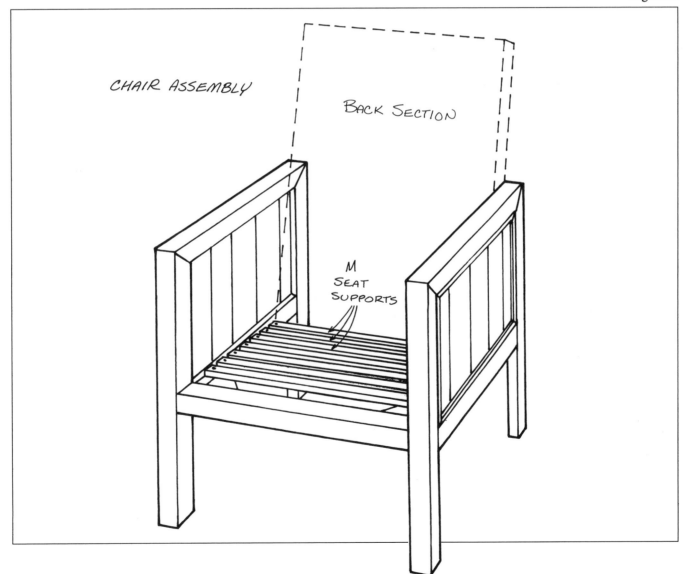

Figure N

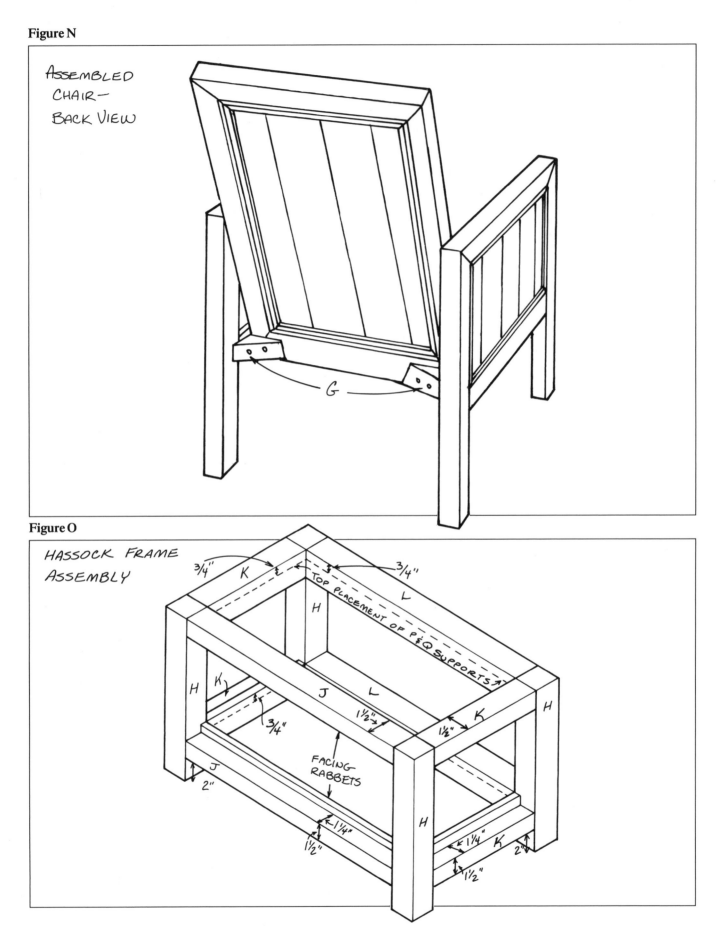

Assembled
Chair—
Back View

G

Figure O

Hassock Frame
Assembly

3/4"   K

3/4"

Top Placement of P & Q Supports

H

L

H   K

H

J   L

H

3/4"

1 1/2"

K

1 1/2"

Facing
Rabbets

J

2"

1 1/4"

1 1/2"

H

1 1/4"   K

2"

1 1/2"

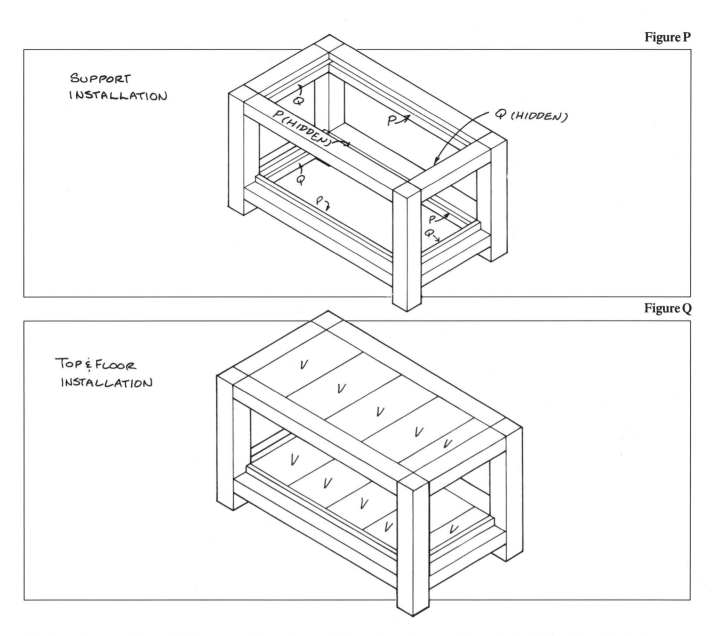

Figure P

SUPPORT INSTALLATION

Figure Q

TOP & FLOOR INSTALLATION

blocks, as shown in **Figure N**. Because of the angle at which the back is installed, you will have to bevel one 3½-inch edge of each glue block to make them fit flush against the back section. Install the blocks and secure with screws, as shown.

6. Drill a pilot hole and install a cushion-glide caster on the bottom of each chair leg. This completes the basic chair assembly. Instructions for making the cushions are provided following assembly instructions for the hassock frame.

Hassock Assembly

The hassock consists of three frame-and-panel walls, with one side left open for access to the interior storage space. The top and floor are composed of panel boards, which rest on support strips attached to the insides of the walls. The assembly is shown in **Figures O** through **R**.

1. Refer to **Figure O**. Note that the J and K rails are rabbeted to accommodate the panel boards. The H legs are not rabbeted and neither are the L spans at the back of the hassock, which

will not have a wall panel. On all four K's and both J's, cut or rout a ½ x 1¼-inch rabbet along one long edge, as shown in **Figure O**.

2. Rip ½ inch from the width of each H leg and L span. This should make them all 1½ inches wide by 1½ inches thick.

3. The hassock frame is shown assembled in **Figure O**. Glue the parts together, following the diagram carefully. Make sure that at each end the upper and lower K's are turned with the rabbets on the outside, facing each other. Likewise, make sure that the two J rails are turned in the same manner. Secure each joint with countersunk screws and cover with plugs.

4. The P and Q support strips are attached to the inside surfaces of the top and bottom rails and spans, as shown in **Figures O** and **P**, to support the top and floor boards. The supports should be placed ¾ below the tops of the frames, as indicated. Glue them in place and secure with screws.

5. The V's serve as the top and floor boards, as shown in **Figure Q**. We did not bevel the edges, as these boards should fit

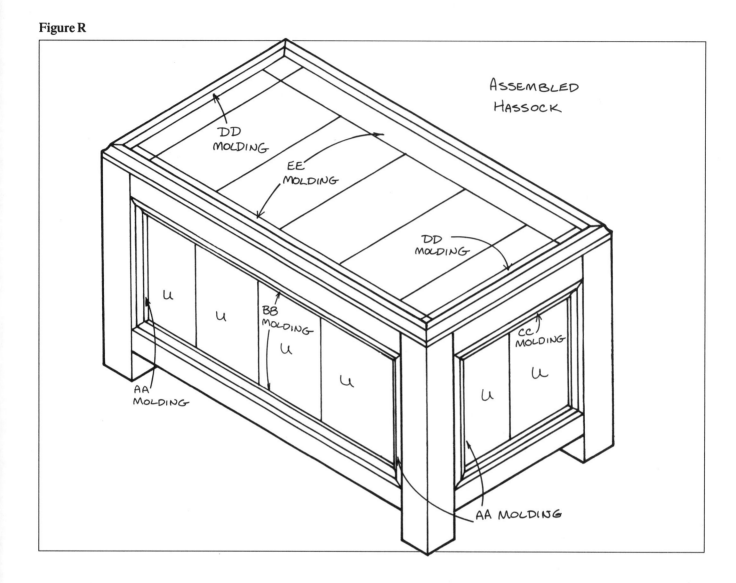

squarely together. There are five **V** boards for the top of the hassock; trim the width of one to make the boards fit within the frame, as shown. If you make it a tight enough fit, there will be no need to glue or otherwise secure the boards in place. You may wish to secure with screws. Use the five remaining **V**'s for the floor, trimming one in the same manner.

6. The **U**'s serve as the panel boards for the two end walls and the front wall, as shown in **Figure R**. They fit into the rabbeted openings and are held in place by keeper frames. Two **U**'s should be sufficient for each end-wall panel; you may need to trim the width of one to get them to fit into the rabbeted opening. They should butt tightly against the unrabbeted **H** legs. (You may wish to bevel the edges, as you did for the chair panel boards.) There's no need to glue the boards in place. Use the remaining four **U**'s for the front wall, trimming one to fit.

7. To form the keeper frame for each end wall, carefully measure and miter at 45 degrees two **AA** and two **CC** molding lengths, as shown in **Figure R**. Make sure you cut the miters the right way in relation to the coved edge of the molding. Secure the keepers with wire brads. For the front wall keeper frame, measure and miter two **AA** and two **BB** molding lengths.

8. We added molding around the top of the hassock, as shown in **Figure R**. It's mostly decorative, but also helps keep the cushion from sliding off. Measure and miter the **DD** and **EE** molding lengths to form the top frame, as shown.

9. Drill a pilot hole and install a cushion-glide caster on the bottom of each hassock leg.

Making the Cushions

1. Cut and label the fabric pieces listed in this step. A cutting layout is provided in **Figure S**.

Description	Dimensions	Quantity
Seat	28 x 60 inches	1
Back	28 x 64 inches	1
Hassock	28 x 38 inches	1
Seat Cap	5 x 25 inches	2
Back Cap	5 x 27 inches	2
Hassock Cap	5 x 14 inches	2

2. The 24 x 25-inch piece of foam rubber will serve as the form for the seat cushion. Place it on top of the 30 x 60-inch piece of quilt batting, as shown in **Figure T**, and wrap the bat-

CUTTING LAYOUT FOR CUSHION FABRIC

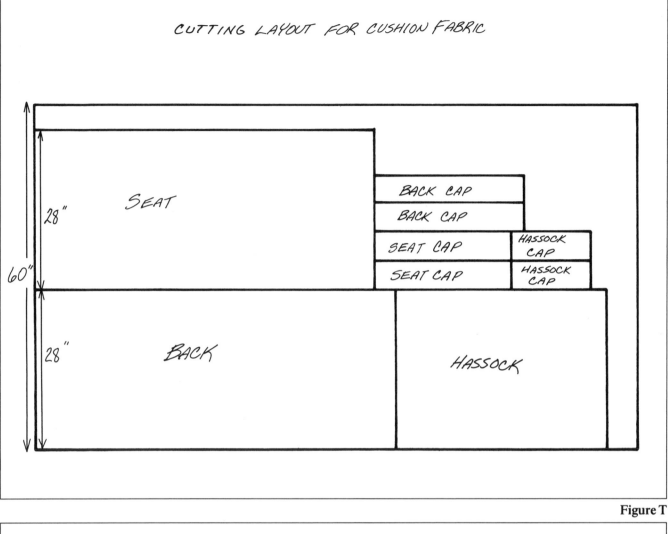

SEAT CUSHION ASSEMBLY

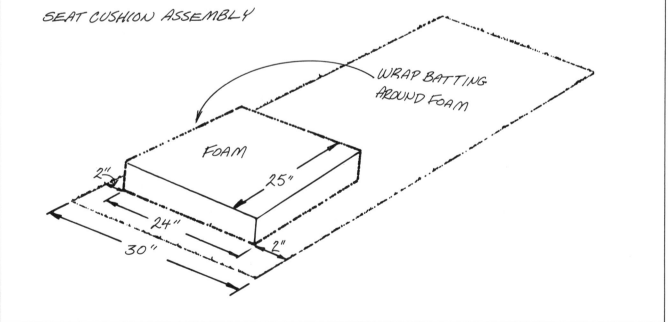

Figure U

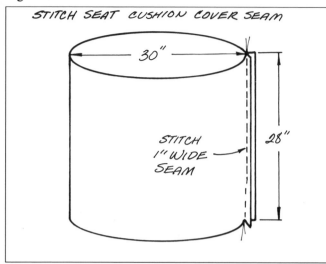

STITCH SEAT CUSHION COVER SEAM

30"

STITCH 1" WIDE SEAM

28"

Figure V

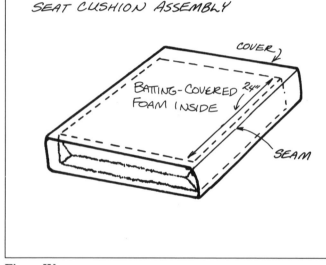

SEAT CUSHION ASSEMBLY

COVER

BATTING-COVERED FOAM INSIDE

24"

SEAM

Figure W

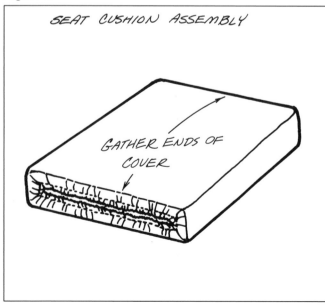

SEAT CUSHION ASSEMBLY

GATHER ENDS OF COVER

Figure X

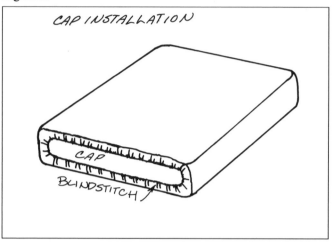

CAP INSTALLATION

CAP

BLINDSTITCH

ting tightly around the foam. Overlap the ends of the batting and baste them together to secure. Neatly fold the open ends of the batting, as you would the wrapping paper on a gift box, and baste. The foam should now be securely encased in batting.

3. Fold the fabric seat piece in half widthwise, with right sides together, and stitch a 1-inch-wide seam along the short edge only (**Figure U**). Press the seam open and turn the cover right side out.

4. Insert the batting-covered foam inside the stitched cover, as shown in **Figure V**. Note how the foam is turned. It will be a tight fit. Adjust the cover so that the seam runs straight along an edge of the foam, as shown.

5. At each open end of the fabric cover, hand baste about 1 inch from the edge of the fabric, all the way around. Pull the basting threads to gather the end tightly around the foam, as shown in **Figure W**. Tie off the gathering threads to secure the gathers temporarily.

6. A fabric cap covers each gathered end of the cushion, as shown in **Figure X**. Round off the corners of the two seat cap pieces. Press a 1-inch hem to the wrong side of the fabric all the way around each piece, clipping the hem where necessary to get it to lie flat. Center and pin one of the hemmed caps to a gathered end of the cushion and blind stitch in place, as shown in **Figure X**. Stitch the second cap to the opposite end. This completes the seat cushion.

7. The back cushion is made in the same manner, using the 24 x 27-inch piece of foam, the 30 x 64-inch piece of batting, the fabric back piece and the two fabric back cap pieces. Note that it is the same width as the seat cushion, to fit between the sides of the chair, but it is slightly longer.

8. The hassock cushion is made in the same manner, using the 24 x 14-inch foam, the 30 x 38-inch batting, the fabric hassock piece and the two fabric hassock cap pieces. It is the same width as the other two cushions, but a lot shorter.

9. Place the seat cushion on top of the seat slats in the chair frame. It will be a tight fit – you'll have to wedge it in place. It should be pushed as far back as possible and should be about even with the front of the chair. Place the back cushion against the back of the chair, resting on top of the seat cushion. Place the hassock cushion on top of the hassock.

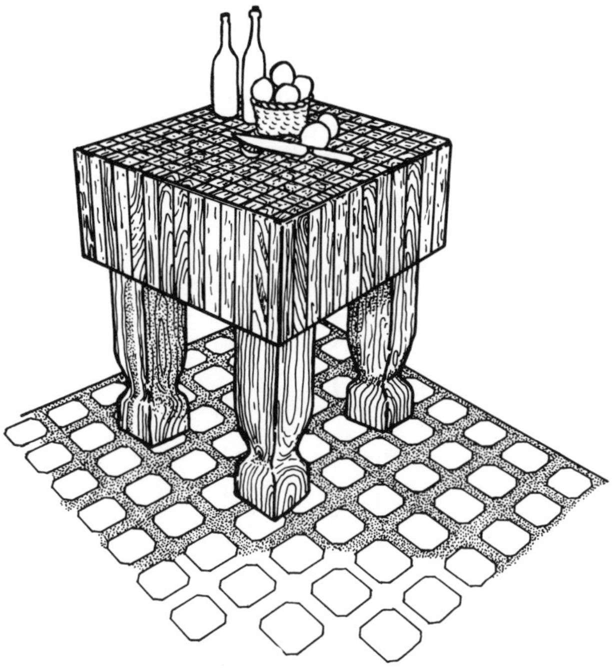

Butcher Block

This classic butcher block provides a large enough work surface to accommodate the wildest kitchen spree. Overall dimensions are 28 x 32 x 28 inches. Built from hardwood, it will last for generations, but you don't need a football team to move it – the massive-looking top is hollow.

Materials

8/4 hardwood: 70 board feet (Note: Standard 8/4 hardwood actually measures 1⅞ inches thick. We used 35 linear feet of 12-inch-wide stock, but you may purchase narrower stock if 12-inch is not available. We used a mixture of oak and maple, for a variegated look on the finished project.)
Pine 1 x 2 or 1 x 4: four 3-foot lengths (These will be used only as router guides.)
Thin plywood or cardboard: 10-inch square (This will be used to make a pattern.)
Sixteen ⅜ x 7-inch lag screws
Carpenter's or waterproof wood glue; and a non-toxic wood finish such as vegetable oil or salad-bowl finish

The butcher block is not very difficult to assemble; cutting the hundreds of blocks of hardwood that make up the top is the most difficult part! You can see how the top is assembled in **Figures F** through **H**. The leg installation is shown in **Figure P.**

Cutting the Parts

Cut the parts as listed below. We have not provided a cutting layout, because chances are the hardwood you purchased is not the same width and length as the stock we started with.

Part	Dimensions in inches	Quantity
Top Block	1⅞ x 1⅞ x 3	169
Frame Block	1⅞ x 1⅞ x 12	56
Leg	1⅞ x 1⅞ x 29	12

Top Assembly

Before you begin work: The center portion of the butcher block top is created by glueing together all 169 top blocks edge-to-edge, forming a 13 x 13-block square. Refer to **Figure A**, which shows four of the top blocks glued together. Note that no adjoining blocks have end grain running in the same direc-

Figure A

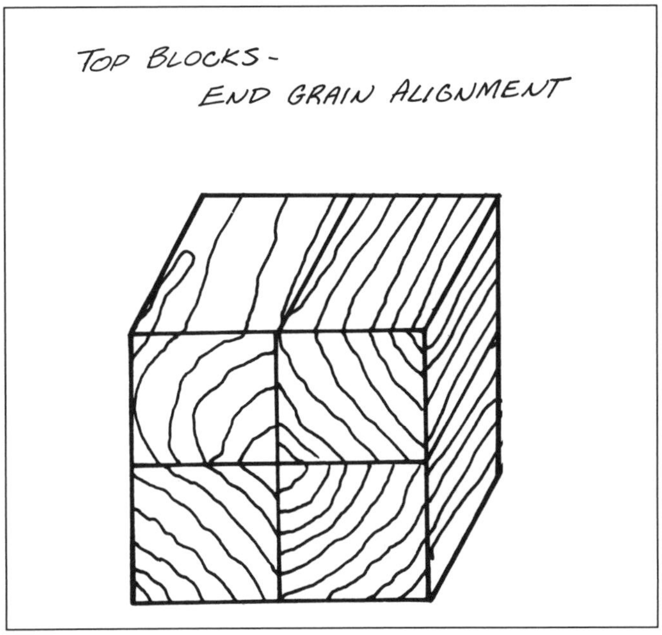

Figure B

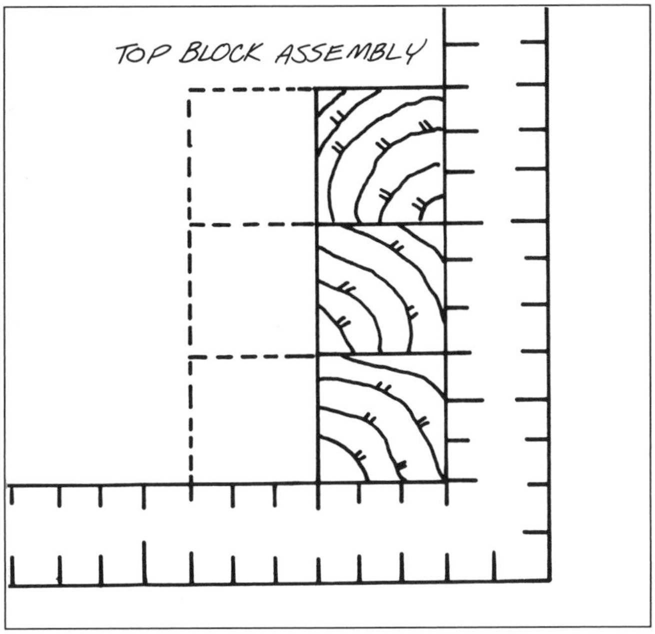

Figure C

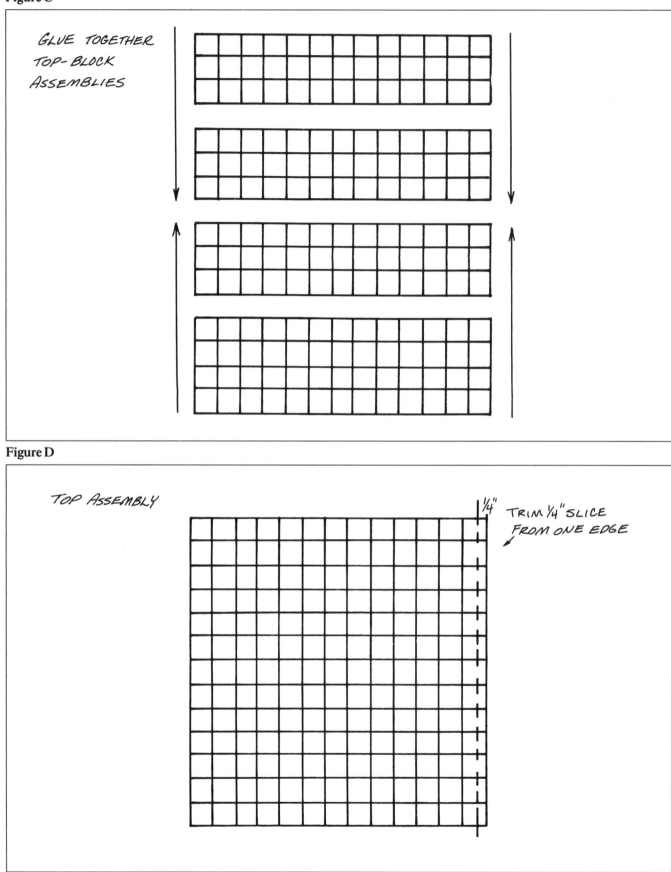

GLUE TOGETHER
TOP-BLOCK
ASSEMBLIES

Figure D

TOP ASSEMBLY

1/4" TRIM 1/4" SLICE
FROM ONE EDGE

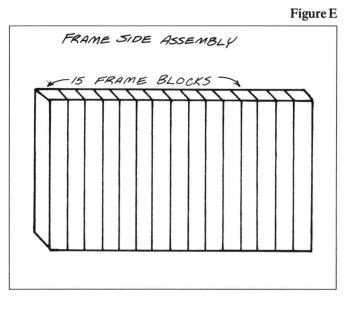

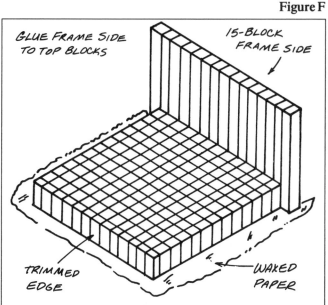

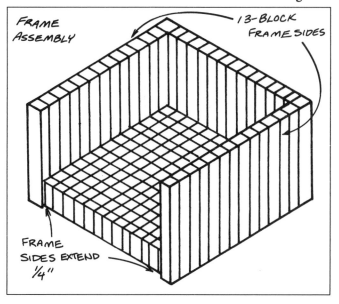

tion. This arrangement not only is attractive, but it increases the strength of the structure through equal distribution of stress.

To make the work go faster once you begin glueing, arrange on a separate table all 169 top blocks as you want them to appear in the finished assembly. You'll be doing a lot of glueing, so cover your workbench with waxed paper to prevent the glue from sticking to it. To insure that the block assembly is square and true, secure a carpenter's square to the workbench and butt the blocks against it as you assemble them.

1. Spread glue on two adjacent edges of a top block. Place it in the corner of the carpenter's square, with the top end down and the unglued edges against the square, as shown in **Figure B**. Spread glue on one edge of a second block and press it in place against the first one. Glue a third block in place, forming a three-block row.

2. Glue three more blocks to those in the first row, as indicated by dotted lines in **Figure B**. Continue working in this manner until you have a rectangle three blocks wide by thirteen blocks long. Clamp the assembly and allow to dry overnight.

3. Repeat steps 1 and 2 to assemble two more rectangular sections of blocks, each three blocks wide by thirteen blocks long.

4. Assemble a fourth rectangle of blocks in the same manner, but make this one four blocks wide by thirteen blocks long.

5. Glue together the four rectangular sections, as shown in **Figure C**. Work on a level surface and turn all of the sections with the tops down, so you'll have less work to do to even and smooth out the top of the assembled butcher block. Be sure all four are flush along the outer edges and the overall assembly is square. Clamp overnight.

6. Cut away a ¼-inch slice from one edge of the assembled top, as shown in **Figure D**.

7. The assembled center section is surrounded by a frame, which consists of the fifty-six frame blocks. To assemble one side of the frame (**Figure E**), glue together fifteen frame blocks edge-to-edge in a straight row. It will help if you place them top ends down along the carpenter's square, beginning in the corner of the square. Clamp the assembly overnight.

8. Repeat step 7 to form a second, identical frame side.

9. Assemble two more frame sides in the same manner, using only thirteen frame blocks for each of these.

10. Refer to **Figure F**. Place the assembled top blocks upside down on a level surface. Glue a fifteen-block frame side upside down against the edge opposite the trimmed edge, as shown. Note that the frame side will extend equally by one block beyond each adjacent edge of the top block section. Clamp the frame side in place.

11. Glue a thirteen-block frame side to each adjacent edge of the top block section, as shown in **Figure G**. Again, make sure all parts are flush along the top surfaces. The shorter frame sides should also be glued to the extending portions of the longer frame side, as shown. This will make the frame flush at the connected corners, but the shorter frame sides will each extend ¼ inch beyond the top blocks at the open end. Clamp in place.

Figure H

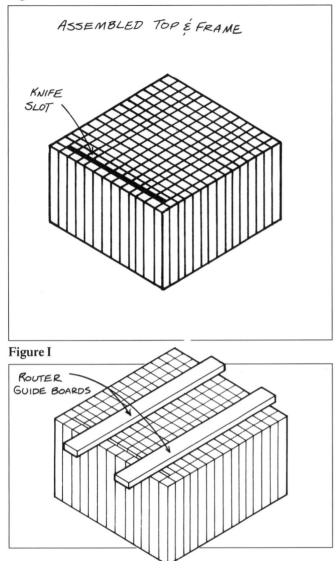

ASSEMBLED TOP & FRAME

KNIFE SLOT

Figure I

ROUTER GUIDE BOARDS

Figure J

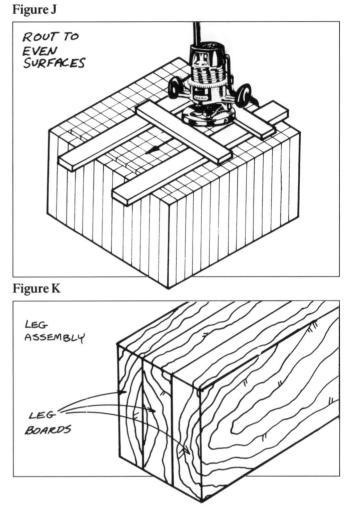

ROUT TO EVEN SURFACES

Figure K

LEG ASSEMBLY

LEG BOARDS

12. Refer to **Figure H**, which shows the assembled top right side up. (You should still be working with it upside down, to insure as level a top surface as possible.) Glue the remaining fifteen-block frame side to the shorter frame sides, flush at the ends, forming a ¼-inch knife slot between the trimmed edge of the top block section and the final frame side. Clamp and allow to dry completely.

Smoothing the Top

1. We used a router with a straight (flat-face) bit to do the initial evening of the top surface. Place two of the pine boards across the top, as shown in **Figure I**. Place the other two boards across the first two. Adjust the boards so that they support the router, as shown in **Figure J**. Adjust the depth of the router bit flush with the lowest block in the assembled top. Use the boards as a guide and move the router over the surface, cutting one row at a time. Move the guide boards as needed until you have routed the entire surface.

2. Rearrange the four guide boards so that the lower and upper boards are perpendicular to their arrangement in step 1. Rout the surface again, one row at a time, moving perpendicular to the direction you did in step 1.

3. Tip the assembly up on one frame side. Rout the surface of the top frame side in the same manner, moving the router across the grain of the wood. Do not make another pass in the other direction.

4. Repeat step 3 to even up the surfaces of the other three frame sides.

5. We used a belt sander to smooth the surfaces of the top and frame sides, using medium-grit sandpaper. Go over all surfaces again, using fine-grit paper. Keep at it until the wood is very smooth.

Leg Assembly

1. Each leg consists of three leg boards laminated and shaped. Glue together three leg boards side-to-side, even along both edges and ends, as shown in **Figure K**. Clamp overnight.

2. Glue and clamp the remaining nine leg boards in groups of three, in the same manner.

3. A full-size pattern for the contoured lower end of the leg is provided in **Figure L**. Trace the pattern and transfer it to a piece of cardboard or thin plywood. Cut out the pattern.

Figure L

LEG

FULL SIZE

LOWER END CONTOUR

Figure M

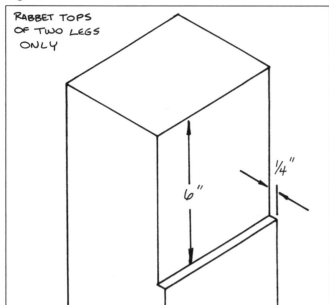

RABBET TOPS OF TWO LEGS ONLY

6"

¼"

Figure N

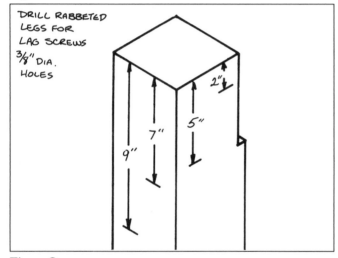

DRILL RABBETED LEGS FOR LAG SCREWS ⅜" DIA. HOLES

2"

5"

7"

9"

Figure O

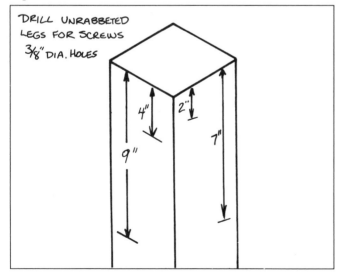

DRILL UNRABBETED LEGS FOR SCREWS ⅜" DIA. HOLES

2"

4"

7"

9"

Figure P

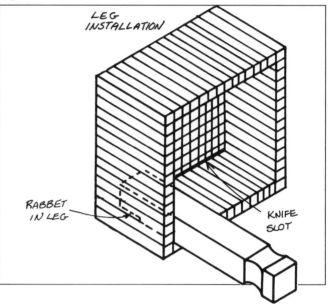

LEG INSTALLATION

RABBET IN LEG

KNIFE SLOT

4. Use the cardboard or plywood pattern as a guide to transfer the contours onto each side of one leg. We used a band saw to cut the leg contours.

5. Repeat step 4 to shape the other three legs.

6. Two of the legs must be modified to allow long knife blades to slide all the way into the knife slot. Cut a ¼ x 6-inch rabbet on one side of a leg, at the square upper end, as shown in **Figure M**. Rabbet a second leg in the same manner, but leave the two remaining legs unrabbeted.

7. Sand the legs smooth.

Leg Installation

1. The legs are attached to the inside corners of the assembled top via the lag screws. Each leg is drilled to accommodate four screws. Refer to **Figure N**, which shows placement of the holes in the rabbeted legs. Drill four ⅜-inch-diameter holes through each of these legs, where indicated.

2. Refer to **Figure M**, which shows placement of the holes in the legs that were not rabbeted. Drill four ⁷⁄₁₆-inch-diameter holes through each of these legs, where indicated. (The slightly larger size of these holes will allow you to level the block to a certain degree.)

3. Tip the assembled top on its side, with the knife slot at the bottom, as shown in **Figure P**. The rabbeted legs are installed against this side, rabbeted side down. Do not use glue, so you can remove the legs if you ever need to transport or store the butcher block. Place one leg against a corner, as shown, butting the upper end against the underside of the top. Use the drilled screw holes as placement guides to drill ⁵⁄₁₆-inch-diameter screw starter holes into the adjacent frame sides. Insert a lag screw into each hole and tighten securely.

4. Install the second rabbeted leg against the adjacent corner in the same manner.

5. Turn the block so that the opposite side is against the work surface. Install the two unrabbeted legs in the same manner.

6. Apply your chosen finish.

Porch Swing

There's nothing quite like a good old-fashioned porch swing to get the family outdoors on a pleasant summer evening. If you don't have a porch, hang it from a tree! The swing is 4 feet long and just under 2 feet high and deep.

Materials

Notes: If you wish to stain your porch swing instead of painting it, choose redwood, cedar or another type of lumber well suited to outdoor conditions (see Tips & Techniques). Be sure to use rust-resistant hardware.

1 x 4 lumber: one 10-foot length and one 8-foot length

1 x 2 lumber: eight 8-foot lengths (Note: No waste allowance is included for the 1 x 2s. Purchase 10-footers in place of the 8-footers if there is more than an inch of unusable wood at the ends of these boards.)

Four heavy-duty eyebolts, 3¼ inches long, each with a flat washer and nut to fit

Two heavy-duty eyebolts, 2 inches long, each with a flat washer and nut to fit

1½-inch-long flathead wood screws

Carpenter's or waterproof wood glue; and finishing materials of your choice

Chain and connecting links: The amount of chain you'll need depends on the height of your porch or tree. For each side of the swing, figure on a single length of chain to reach from the ceiling or branch down to a few inches above the top of the swing, plus another 7 feet to form an inverted V-shape. If the chain must be wrapped around a tree branch, you'll need that much extra on each side. Be certain that the chain is heavy enough to hold the weight of four adults, just to be on the safe side. In addition to the chain, you'll need six connecting links, at least as heavy as the chain, to connect the chain to the swing. You'll also need hardware to connect the chain to the ceiling, or two more connecting links to secure it around the tree branch.

This simple swing can be assembled in just a few hours. There are no complex joints or tricky cutting procedures. The assembly is shown in **Figures C** through **G**.

Cutting the Parts

1. Cut from 1 x 4 lumber the lengths listed in this step and label each one with its code letter, for reference during assembly. All parts are the full thickness and width of the stock – ¾ x 3½ inches. (All of the parts will be shaped or otherwise modified in later steps.) A cutting layout is provided in **Figure A**, showing how we used the lengths of 1 x 4 specified in the materials list.

Code	Description	Length	Quantity
A	Back Support	21 inches	2
B	Seat Support	19 inches	2
C	Seat Support	21 inches	2
D	Armrest	20 inches	2
E	Post	13 inches	2

Figure A

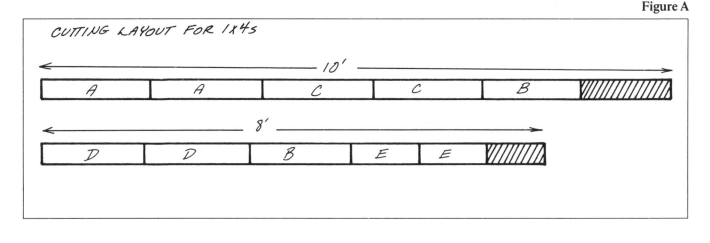

CUTTING LAYOUT FOR 1x4s

10'

| A | A | C | C | B | |

8'

| D | D | B | E | E | |

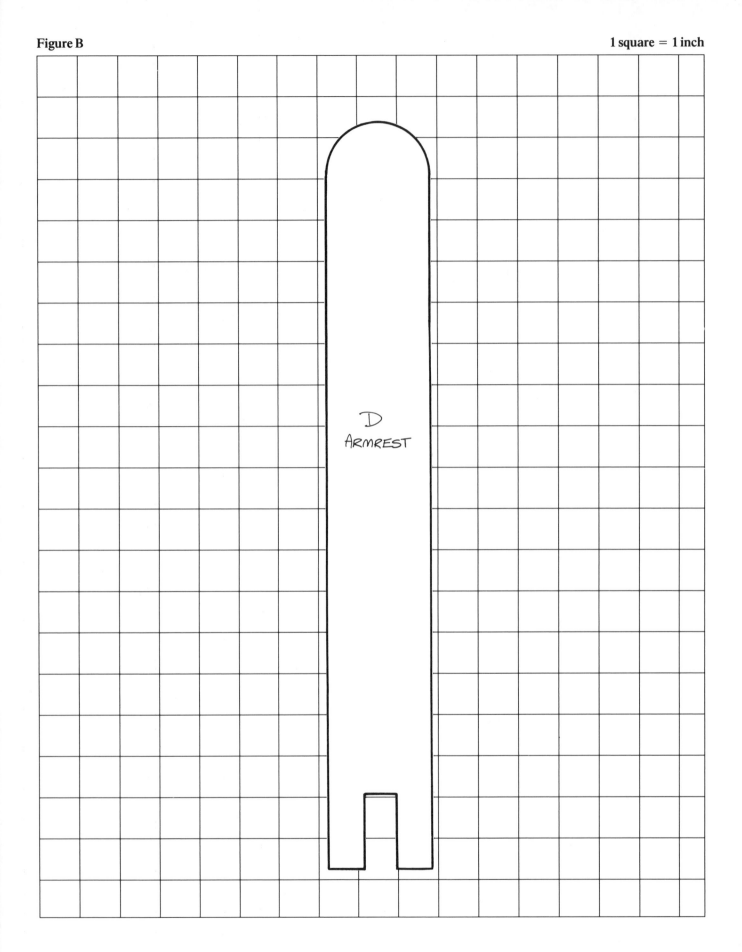

D
ARMREST

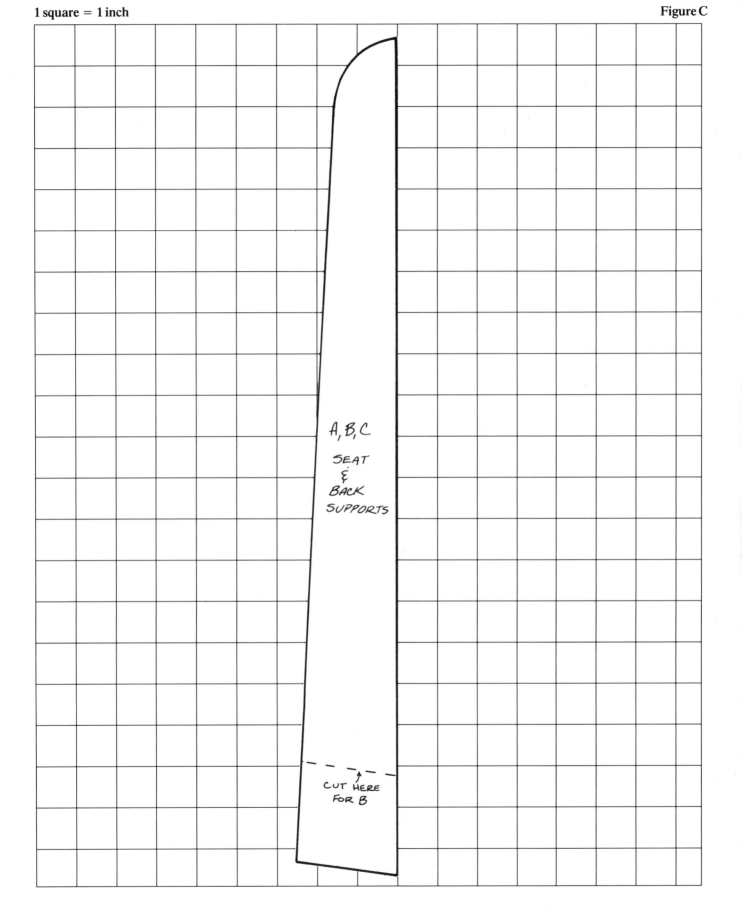

A, B, C

SEAT
&
BACK
SUPPORTS

CUT HERE
FOR B

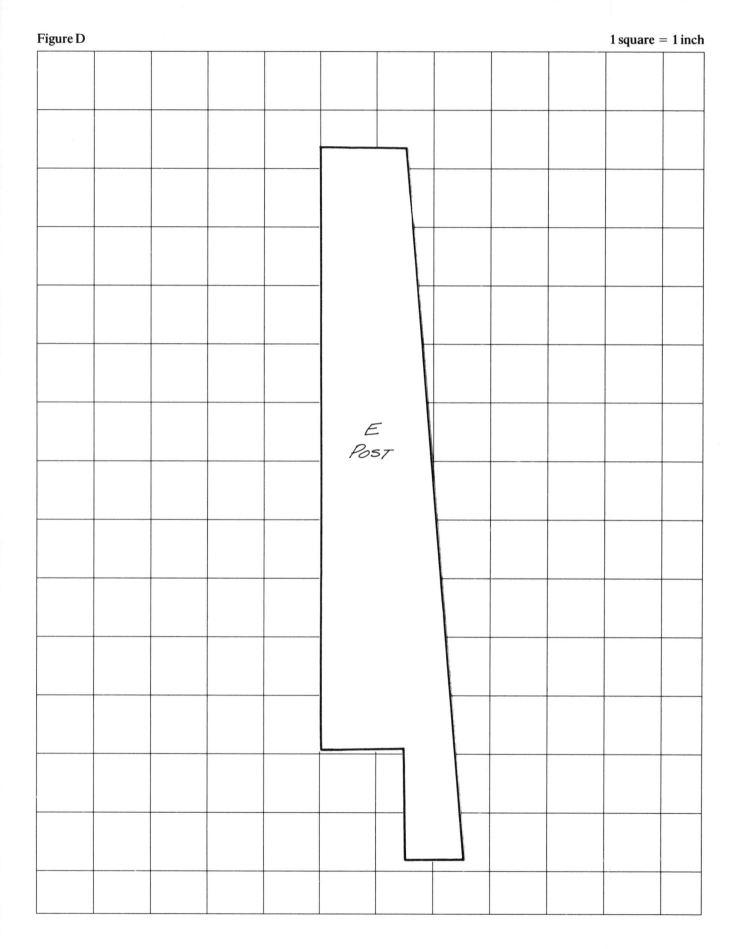

E
POST

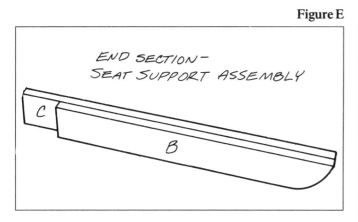

END SECTION— SEAT SUPPORT ASSEMBLY

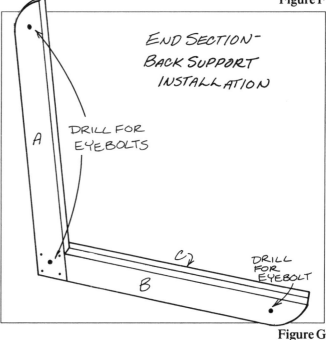

END SECTION— BACK SUPPORT INSTALLATION

DRILL FOR EYEBOLTS

DRILL FOR EYEBOLT

Figure G

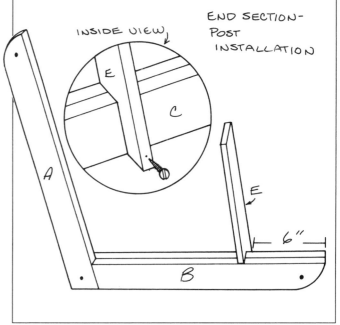

INSIDE VIEW

END SECTION— POST INSTALLATION

6"

2. Scale drawings for all of the 1 x 4 parts are provided in **Figures B, C** and **D**. Enlarge the drawings to make full-size patterns. (Refer to the appropriate section of Tips & Techniques if you need some hints on how to go about this.)

3. Note that there is a single pattern for all of the A, B and C supports. They are all identical, except that the B's are a bit shorter than the A's and C's, as indicated on the scale drawing. Transfer the appropriate outlines of the pattern to the respective A, B and C lengths of 1 x 4. Cut the contours.

4. Transfer the outlines of the full-size D armrest pattern to the two D boards that you cut in step 1. Cut the contours.

5. Transfer the outlines of the full-size E post pattern to the two E boards that you cut in step 1. Cut the contours.

6. The sixteen slats that form the seat and back of the swing are lengths of 1 x 2 lumber (see **Figure I**). We cut each of the eight 8-foot lengths of 1 x 2 in half, giving us sixteen slats, each just slightly shorter than 4 feet long. All of the slats must be exactly the same length. If you purchased 8-foot lengths of 1 x 2, and any of them contain cracked or otherwise unusable portions at the ends, cut off the bad parts. Cut the shortest resulting 1 x 2 in half and use these two lengths as guides to cut fourteen more slats from the remaining 1 x 2s. As we said in the materials list, if there is very much more than an inch or so of unusable wood, the slats (and therefore the swing) will be shorter than it should be. If you purchased 10-foot instead of 8-foot lengths of 1 x 2, cut two 4-foot lengths from each one. Label all of the slats F.

7. Sand all of the parts.

Assembly

The swing consists of two mirror-image end sections joined by the sixteen slats. Each end section consists of one A, one B and one C support, a D armrest and an E post, which supports the armrest at the front (see **Figure H**).

1. Glue a B and C support together, flush along both long edges, as shown in **Figure E**. The C support will face the center of the swing. Secure the assembly by inserting two screws through the C into the B.

2. Refer to **Figure F**. Glue an A support to the B-C assembly, fitting the lower end of the A into the gap between the angled ends of the B and C supports. Note that the lower end of the A is flush with the lower edges of the B and C. The end of the C should be flush with the back long edge of the A. To

secure, insert four screws through the A into the C support, where indicated in **Figure F**.

3. Drill three ⅜-inch-diameter holes through the A-B-C assembly, where indicated in **Figure F**, to accommodate the eyebolts that will secure the chain.

4. Refer to **Figure G**. Glue an E post to the seat-support portion of the assembly, fitting the notch against the C support and over the B-C boards, as shown. Note that the post should be 6 inches from the front end of the seat support. Secure the post by inserting a single screw through the lower extension into the C support, as shown in the detail diagram.

Figure H

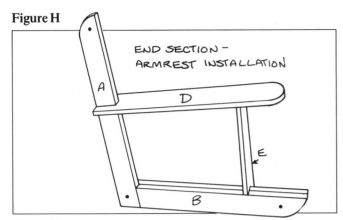

END SECTION –
ARMREST INSTALLATION

A
D
E
B

Figure I

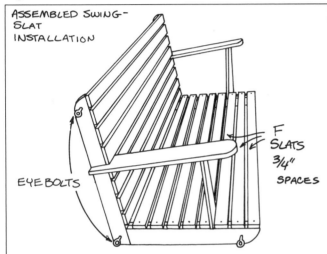

ASSEMBLED SWING –
SLAT
INSTALLATION

F
SLATS
3/4"
SPACES

EYEBOLTS

5. The armrest installation is shown in **Figure H**. Fit the notched end of the D armrest around the A back support. Adjust it so that it looks relatively level when the front end is resting on top of the E post, as shown. Glue the armrest in place. To secure, insert one screw down through the armrest into the E post. Insert another screw through the back extension of the armrest, from the C side of the assembly into the A support.

6. Install an eyebolt in each drilled hole, inserting them from the outside of the assembly (see **Figure I**). Use the longer bolts at the bottom and a shorter one at the top. Secure each bolt on the inside with a washer and nut.

7. Repeat steps 1 through 6 to assemble a second, mirror-image end section.

8. Refer to **Figure I**. Align the two end sections about 4 feet apart and place one F slat on top, at the front. Align the front edge of the slat flush with the front ends of the end sections, as shown, and adjust the end sections so that the ends of the slat are flush with the outer surfaces. To secure, insert a single screw down through each end of the slat into the seat support below.

9. Attach a second slat ¾ inch behind the first one, as shown in **Figure I**. Attach a third slat ¾ inch behind the second one; it should butt against the front of the E post. Attach the fourth slat butted against the back of the post. Attach four more seat slats in this manner, allowing ¾ inch between slats, as shown.

10. Use the eight remaining F's as back slats, attaching them to the A back supports in the same manner.

11. Apply your chosen finishing materials and allow to dry.

12. The chain configuration is shown in **Figure J**. Use the connecting links to join the chain to the eyebolts and to attach the V-shaped portion of the chain to the vertical portion.

13. Hang the swing and adjust the chain so that the swing hangs evenly.

Figure J

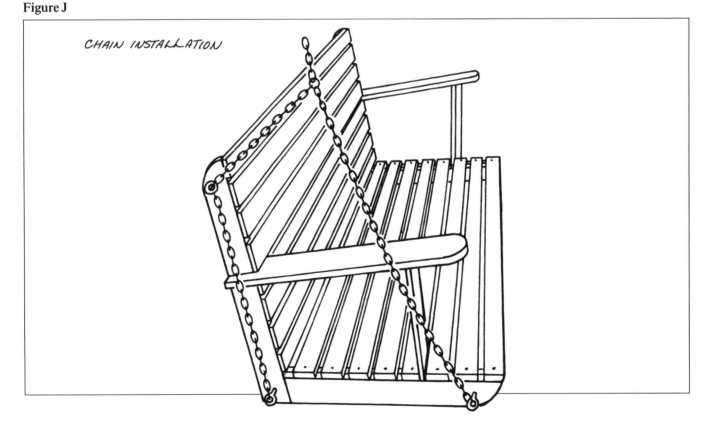

CHAIN INSTALLATION

Rolling
File Organizer

Here's the perfect solution to home paperwork organization. This handy, rolling organizer is easy and inexpensive to build and will hold a surprising number of files, with room underneath for extra storage. Overall size is 15 x 20 x 24 inches.

Materials

Notes: We used ¾ oak for this project, but it can be very handsome in pine if you pay special attention to finishing. Amounts of lumber listed here are based on standard softwood dimensional lumber sizes. If you wish to use hardwood, refer to Tips & Techniques for a discussion of converting linear feet of dimensional lumber to the board feet amounts required for purchasing hardwood. All of the parts are quite narrow (3 inches

or less), so the width of the stock doesn't matter too much.

1 x 4 lumber: one 8-foot length and two 6-foot lengths
1 x 2 lumber: one 10-foot length
¼-inch better-quality plywood: 14 x 20-inch piece
Four shank-type swivel casters
Flathead wood screws in ¾- and 1¼-inch lengths
¾-inch-long wire brads
Carpenter's wood glue; and Danish oil or other finishing materials of your choice

Optional:

If you want to cover the files or use the unit as a small table, you can add a removable lid. You'll need an additional 15 x 24-inch piece of ¼-inch plywood and a 1-foot length of ¼-inch dowel rod.

If you want to cover the openings in the sides, front and back of the unit, use fabric or plywood. If you use plywood, you'll need two 14 x 19-inch pieces and two 9-inch squares, plus some ¾-inch wire brads or staples. If you use fabric, you'll need two 16 x 21-inch pieces and two 11-inch squares. Purchase 2 full yards for an overall cover.

This project shouldn't take more than an afternoon or two to assemble. It contains two identical side sections, identical front and back sections, a floor-support assembly and rabbeted file-support rails. The assembly is shown in **Figures D** through **H**.

Cutting the Parts

1. The main parts are cut from 1 x 4 lumber that has been reduced to 3 inches wide. Rip all three lengths of 1 x 4 to 3 inches in width. Do not reduce the ¾-inch thickness. (Save the leftover ripped strips for use in step 2.) Cut from the 3-inch-wide stock the parts listed in this step and label them with their code letters. A cutting layout is provided in **Figure A**.

Code	Description	Length	Quantity
Side Sections:			
A	Rail	24 inches	4
B	Stile	12¼ inches	4
Front-Back Sections:			
C	Rail	13½ inches	4
D	Stile	6¼ inches	4

Figure A

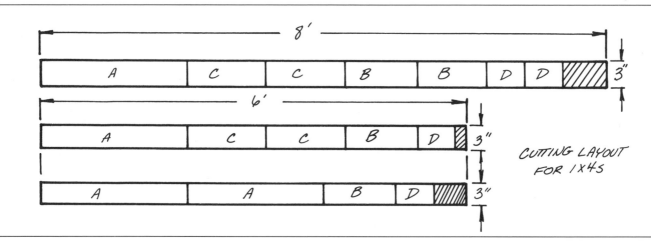

CUTTING LAYOUT FOR 1X4S

Figure B

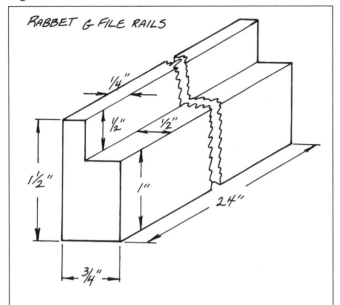

RABBET G FILE RAILS

Figure C

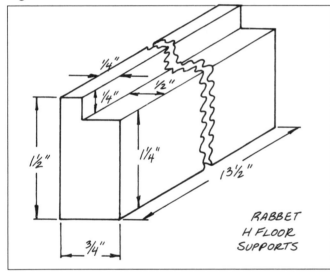

RABBET
H FLOOR
SUPPORTS

Figure D

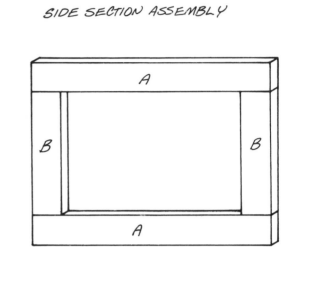

SIDE SECTION ASSEMBLY

Figure E

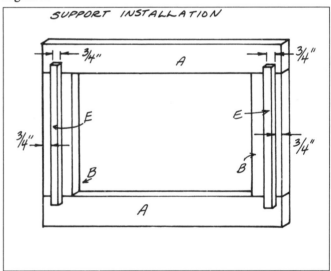

SUPPORT INSTALLATION

2. The parts listed in this step are cut from the narrow strips left over from step 1. All of these parts are ⅜ inch thick by ¾ inch wide by the lengths listed below. The leftover strips from step 1 should be ⅜ x ¾ inch, by 6 or 8 feet. Cut the specified lengths and label them with the code letters listed.

Code	Description	Length	Quantity
E	Long Support	13¾ inches	4
F	Short Support	8 inches	4

3. The parts listed in this step are lengths of 1 x 2 lumber. All are the full thickness and width of the stock – ¾ x 1½ inches. Cut and label the parts as listed.

Code	Description	Length	Quantity
G	File Rail	24 inches	2
H	Floor Support	13½ inches	2
J	Floor Support	18 inches	2

4. The two **G** file rails are rabbeted to accommodate hanging file folders. Refer to **Figure B**. Cut or rout a ½ x ½-inch rabbet along one long edge of each file rail, as shown.

5. The **H** floor supports are rabbeted to accommodate the plywood floor. Refer to **Figure C**. Cut or rout a ¼ x ½-inch rabbet along one long edge of each **H** support, as shown. Do not rabbet the **J** floor supports, but rip them to 1¼ inches wide. Do not reduce the ¾-inch thickness or the 18-inch length.

6. For the floor, cut a 13⅜ x 18⅞-inch piece of ¼-inch plywood. Sand all parts.

Assembly

1. An assembled side section is shown in **Figure D**. Glue together two **A** rails and two **B** stiles, butting the ends and edges as shown.

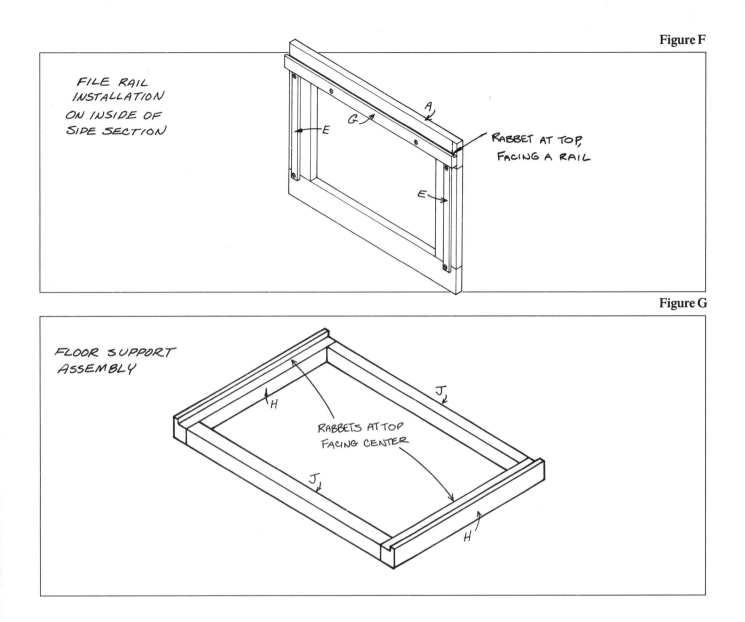

FILE RAIL
INSTALLATION
ON INSIDE OF
SIDE SECTION

G

E

A

RABBET AT TOP,
FACING A RAIL

E

FLOOR SUPPORT
ASSEMBLY

H

J

RABBETS AT TOP
FACING CENTER

J

H

2. Two E long supports are used to reinforce the joints of the assembled side section, as shown in **Figure E**. They are attached to what will be the inside surface. Note that each one is ¾ inch from the outer edge and extends evenly beyond the upper and lower ends of the B stile to which it is attached. Glue the long supports in place and secure with screws inserted through the supports into the A rails and B stiles.

3. Assemble a second, identical side section.

4. The front and back sections are identical to the side sections, but not as large. Assemble two C rails and two D stiles, butting the edges and ends as you did the A rails and B stiles for the side sections. To reinforce the joints, attach two F short supports to one side of the assembly, as you did the E long supports for the side sections. Again, each support should be ¾ inch from the outer edge and should extend equally beyond the upper and lower ends of the D stile to which it is attached. Secure the supports with screws inserted through them into the C rails and D stiles.

5. Assemble a second, identical front-back section.

6. Glue a rabbeted G file rail to the inside surface of one side section, as shown in **Figure F**. The lower edge of the file rail should butt against the tops of the two E long supports. The file rail should be turned with the rabbet facing the side section and opening at the top, as shown. Secure with two screws inserted through the G file rail into the A rail. Attach the second file rail to the inside surface of the other side section.

7. To assemble the floor-support frame, glue together the H and J floor supports, as shown in **Figure G**. Note that the rabbets face center, at the top. Secure each joint with a screw inserted through the H support into the adjacent J support.

8. The assembled file organizer is shown in **Figure H**. Glue the front and back sections between the side sections, flush at the ends. Note that the front and back sections do not extend above or below the side-section stiles. Be sure all four sections are turned with their inner surfaces facing center (all supports should be on the inside). Secure by inserting screws through the side-section stiles into the edges of the front and back sections. Countersink the screws and cover with plugs.

Figure H

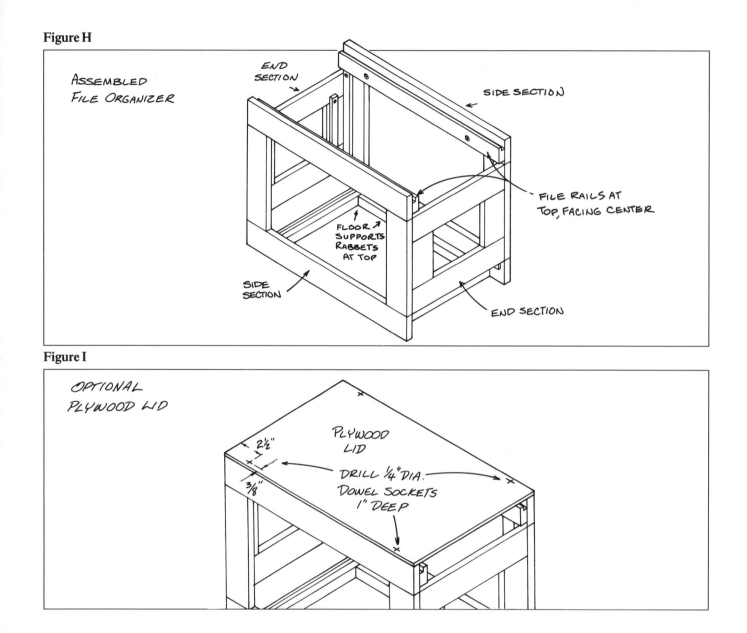

ASSEMBLED FILE ORGANIZER

END SECTION

SIDE SECTION

FILE RAILS AT TOP, FACING CENTER

FLOOR SUPPORTS RABBETS AT TOP

SIDE SECTION

END SECTION

Figure I

OPTIONAL PLYWOOD LID

PLYWOOD LID

DRILL ¼"DIA. DOWEL SOCKETS 1" DEEP

2½"

3/8"

9. Glue the assembled floor-support frame between the two side sections, flush at the bottom and with the rabbets at the top, as shown in **Figure H**. The frame should be centered between the ends of the side sections. Secure it with a few screws. Glue the plywood floor into the rabbets on top of the support frame and secure with a few wire brads.

10. To install the casters, turn the unit upside down. On the lower edge of each side-section bottom rail, drill two sockets to accommodate the caster shanks, placing them about 2½ inches from each end of the rail and centered on the edge. Follow the manufacturer's instructions to install the casters.

Options

1. If you want to make a removable cover, cut a 15 x 24-inch piece of ¼-inch plywood. Place it on top of the unit, flush along all edges. Temporarily clamp it in place.

2. Dowel pegs will be used to hold the cover on the unit. To accommodate the pegs, drill four ¼-inch-diameter holes through the plywood cover, placing them ⅜ inch from the long edges and 2½ inches from each end, as shown in **Figure I**. Continue drilling straight down into the side-section rails, making the total drilling depth 1 inch. Be sure to drill in a very straight line, or you'll break through the rails.

3. Cut four 1-inch lengths of ¼-inch dowel rod. Remove the cover from the file organizer and glue a dowel peg into each socket in the side-section top rails. Replace the cover, guiding the pegs through the holes.

4. Sand and finish the plywood cover and the extending upper ends of the pegs.

5. If you want to cover the openings in the unit, cut a piece of plywood or fabric slightly larger than each opening. For plywood covers, sand the pieces and attach to the inside surfaces of the walls, using staples or wire brads. For fabric covers, press and stitch a narrow hem along each edge before stapling over the openings.

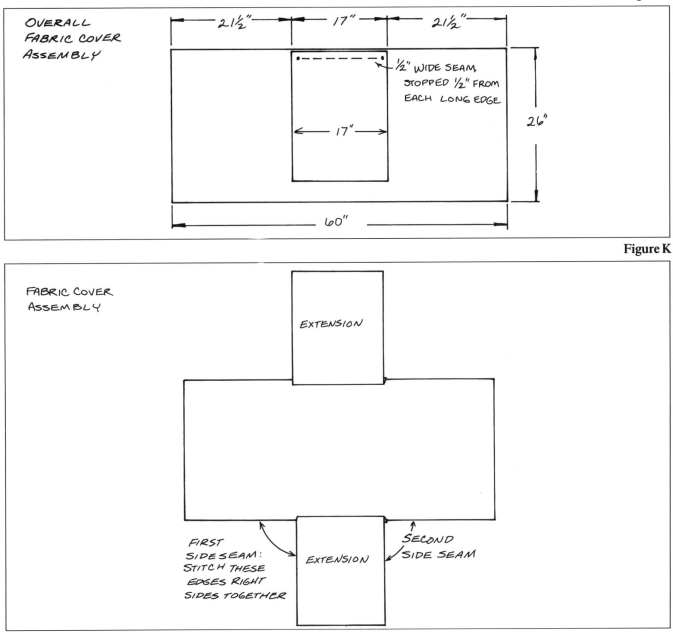

Overall Fabric Cover

It's very easy to make a box-like fabric cover to conceal or protect the entire unit. An illustration of the overall cover is provided in **Figure L**. It will keep most of the dust out of your files and, if made from an attractive fabric, will compliment your decorating scheme.

To make an overall cover, you'll need 1¼ yards of 60-inch-wide fabric or 1¾ yards of 45-inch fabric. Use medium- to heavy-weight fabric for the best result.

1. Cut one 26 x 60-inch piece and two 17 x 22½-inch pieces from the fabric you have chosen.

2. Place the large fabric piece right side up on a flat surface and place one of the smaller pieces right side down on top. Align one end of the smaller piece at the center of a long edge of the larger one, as shown in **Figure J**. Stitch a ½-inch-wide seam, starting and stopping ½ inch from the long edges of the smaller fabric piece, as shown. Turn the smaller piece outward and press the seam.

3. Repeat step 2 to stitch the remaining smaller fabric piece to the larger one, directly opposite the first smaller piece. When stitched and turned outward, the assembly should look like the one shown in **Figure K**.

4. There are four side seams, which are formed by joining the long raw edges of the two smaller extensions to the adjacent portions of the long edges of the larger piece. The two edges that are joined to form the first side seam are indicated in **Figure K**. Fold and adjust the assembly to align these edges, placing

Figure L

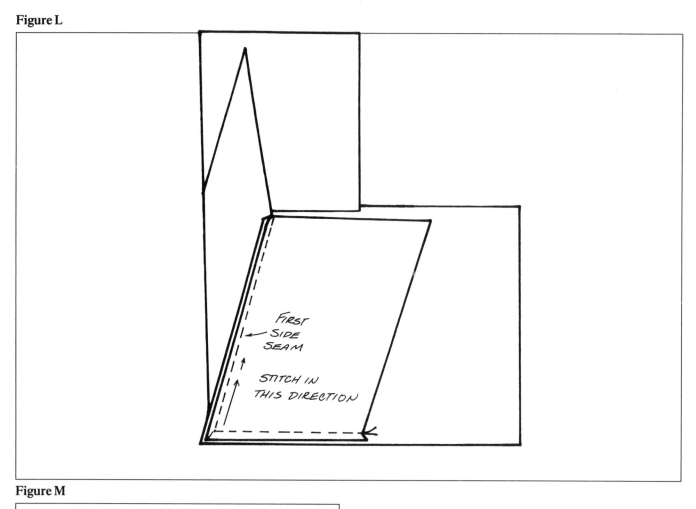

FIRST SIDE SEAM

STITCH IN THIS DIRECTION

Figure M

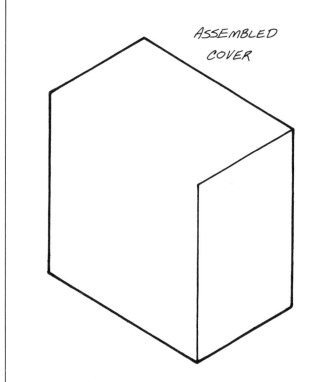

ASSEMBLED COVER

the fabrics right sides together, and pin the seam. Start at the corner where the extension is already attached to the larger piece and stitch a ½-inch-wide seam all the way down to the lower ends, as shown in **Figure L**. Press the seam.

5. Repeat step 4 to stitch the second side seam, joining the opposite long edge of the same fabric extension to the adjacent edge of the larger fabric piece.

6. Repeat step 4 to stitch the last two side seams, joining the long edges of the other fabric extension to the adjacent edges of the larger fabric piece.

7. Turn the assembly right side out. It should now look like the illustration in **Figure M**.

8. If you are going to use the covered file organizer as a table, you will need to install a removable plywood lid that will fit underneath the fabric cover. To do this, follow the instructions in steps 1 through 4 under the heading "Options." If you will not be using the unit as a table, but just want a fabric cover, you can do without the plywood lid.

9. Slip the assembled fabric cover down over the file organizer. (If you made a plywood lid, it should be in place.) Pin up a hem around the raw lower edges of the cover.

10. Remove the cover from the unit. Press a ¼-inch hem allowance to the wrong side of the fabric all the way around the lower edge. Fold the pressed edge under again, along the marked hem line, and pin in place. Stitch the hem by hand or by machine.

Modular Bookcase

Build to fit! This simple structure can be modified to create custom-designed shelving to fit your needs and available space. It is extremely easy to assemble and can be made for next to nothing, if you use construction-grade 2 x 4s and paint them nicely. Better-quality 2 x 4s are not that much more expensive and can be stained.

Materials

Note: This materials list indicates the amount of lumber required to build a single bookcase module 6 feet tall, 4 feet wide and 10 inches deep. It is intended only as an example. When you've determined the size and shape of the bookcase you wish to build, you'll need to work up a list of materials.

2 x 4 lumber: six 8-foot lengths
1 x 8 lumber: four 8-foot lengths
2¼-inch-long flathead wood screws
Carpenter's wood glue; and finishing materials of your choice

Please read through the instructions for the bookcase module that we built. Once you understand the basic assembly, you can more easily determine overall size and design of the unit you wish to build. At the end of the instructions for our module, you'll find a section of hints and considerations to keep in mind as you design a custom unit for your home.

Before reading the instructions for the single module, refer to **Figures E** and **F** on pages 127 and 128. These illustrations will give you an idea of how the single module can be modified or combined with other modules to create a custom bookcase. You'll find that the basic design is so simple, it lends itself easily to a wide variety of shapes and sizes.

Cutting the Parts

1. Cut the lengths of 2 x 4 lumber listed in this step and label them with their code letters. All parts are the full thickness and width of the stock – 1½ x 3½ inches. A cutting layout is provided in **Figure A**, showing how we used the 2 x 4s specified in the materials list.

Code	Description	Length	Quantity
A	Post	72 inches	4
B	Foot	14 inches	2
C	Spacer	7⁵⁄₁₆ inches	26

2. The two B feet are tapered to make the bookcase lean just slightly toward the wall. This will eliminate the possibility of the unit falling over into the room, without having to attach it to the wall. The B's are also beveled at the ends. An edge view

Figure A

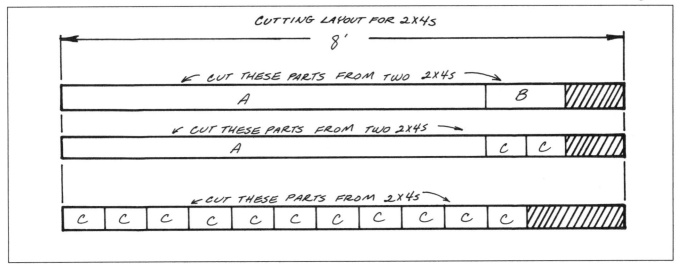

Figure B

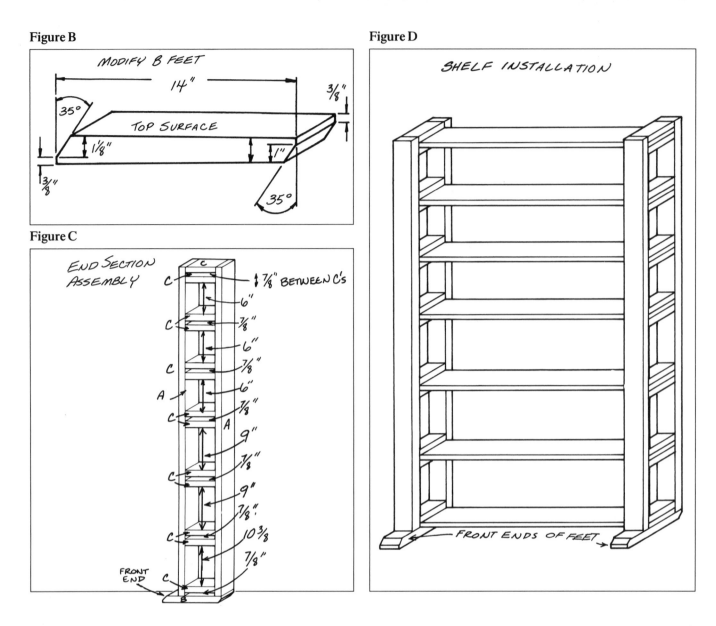

Figure C

Figure D

of one foot is provided in **Figure B**. To taper it, plane or sand the top surface only, reducing the thickness at the back end by about ⅛ inch. Do not reduce the thickness at the front end. Now bevel the front end at an angle of about 35 degrees, beginning ⅜ inch from the bottom surface, as shown. Bevel the back end at about the same angle, beginning ⅜ inch below the top surface, as shown. Modify the other B foot in the same manner.

3. In this unit, each shelf is a 4-foot length of 1 x 8 lumber. They are the full thickness and width of the stock – ¾ x 7¼ inches. Cut each 1 x 8 in half.

Assembly

The module consists of two end sections, which look like ladders, and the shelves.

1. One end section is shown in **Figure C**. It consists of two A posts attached to a B foot at the bottom and separated by C spacers, which support the shelves. In this unit, we have seven

shelves. A shelf end fits between each pair of closely spaced C spacers. (At the bottom, the B foot also serves as the lower spacer for the bottom shelf.) Glue thirteen spacers between two posts, spacing them as shown. Secure each spacer with two screws at each end.

2. Glue the assembled ladder to the B foot, aligning it as shown in **Figure C**. Secure each post with at least two screws inserted up through the foot.

3. Build a second, identical end section.

4. Align the end sections 41 inches apart, making sure that the front ends of the two feet face the same direction. Insert the shelves, as shown in **Figure D**. We left the shelves unattached, as it is very unlikely that the ladders will move enough to dislodge them. You may wish to secure them with screws.

This completes the assembly of the basic bookcase module. Now it's time to give some thought to the size and configuration of the bookcase unit you want to build.

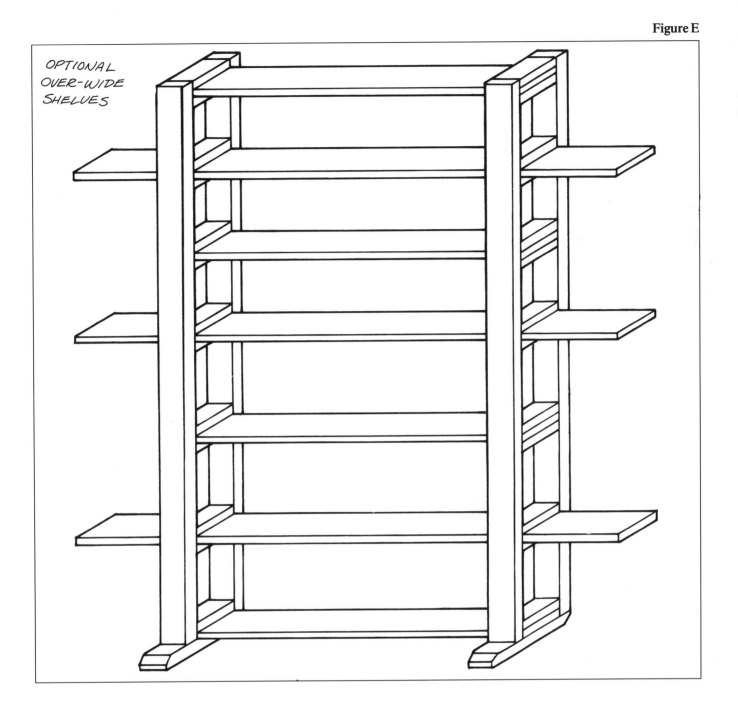

OPTIONAL OVER-WIDE SHELVES

Designing a Bookcase

1. Before getting down to work, there are a few things to keep in mind. First, the shelves need not all be the same length. Some may be allowed to extend a foot or so beyond one or both end sections, as shown in **Figure E**.

2. If you want a bookcase wider than 4 feet, it should be composed of more than one module. A shelf that is supported at intervals wider than about 4 feet will be too likely to sag in the middle. An example of a multi-module bookcase is shown in **Figure F**. Note that adjoining modules share end sections. This cuts down on unusable shelf space, overall weight and cost.

3. No matter what size unit you design, you can stick with 2 x 4 lumber for the posts, spacers and feet and still come out with a sturdy, handsome bookcase. If you want a really massive appearance, you can use 2 x 6 lumber for these parts, but it will mean a lot of wasted space and a very heavy bookcase. For the shelves, you can use wider or narrower 1-by stock, depending on the depth you want. For a very deep bookcase, use 1 x 12 lumber or plywood for the shelves.

4. Now to get down to work: Measure the horizontal and vertical wall space where you want the unit to go. Sit down with pencil and paper and make some rough sketches of how you want the unit to look. Will there be more than one module? Will

Figure F

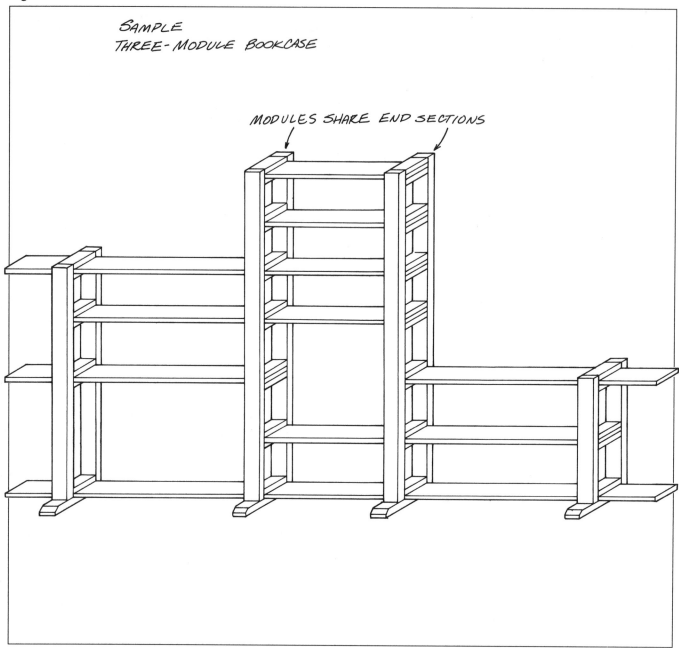

SAMPLE
THREE-MODULE BOOKCASE

MODULES SHARE END SECTIONS

all modules be the same height? Width? How many shelves? How much space between shelves do you need? How deep?

5. When you have answered all these questions and made a diagram of your desired bookcase, make a separate, detailed diagram of each end section, referring to **Figures C** and **F** for examples. (Graph paper will make this job easier.) If your unit has more than one module, be sure to include in each end-section diagram all of the spacers that will be required for the shelves on both sides of that section (see the end section shown in **Figure F**). Keep in mind that the two spacers that form each pair should be ⅞ inch apart, but the spacing between pairs is what determines shelf height. (The usable distance between one

shelf and the next will be 3 inches greater than the distance between the spacer pairs.)

6. Make a list of all parts, specifying their lengths. The spacers should be cut ¹⁄₁₆ inch longer than the width of the shelves. The feet should be cut 6¾ inches longer than the spacers.

7. Add up all the lengths of 2 x 4 and add about ten percent for a waste allowance. Purchase at least this much 2 x 4 lumber. Do the same for the 1-by lumber (1 x 8, or whatever width you have settled on for your bookcase shelves).

8. Refer to your list of parts as you cut the lumber to length. Be sure to modify the feet as described for our sample unit.

9. Refer to your diagrams as you assemble the bookcase.